Eyes on the
Sporting Scene,
1870–1930

Eyes on the Sporting Scene, 1870–1930

Will and June Rankin, New York's Sportswriting Brothers

Pamela A. Bakker

McFarland & Company, Inc., Publishers
Jefferson, North Carolina, and London

LIBRARY OF CONGRESS CATALOGUING-IN-PUBLICATION DATA

Bakker, Pamela A.
Eyes on the sporting scene, 1870–1930 : Will and June
Rankin, New York's sportswriting brothers / Pamela A. Bakker.

p.   cm.

Includes bibliographical references and index.

ISBN 978-0-7864-7314-4
softcover : acid free paper ∞

1. Rankin, Will, 1849–1913. 2. Rankin, June, 1851–1930.
3. Sportswriters — New York (State) — New York — Biography.
4. Baseball — United States — History — 19th century.
5. Baseball — United States — History — 20th century. I. Title.
GV742.4.B36 2013   070.4'497960922 — dc23   [B]   2013003028

BRITISH LIBRARY CATALOGUING DATA ARE AVAILABLE

© 2013 Pamela A. Bakker. All rights reserved

*No part of this book may be reproduced or transmitted in any form
or by any means, electronic or mechanical, including photocopying
or recording, or by any information storage and retrieval system,
without permission in writing from the publisher.*

On the cover: *left* Will and *right* June Rankin; *center detail*
baseball daily newspaper *Official Record*, June 15, 1886
(all courtesy Rankin family archive);
bottom sports illustrations clipart.com

Manufactured in the United States of America

*McFarland & Company, Inc., Publishers
Box 611, Jefferson, North Carolina 28640
www.mcfarlandpub.com*

In memory of
William McDowell "Will" Rankin and
Andrew Brown "June" Rankin V.

Dedicated to
the granddaughters of June:
Ruth Rankin Leaper and Lois Rankin Prior;
their children, grandchildren and great-grandchildren;
and to my children:
Alissa, David, and daughter-in-law Ashley;
and my granddaughter, Payton

reporters type in cigar filled rooms
leaning in to watch the game
a tip, a ball, a strike, a run
immortal player, recorded name
— Pamela Bakker 10/24/2011

Table of Contents

Acknowledgments viii
Preface 1

ONE. Family Origins (1715–1859) 5
TWO. The Horror of the Civil War (1849–1865) 13
THREE. New York, New York (1865–1870) 26
FOUR. Follow the Ball (1870–1879) 38
FIVE. Rising to the Top (1880–1884) 58
SIX. Celebrities in Baseball (1885–1889) 78
SEVEN. A Decade of Change (1890–1899) 106
EIGHT. Origins of Baseball (1885–1906) 122
NINE. A Century Turns (1900–1910) 139
TEN. Working to Death (1910–1913) 161
ELEVEN. June Writes Alone (1913–1930) 167

Appendix 179
Notes 185
Bibliography 201
Index 209

Acknowledgments

I would like to express a special thanks to my family for their support and encouragement. My children, Alissa and David, never wavered in their belief in the book. My siblings Kit Canepi and Bob Leaper were excited by the project, and Diane Donohue helped me in the area of providing research access and in editing. Also, a special thank you goes to the granddaughters of Andrew: my mother, Ruth Rankin Leaper, and aunt, Lois Rankin Prior, who held the special family stories. Arthur Rankin, great-grandson of William M. McDowell, provided his part of the family genealogy information and showed that, even through many generations and distance of location, a family still has ties as a family. The National Baseball Hall of Fame Museum and Library gets the credit for connecting our two branches of the family together.

In the area of reference material, special thanks goes to the Cleveland Public Library for holding some of William's collections and their assistance in helping me to understand the 40 cases of baseball scrapbooks and scores in their possession. Also, their online microfilm of many of Will's scrapbook volumes assisted me greatly. When William M. Rankin died in 1913, he had the largest baseball library in existence. Some of that library went to Charles Willard Mears, 1874–1942, and a few of his scrapbooks are now held by the Cleveland Public Library as the Charles W. Mears Baseball Collection of the Cleveland Public Library. In the collection are Will's personal letters, some of his columns, baseball histories, scores from papers and things he found of interest beginning from the mid–1850s to the end of his life in 1913.

Both brothers wrote for many of the 19th century New York newspapers. The New York Public Library has a wonderful collection of newspapers for which both brothers wrote. They also provided one of the club photos for the book and microfilm of one of June's books.

Thank you to Brian Jennings of the Nyack Public Library, Nyack, New

York, for looking through their collection of county baseball photos, and for work being done on the online version of the *Rockland County Journal,* a paper for which Will wrote, covering baseball from 1870 to 1873. It contained his baseball columns, and notices on a number of family members from the late 1860s on. It also mentioned the early baseball clubs on which both Will and June played.

Thank you to Susan Halpert, reference librarian at Houghton Library, Harvard University, for research tips and ideas, and a special thank you goes to Arlene Balkansky, reference specialist at the Newspaper and Current Periodical Reading Room of the Library of Congress, for help and guidance. She went beyond the call of duty in tracking down periodicals.

The Brooklyn Public Library has the *Brooklyn Daily Eagle* online, a paper for which both brothers wrote and which carried many comments about the family. The brothers lived in Brooklyn and became friends with many of the newspapermen from that paper. Thank you to all of the libraries faithfully saving newspapers and microfilm so that others might have an opportunity to read writers from the past. Thank you, too, to the groups who collect and sell original copies of vintage newspapers, enabling others to own hard copies for their own enjoyment.

Freddy Berowski at the National Baseball Hall of Fame and Museum, Abner Library, Cooperstown, New York, was helpful in listing their scrapbook on William Rankin and the small file, and the two baseball books in their library written by June Rankin. John Horne in the photo archives supplied a number of photos of early clubs—the New York Reporters Base Ball Club, the Mutuals, the Metropolitans, and the Giants—and photographed June Rankin's two books. Tim Wiles, director of research, not only sent me the file on Will Rankin, but through that act connected me to Will's heirs, enlarging my family circle.

Thank you to Nancy Stulack, museum librarian at the United States Golf Association Museum Library in Bernards Township, New Jersey, for help in tracking down Andrew Rankin's golf magazine. The museum has two very rare copies of Andrew's *The Official Golf Record,* published in 1906. They also provided a photograph of one for the book. The library also has an online search center which was very helpful in finding commentary about Andrew in early golf magazines. Also, thank you to Dr. William Quirin of Adelphi University for trying to help locate the names of the New York Newspaper Golf Writers through the Metropolitan Golf Association.

The website Baseball Almanac/Baseball Fever has an online "Meet the Sport Writers" page which gives others an opportunity to see photos of the brothers and small obituary notices. The LA84 Foundation has wonderful searchable resources in the area of golf and baseball, particularly *Sporting Life*, which carried a large number of articles on the brothers.

Much praise goes to the Society for American Baseball Research (SABR) which offers resources for those looking for historical reference material. Thank you particularly Jacob Pomrenke for emailed material on William Rankin. Members of this organization have contributed tirelessly to the wealth of knowledge on the sport, and their interest has helped many researchers particularly in the area of 19th century baseball.

Preface

Will and June Rankin were famous 19th century New York sportswriters. Will's full name was William McDowell Rankin, and he was best known for his work on the *Brooklyn Daily Eagle* and as the baseball editor of the New York *Clipper* during the 1880s. However, he actually wrote for a very long list of newspapers and magazines over a much longer span of time. He was an authority on baseball, untangling many tricky questions sent into newspapers about particular plays or historic games. His knowledge of the game began in the mid–1860s to early 1870s when he played for clubs in Rockland County, New York, first as an amateur and then as a semi-pro catcher. He also was the first official scorer serving the National League and the New York Mutuals in 1876. Later he was scorer for the Brooklyn Club (Dodgers) at their inception.

His brother, June, was named Andrew Brown Rankin V. He was best known as baseball editor of the New York *Sunday Mercury* and the New York *Herald* in the 1880s, however he also wrote over a longer span of time and for a number of newspapers and journals as well. He had played baseball on the same clubs with his brother first as a pitcher and second baseman, and also in left field. June wrote two baseball books and three sports newspapers. He also played on the New York Reporters Base Ball Club. June served the New York Metropolitans and New York Giants as scorer at their inceptions. Following the Baseball Wars between the National League and Players League, June covered boxing as it emerged as a gentleman's sport and golf as it emerged in America through the development of organizations like the USGA. June played on the New York Newspaper Men's Golf Club as well.

Together, the Rankin brothers covered sports from 1870 to 1930. They left volumes of material in print documenting the evolution of many sports during the post–Civil War period. These men are members of my family. June was my maternal great-grandfather. When I was a child in the 1950s, I heard stories about Jun or June, short for Junior. We had photos of him alone and with his family. We had photos of a young Will Rankin. My grandfather used to say that they were both celebrities in their day. However, I did not really discover the full details of their lives until I reached adulthood and took on the mantle of family genealogist, a mantle begun by their sisters. Few even knew they had sisters, yet in the family the sisters were powerful forces because they raised my grandfather.

The project of putting a book together began after writing a chapter on June and Will's father, Andrew Nerva Rankin, Esq., for the Chambersburg Historical Society for a Civil War anniversary journal. He had been a justice of the peace, editor and owner of the *Repository and Transcript* newspaper, an abolitionist, and a community organizer during the war. I began looking seriously at the two sons who had been larger-than-life characters in the 1880s, particularly in the world of baseball. Meeting ancestors through newspaper commentary is always a little strange, yet some of the characteristics exhibited in their comments are still found in the family line today, particularly a love of history, writing, and community involvement. It was a gift to find so much material still in existence, which is one of the benefits of working with newspaper columnists.

The initial launch of the project actually came after I asked the question of those doing the SABR Baseball Biographies Project, "Has a biography been written on the lives of William and Andrew Rankin?" The immediate email responses I received from people like Frank Ceresi, Dan O'Brien, and John Thorn, with attachments, encouraged me to write the book. The warmth with which I was received, and the rapid responses to my somewhat innocent questions, was truly touching. Their willingness to help direct a person new in their area of expertise shows the type of people who love writing about the early game. I am also a member of SABR. I am especially grateful to John Thorn for his gift to baseball history in his writing.

As I began to write, I did find current authors mentioning the brothers, but a few confused one brother for the other in listing things they did or said, and some had no idea that a quote from a newspaper at a given time might actually have come from one of them. Editors usually wrote copy, and both wrote for organizations like the *Associated Press* and early *United Press*. Andrew often was blurred into William, and nobody seemed to know the list of things that each had done in the world of sports, or their full list of publications. They also did not know that they had played baseball and had been official scorers for the early New York and Brooklyn clubs. Many old time reporters simply referred to them as "the Rankin brothers from New York," confident that everyone knew them.

It is my hope that the reader sees the real-life men behind the articles and statistics. The title of the book is really a little misleading in just focusing on sports, though that was surely what they did, because their lives also reflected the sweeping changes happening within the United States following the Civil War. They were from an American family, and reflected the world around them as they moved from candlelight and horse and buggy to electric light and first flight. June and Will were men set within a time period, experiencing the pains of the nation and recording the events of the day as they lived their lives and raised their families. Baseball, and other sports, became a way of life for them in those early years, and they helped America feel part of the joy of the game.

ONE

Family Origins (1715–1859)

Baseball has been called America's national sport. It is difficult to imagine a time without baseball, and it is equally difficult to imagine the game in its beginning stages in simple fields and ballparks without slick advertising. Most people are accustomed to watching the game live or televised and are not dependent upon reading about it in print or trying to think out the innings in the mind's eye while looking at teletype or a scoreboard posted over a newspaper office. The popularity of the sport increased over time, but it was largely due to the coverage of games printed in the post–Civil War newspapers. The faithful recording of events and statistics by unsung heroes helped Americans feel as though they were part of the game while carrying out their daily lives during the Industrial Revolution with its long days and low wages.

Two journalist brothers became legends in their day as they recorded the faltering beginnings of the sport on ink-pressed paper. There were no instant replays to double check a call, no typewriters, no telephones or electric lights for that matter, when they began to write. It was simply a man writing what he saw, or what another could remember to tell him, and then delivering the material by hand, or sending it by telegraph, to the paper in question. William McDowell "Will" Rankin, and his brother, Andrew Brown "Jun" or "June" Rankin V, were two men sitting by the sidelines keeping track of the game at a time when the nation was trying to recover from the emotional damage done during the Civil War. They were both tied to the struggles in the founding of America in many ways.

Will was born on May 20, 1849, in Greencastle, Franklin County, Pennsylvania. His brother, June, was born on September 20, 1851, in nearby Welsh Run. Both brothers were sandwiched between two older sisters, and two younger sisters. All the sisters outlived William, and the two younger ones outlived Andrew. The sisters were the first genealogists in the family and left little details that they had discovered about their family of origin.

Their family foundations within Franklin County, Pennsylvania, went all the way back to the early 1700s. On their mother's side, Elizabeth McDowell Rankin, they were related to founding family William and Mary Irvine McDowell. William was born in 1680 and left Ulster, Northern Ireland, with other Ulster-Scots in 1715, under a series of persecutions instituted by the British. The plantations in Ulster, settled by both the Scottish and English, had produced excellent linen and woolen products. The British passed laws forbidding the exportation of those products to the colonies, and later the importation of products from the colonies to Ulster, thereby suppressing their competition. Rents were also raised on tenants.

The Test Acts of 1673 and 1678 had forced subjects of the crown to take Communion in the way of the Anglican Church, using the *Book of Common Prayer*. Subjects were to denounce all other forms in order to be able to take public office, a move aimed particularly at Roman Catholics, dissenting Protestants (into which the Scotch Presbyterians fell), and Jews (who were a small minority). The Presbyterians held to the Bible with their *Westminster Confession of Faith and Catechisms*. Presbyterian ministers were driven out, and many Scots were martyred as they resisted during the enforcement of the acts. The Test Acts would not be repealed until 1828. Also, Scotland and England had been two separate countries. The British passed the Act of Union of 1707 to create a Great Britain. Politics and religion were seen as one. The Presbyterian faith was built on representative democracy, gathered into assemblies with self-rule. The Anglican Church had a bishop structure, which worked well with a king. The two styles of church government did not work well together, especially because the Reformed faith sought to do away with a bishop structure with power being in the hands of just one person.

A quarter of a million Ulster-Scots migrated in five waves to the American colonies, often following their pastors, between 1717 and 1718, 1725 and 1729, 1740 and 1741, 1754 and 1755, and 1771 and 1775. Most of the Scottish entered America through one of three ports in Philadelphia and Chester, Pennsylvania; or New Castle, Delaware.[1] William settled first in Chester, Pennsylvania, seeking to obtain religious freedom as a Presbyterian, and also seeking economic prosperity. He arrived right before the first wave of Ulster-Scots.

William McDowell moved his wife and 11 children to the Cumberland Valley in 1735 to Peters Township in what would be Franklin County, Pennsylvania. Scottish families often had ten or more children. It was quite common. The Cumberland Valley lay next to the Appalachian Mountains. The McDowells settled at the foot of Mt. Parnell, on the banks of the Conococheague Creek, after obtaining a land warrant for 800 acres from William Penn's heirs. It was frontier country at the time; very hostile and dangerous.

They cleared the land and farmed on the now famous McDowell Road, site of McDowell's Fort (1753–1754), which was built by William's son John. William McDowell was a Covenanter Presbyterian, which was the more conservative branch, believing in the biblical role of elders governing not only the church, but the community as well. This was similar to the Puritans in New England and Dutch in New Netherlands. All based their community structures on John Calvin's system used in Geneva, Switzerland. The church was to speak in the public square. William, after fleeing to Wright's Ferry from a American Indian attack, died and was buried at Donegal Church in Lancaster County.

John McDowell built a mill on the corner of the family property. It was a rude log construction and became an enclosed fort with a two-story log house thirty yards from the mill. The house was built with many portholes in it to use for defense. It was named Fort McDowell. It became part of a "Plan for the Defense of the Frontier of Cumberland County," which was issued in 1754 for Colonel John Armstrong. The fort was patrolled daily with a night watch set in place. John's mill at the time was considered the most important pass and the most exposed. It was one in a string of forts used by the British to protect settlers from American Indians and wild animals during the French and Indian War. The Cumberland Valley saw quite a bit of bloodshed during this period. The natives were largely Iroquois, Lenape and Shawnee. The McDowells were said to have learned the American Indian dialect which they reported was not difficult.

Fort McDowell served as a supply post for the British before Fort Loudon was built a few miles north.[2] It stored munitions for General Braddock's expedition against Fort Duquesne and was considered a principal magazine by Sir John Sinclair, quartermaster general under Braddock. Wounded soldiers used it as shelter after the failed mission. It also served as a place where the British enlisted 300 provincials to destroy Kittanning, the American Indian town in the upper Ohio Valley. Some of those fighting with the British in those battles would later enlist to fight against them during the Revolutionary War, officers Hugh Mercer and John Steel being among them. The fort was still in place when Will and June were children, but owned privately. Nothing remains of the fort now except a historical marker, but the land is still sweeping farmland with a beautiful view of the mountain. A stone monument was dedicated there October 5, 1916, by the Enoch Brown Association.

It was a strategic place connecting the British military road from Pennsylvania to the Braddock Road. General Braddock had demanded that the provincial government enlarge the bridle path into a road suitable for wagons, resulting in its being named Braddock Road. It extended from the McDowell mill to the three forks of the Youghiogheny River, a tributary of the Monongahela River. The river was used by the military as well.

Later, the McDowells joined the patriots in fighting against the British, first during the Revolutionary War and then the War of 1812. Elizabeth's grandfather was the famous patriot Nathan McDowell who served as a private from July 29, 1777 to 1778 and in 1780, under Captains James and Samuel Patton. He was 19 years old when he first fought in the Revolutionary War under Philadelphia-born General Josiah Harmar (1753–1813). After the war, he was an ensign in Colonel Josiah Harmar's Regiment of the Western Frontier.[3] President George Washington sent Harmar's Regiment into the Northwest Territory to subdue American Indians. In 1785 Nathan distinguished himself in one of the conflicts. Harmar, however, was ultimately defeated. Nathan had also been one of those who signed the petition to form Franklin County, Pennsylvania, in July 1784, the year slavery was outlawed in Pennsylvania, with the county seat at Chambersburg. McDowells would serve as attorneys and judges within the community.

Most able-bodied men would continue to serve in the militia following the Revolutionary War with some placed as officers, commissioned to hold regular encampments and muster days. Residents were to bring their rifles. If they did not have one, they were to bring a cornstalk with which to practice. They gained the name "cornstalk militia" because of this. Will and June's paternal grandfather would serve as an officer in the militia.

On Will and June's father's side, Nathaniel Rankin was born in 1765 in Ulster, Northern Ireland, and left from Belfast as a young lad. In the 1790 census, the first census in the newly formed United States of America, he was living in Greencastle (Green Castle), Pennsylvania, and by 1793 he had a post office box in Chambersburg.[4] Chambersburg had the first post office in Franklin County, which had only opened in June 1790. From Chambersburg, mail was distributed on horseback to spokes in Shippensburg, Greencastle, and Mercersburg and then from Mercersburg to Hagerstown. It took a full week to run the delivery system. Initially, Chambersburg was an enclosed fort, but by 1764 the community was laid out and houses built.

Nathaniel was married to Ann Brown, who had been born in Ulster in 1768 and also came to Pennsylvania as a young child. Her father had purchased land in Westmoreland County, Pennsylvania, and then sent for the family to join him, but unfortunately he died on the way to the Baltimore port. Ann's mother brought the children to Mercersburg where they lived with friends.[5] A widow Brown is on the 1786 Taxable List for Peters Township in Mercersburg.

Greencastle was a section within Antrim Township, south of Chambersburg, which had 60 houses built on the 246 lots by 1794, mostly clustered on Baltimore and Carlisle streets, called pikes, radiating north and south, and east and west with the town square in the center. The population at that time was about 400 people. The roads crossing it were called chief roads in the area, connecting north with Chambersburg; south with Maryland, Virginia, Washington, D.C., and Baltimore, Maryland; west with Pittsburgh; and east with Harrisburg and Philadelphia. Pack horses loaded with goods and supplies continually made their way past the newly established homesteads. Later, the son of Nathaniel and Ann Rankin would have a house on Carlisle Street during the Civil War, just two houses north of the town square on the eastern side. His son lived next door within the same block. It would not be too far a stretch to believe that one of the two houses on Carlisle Street had been Nathaniel's original plot. Most of those living in Greencastle proper farmed acreage in outer Antrim Township, had trades, or did both.

George Washington stayed in Chambersburg and passed through Greencastle during the Whiskey Rebellion, which had begun in 1791 when taxes were placed on whiskey. This climaxed in 1794. The local residents, mostly Scotch-Irish and German, did not receive the news well, especially since many of them had stills on their farms. There was no temperance movement. Washington arrived from Philadelphia on October 11 or 12, 1794, with General Henry Knox, secretary of war; General Alexander Hamilton, secretary of the treasury; Judge Richard Peters; and others. Commissioners eventually negotiated a resolution. Nathaniel and Ann Rankin were living in the small town when the events were happening. It would have been hard to have missed the disquieted mob and presidential entourage while living on the main road Washington used to return to Virginia. He also stopped in the town center, and they lived right by the town square.

Ann Rankin's father was cousin to Enoch Brown, the schoolteacher who had been clubbed, scalped and murdered, along with eleven of his students with one living, by three American Indians following Braddock's defeat during the French and Indian War. This was during the Pontiac Rebellion on July 26, 1764. It was known as the Enoch Brown Incident. The teacher tried to give himself in place of the students as the intruders pushed their way into the log schoolhouse, but he lost his life as did eight boys and two girls. The act perpetrated by the warriors was later denounced by their tribal elders. The bodies of the victims were quickly buried in a large box by the area settlers who were horrified by the brutality of the scene. Later on August 4, 1843, an expedition was launched to find the spot. It was led by Will and June's grandfather, Andrew Brown Rankin III, Esq. Their father, a young man at the time, was also present. The group found the shallow grave in the woods, which verified the written accounts. Later, a small park and monument were dedicated there, on August 6, 1885. Andrew Nerva Rankin attended that service. The park is now known as Enoch Brown Park in Antrim, Pennsylvania.[6]

Andrew Brown Rankin III, Esq., born 1791, was the paternal grandfather of Will and June. Andrew III enlisted to fight in the War of 1812 after Washington, D.C., was burned by the British. His unit, under Captain Andrew Robson, was formed in 1814 to defend Baltimore, but they did not see action.[7] Andrew later served as major (later colonel) in the Second Battalion, 6th Regiment of the Militia of the Commonwealth of Pennsylvania in the 2nd Brigade of the 11th Division of men from Cumberland, Perry and Franklin counties during the period between the War of 1812 and the Civil War. Little is known about the work of the militia during this period, other than simple practice drills with community residents. State militias would become the foundation for the National Guard.

Andrew III then served as justice of the peace in Antrim and Greencastle with records showing him in that position as early as 1821.[8] He was repeatedly elected, serving a total of 50 years. Andrew III was a saddler by trade and maintained his business until retirement. People living in the early 1800s usually had a trade while serving in public office. In addition, he served on just about every committee in the community, including as the president of the Mercersburg, Greencastle and Waynesboro Turnpike Company. The pike was forty-two miles in length. Andrew III was a member of the Whig Party initially, George Washington's party, and then a member in the newly formed Republican Party. Andrew III had two properties: one was a farm west of the center of Greencastle. It was listed on an 1858 county map. The other property was by the town square, as per a Civil War map. It may have been used as the legal office by Andrew. That one may have originally been his father's property.

Andrew III married Margaret Ritchey, daughter of John Ritchey and Lady Elizabeth Acheson, of the Market Hill, Northern Ireland, Acheson family. Archibald Acheson had been the Earl of Gosford Castle, a near-royal. John was Elizabeth's tutor in Ulster, and a marriage was not supported by her father who deemed "the Scotch man" not desirable. She was close to 17, and John was much older. She was given 100 pounds sterling from her father but lost her part of the inheritance. The Ritcheys moved first to Belfast and then traveled to America, settling in Franklin County, Pennsylvania, in 1790. There were other Ritcheys already in the area, engaged in commercial businesses and serving in various offices. One of those Ritcheys helped sell property owned by George Washington's widow. The property was purchased by a McDowell. Those Ritcheys all claimed to have come from the Glassdrummond

Ritchey estate in Southern Armagh, Northern Ireland. It is not known if John Ritchey came from the same estate. Other Achesons also would leave Armagh for this particular area as members of a parallel line to Archibald Acheson. The Rankin family was insistent that Elizabeth was the daughter of Archibald Acheson, though the daughter of Civil War hero Colonel John Lindsay Ritchey stated that Elizabeth was daughter of Thomas, the son of Archibald. No proof of either was ever presented. It was simply stated as fact. The belief that this Rankin family was directly related to Archibald Acheson would later imprison the sisters of Will and June, and keep them isolated.

Andrew Brown Rankin III, Esq., and Margaret Ritchey Rankin had ten children. The first daughter, Ann Brown Rankin, married an attorney and member of Congress, David F. Robinson, Esq., D.F. for short. The first son, William Ritchey Rankin, was a lawyer who for a time was in partnership with D.F. and then became a famous Ohio criminal attorney and judge. Elizabeth Acheson Rankin married William Fleming from another founding family. Andrew Brown Rankin IV, father of Will and June, was born fourth. Margaret Jane Rankin married the minister's son, John Ruthrauff. Edmund Davidson Rankin married Adeline Reed and lived next door to Andrew III. Martha Fisher Rankin married Dr. M.F. Robinson, the brother of D.F. John and Mary died as teenagers on the same day, which may have been from an illness, and then another John was born.

The county was initially serviced with Concord stagecoaches, which ran from Chambersburg to Pittsburg, beginning in 1804. But, the railroad would make that mode of travel unnecessary. Chambersburg had three railroad lines running through it. The Cumberland Valley Railroad was established in 1831 and opened between Harrisburg to Carlisle and by 1837 connected to Chambersburg. The company took over the old Franklin Railroad. The Mont Alto Railroad and Southern Pennsylvania Railroad were the other two companies functioning in that town, making the county seat a place of daily activity. This strength in transportation would later prove a source of problems.

Andrew Nerva Rankin, Esq., born in 1821, was the father of Will and June. He was initially named Andrew Brown Rankin IV, but he legally changed his middle name in adult years to reflect an unknown man he admired. He was later justice of the peace in Antrim and Greencastle, served on just about every committee like his father, and was eventually the president of the same turnpike company. He also was a founding member of the Independent Order of Odd Fellows, Conococheaque Lodge, Number 228. It was organized in 1848 in Chambersburg. The Odd Fellows were given the name in 17th century England due to their willingness to band together to give aid to those in need, without recognition. Apparently, it was considered odd to care for others at the time. The lodge believed in a supreme being and love and truth while working within local communities. During the Civil War their lodge became a hospital for the Union soldiers.

Andrew Nerva Rankin purchased the Republican Chambersburg Repository and Transcript newspaper in 1859 (though some papers list him as owning it as early as 1856, which may be a better date).[9] He wrote strong pro–Union, anti-slavery texts until 1863 when he sold the paper. He was aggressive in his commentary, which was targeted at his divided white community, the opposing political party, his own waffling political party, and southern slave owners in general. All of this made him a number of enemies as he often used inflammatory language, which did not always show sensitivity.[10] His focus seemed to be always on winning an argument, hurling back like language, and not on being nice, per se, or politically correct. It served him well in the legal field.

Two

The Horror of the Civil War (1849–1865)

Franklin County, Pennsylvania, is situated just north of the Mason-Dixon Line. It bordered Maryland and West Virginia to the south and was close to the northern border of Virginia. Towns like Greencastle, where Nathanial and Andrew Brown Rankin III lived, touched the Mason-Dixon Line at their southern edges. Andrew III lived, or had an office, on the eastern side of Carlisle Street, just two houses north of the town square. It was a major north-south road leading to Chambersburg in one direction and Maryland in the other. Since Andrew III and later Andrew Nerva Rankin (IV) both served as justice of the peace in Greencastle and Antrim, they both dealt with the continual issue of slavery, escaped slaves and aggressive bounty hunters. Franklin County was ranked number five in the number of free blacks in the country.[1] According to the census, Andrew III also had an African American woman working for him as a housekeeper who had been born in Maryland. She most likely had been born into slavery. In Pennsylvania, she was a free black earning a living, but danger for her was only a few miles away.

Once married, Andrew Nerva Rankin eventually moved his family a few miles north of Greencastle to Chambersburg. Chambersburg was 14½ miles north of the Mason-Dixon Line. Andrew Nerva and his wife, Elizabeth, had two older daughters: Mary Adella, called Adda, born in 1844, and Margaret Virginia, called Margie, born in 1846 in Greencastle. Adda, with her dark brown hair, took a liking to elocution and doing recitations; after all her father was forever campaigning during her youth and invented an Annunciator. Margie, however, was deaf and fairer in complexion. Deafness and loss of hearing would surface in the family line from time to time.

William McDowell Rankin, called Will, was born May 20, 1849, in Greencastle, and Andrew Brown Rankin V, called June, was born in nearby

Welsh Run on September 20, 1851. At this time, most births were done at home, or in a neighbor's home. Some of the births were assisted by a family member and some by a local physician. Will was named not only after his uncle William Rankin, but also after his grandfather William McDowell, and the series of William McDowells before him dating back to at least the late 1600s. There were so many Andrews in the family, however, that each ended up with a different nickname and number to distinguish one from the other. The formal name Andrew was used for Andrew III; A. Nerva or Andrew N. was used for Andrew IV; Jun or June — short for Junior — was used for Andrew V; and later Andrew VI would be Drew; and Andrew VII would be Andy.

In 1852, Andrew Nerva Rankin (IV) helped draft the Franklin County Agricultural Society constitution, and served on the county executive committee as corresponding secretary. The community was largely an agricultural community but also had industrial workers and tradesmen. Andrew Nerva was involved in the Farmers and Mechanics Industrial Association of Franklin County as well.[2] This naturally fed into his interest in inventing and things mechanical. He began securing patents when William was three and June was one. His patents in Pennsylvania tended to deal with things used in law enforcement, perhaps after watching what frustrated his father and oldest brother in their work. He was admitted to the Pennsylvania Bar on April 14, 1852.

The family was complete with the birth of two younger daughters: Sarah Elizabeth, called Lizzie, born in 1853, and Arie Alcesta, called Etta, born in 1858. Lizzie took a

Andrew Nerva Rankin, Esq., and Elizabeth McDowell Rankin were the parents of William and Andrew Rankin. Andrew Nerva, pictured, served as justice of the peace in Greencastle and Antrim, Pennsylvania. He was the owner and editor of the Chambersburg *Repository and Transcript* from 1856/1859 to 1863. He was also an inventor and held numerous patents (photographgraph provided by Lois Rankin Prior. Used by permission, Rankin Family Archives).

liking to dance; interpretive and formal, not ballet. Etta loved music, especially the piano. William and June, with four sisters, became each other's playmate. All the children were encouraged to be articulate, well educated, and very strong willed.

Andrew Nerva Rankin became the owner and editor of the *Repository and Transcript* newspaper in Chambersburg, from 1856 to 1863. The paper was located in a building on the town square which was adjacent to the 1843 Franklin County Courthouse.[3] The square was actually called The Diamond. He wrote abolitionist commentary and aggressively attacked the Confederate states. The *Repository and Transcript,* in its early stages, had been the Chambersburg *Gazette*, the paper that recorded Nathaniel Rankin as having a post office box in 1793. The paper actually began on July 14, 1790, as *The Western Advertiser and Chambersburg Weekly* on July 14, 1790. It became the Chambersburg *Gazette* on September 12, 1793; Franklin *Repository* on April 25, 1796; *Repository and Whig* in the 1840s when post riders were hired by the paper to deliver it weekly to residents; the Franklin *Intelligencer* on July 4, 1849; the *Repository and Transcript* on July 5, 1853, and had that name during Andrew's term of ownership. It would return to the Franklin *Repository* title when he sold it in 1863; and in 1869 it took on the title *Public Opinion* and is still in print under that name.[4] They have an old 1800s printing press in their lobby. The paper is currently owned by a partnership between Gannett and MediaNews Group.

Andrew Nerva was an emotional and sometimes snippy writer. He had a nemesis: the editor of the Democratic *Valley Spirit* newspaper in town, which was pro–South. The two became quite personal in their commentary and were polar opposites in politics. There was a constant volley in print. Whenever Andrew and his friends left on a political rally by train, the *Valley Spirit* editor wrote that the people should rejoice because he was gone for a while. These two papers chronicled the development of the Republican and Democratic parties and the mindset of people in this mid–1800s era.

Andrew Nerva Rankin actually invited Frederick Douglass to speak at his paper in 1859, but found him to be too extreme in his willingness to throw out both parties if neither acted to end slavery. Andrew seemed to feel that his party was trying to do that, and may have been looking for gratitude. He did not appear to understand the full level of frustration felt by many in the African American population. This meeting at the newspaper was the same night when Douglass met with John Brown at an abandoned quarry outside of Chambersburg on August 19. John Brown, disguised as Isaac Smith, was staying in Chambersburg without anyone's knowledge. Brown, as Smith, had disguised himself as an iron mine developer while planning his action. Douglass had come to the town for that meeting and ended up speaking in town by default. Douglass tried to dissuade Brown from the Harpers Ferry Raid, which he felt was suicidal, but he failed.

In the raid, John Brown attempted to seize the United States Arsenal at Harpers Ferry, Virginia, on October 16, 1859, with twenty-one men representing both white and black, and with his sons. His plan was to take the stolen weapons and distribute them to slaves who would then be encouraged to join a battle against their slave owners. Those who took part in the raid were John Brown with his three sons Watson, Oliver and Owen; Aaron D. Stevens; Edwin and Barclay Coppie; Albert Hazlett; John E. Cook; Stuart Taylor; William Lehman; William Thompson; John Henri Kagi; Charles P. Tydd; Oliver Anderson; Jeremiah Anderson; Dolph Thompson; along with four African Americans named Dangerfield Newby, Shields Greene, John Copeland, and Lewis Leary.[5] However, they were discovered, and the United States Marines led by then–Colonel Robert E. Lee pursued them. Lieutenant J.E.B. Stuart was also part of this action. Both these men would leave scars on Chambersburg in the near future. John Brown was ultimately hanged on December 2, 1859. And Andrew Nerva Rankin was maliciously accused of being part of that event by the *Valley Spirit* newspaper's editor, which he emphatically denied in his paper. He thoroughly denounced the raid, which he knew nothing about. Connecticut-born John Brown was not related to the Browns in the Rankin family in any way.

Though Andrew did not seem to fully understand the frustration expressed by Frederick Douglass at the time of his meeting, and did not show sensitivity to his feelings, Andrew did become increasingly swept into the issues involved in abolition. The meeting, though perhaps shocking for Andrew, may have served to open his eyes to the severity of the situation, and during 1859 Andrew went on to write about the illegal importation of slaves in Savannah, the foolishness of a law on the books in the South giving more jail time to those assisting slaves in escape than those committing murder, and other issues like hangings of blacks on trumped up charges. These things might show a slow evolution in his thinking which might have been due to the impact made upon him by his uncomfortable encounter with Douglass.

Though aggressively anti-slavery, Andrew Nerva Rankin had often appeared to miss sensitivity to African Americans in his columns due to his focus on using mocking language to correct the white slave owners a few miles south in the land of the lash, and he would chide members of both political parties for waffling and being inconsistent, while sometimes being inconsistent himself. It appears that he assumed his audience was made of white, likeminded people who saw slavery as immoral and evil. Though he might not

Two. The Horror of the Civil War (1849–1865)　　　　17

have fully understood what equality could mean for African Americans, he did put his life in danger by his commentary in print, and he slowly moved from verbal activism to physical activism in the abolitionism movement.

In May 1860, he wrote on the need for a Republican president to encourage southerners to regain their birthright by throwing off the "Slave Oligarchy." In July, he wrote against importing slavery into the new territories. In August, he wrote about the debasing nature of slavery even on slave owners, and called it "heathenish degradation," wondering how a Christian could ever deliberately refrain from using everything in their power to stop it. He went on to write that the only way it would end effectively would be to make it against the law.[6]

That year, Andrew Nerva Rankin helped form a branch of, and was a member of, the paramilitary, pro–Union Wide Awakes. The Wide Awakes (or Know Nothing movement) supported Abraham Lincoln and were considered "well drilled," and a type of "political police" which escorted "party speakers" and preserved "order at public meetings."[7] The county had 100 men total in the Wide Awakes movement, many of them young.[8] They were structured with captains and lieutenants and often referred to as a type of militia as they drilled with their lanterns on poles. Andrew Nerva Rankin accompanied, fully armed and in black cap with cape, political speakers to their engagements along the northern border states for their protection. Many speakers had been harassed and mauled by the locals. He often traveled with them in parties by train. Some historians have actually pointed to the rallies created by the larger Wide Awakes organization as being a major contributor to pushing the country towards the Civil War. Southerners, in general, feared them. Groups like the Wide Awakes were among the first volunteers in the Union Army when war was declared.

Andrew Nerva also campaigned heavily for Lincoln and became a community activist for his election, raising a Lincoln Pole outside the newspaper office. The raising of Liberty Poles dated back to the Revolutionary War. This one was described as being "over 100 feet in height, topped with a small streamer of red, white and blue; 12 feet from the top was a blue streamer with the names of Lincoln, Hamlin and Curtin in white letters. 12 feet lower was the American flag."[9] Lincoln was elected in the North on November 6 of that year. The town was uneasy at this time with political conversations the norm. The majority of the town had voted for Lincoln, but a large percentage had not. William was 11 and June was 9.

Chambersburg was organized in grid blocks. It had 4700 residents radiating out from the town center. The Rankin family, in the 1860 census, was living next door to the A.H. McCullough family. The Rankins had six children and the McCullough family had four girls, though they were mostly teenagers, the youngest being close in age to Andrew Nerva's oldest daughter, Adda. A.H. was the general ticket agent for the Cumberland Valley Railroad and in the same agricultural society as Andrew. Chambersburg had three railroad lines running through it, making it a good communication center. The Cumberland Valley line ran from Harrisburg to Chambersburg; then to Hagerstown, Maryland; and on into the Shenandoah Valley ending in Winchester, Virginia. McCullough and Rankin also shared a background in law, were members of the same political party, and Presbyterians.

A.H. McCullough was married to Elizabeth Brown, but it is unknown if she was related to Andrew's grandmother. However, they do have the same family number on the census. A.H.'s father had been editor of the Franklin *Repository* in the early 1800s. Also, during the July 26, 1764, Enoch Brown Incident, one of the boys who had been scalped, but lived, was a very young Archibald "Archie" McCullough, which may have tied their families back many generations. Other McCullough children had also been kidnapped from their home by five Delaware Indians, who adopted them, prior to that incident. They were able to relate the American Indian side of the story with the tribal elders condemning the deed. The census shows the Rankin family doing well in Chambersburg. Andrew Nerva's real estate was valued at $9,000 and his personal net worth was $7,000. It is hard to tell if he gained any income from his inventions, but he did appear to have a high standing within the community. His paper made frequent contributions to community causes, so it must have had success in its circulation.

During the boyhood of Will and June, it is unknown if they were exposed to ball games like round town ball, Philadelphia town ball, or bandy wicket, all of which had been played in Pennsylvania before the Civil War. Their father did travel extensively within the state. He did receive newspapers from the surrounding cities, especially Philadelphia and New York, though his focus was on political coverage. The telegraph in town also linked to New York City. The New York Knickerbockers had been formed in September 1845, and a host of New York City, Brooklyn, Long Island, and New Jersey clubs joined suit from 1854 through 1857. Philadelphia's Olympic club had switched from townball and cricket to the New York style of baseball in 1859 and Philadelphia's Athletics club switched in April 1860,[10] however, most of the material written about the brothers points to their experiencing baseball in New York.

Will and June were both very athletic and would likely have known the game of cricket, which was widely played in America at the time. The Chambersburg area was known for good trout fishing, hunting, and hiking along

Two. The Horror of the Civil War (1849–1865)

the Appalachian Trail, and children generally played by the Conococheague Creek, or the Conegogig Creek by the Great Falling Spring. The Conococheague feeds into the Potomac River. Perhaps the brothers joined their peers in those activities, though children generally did chores and assisted parents in their daily duties. There were reports of June being an excellent ice skater later in life which might have related to a childhood activity in the winter. One of the first baseball games played in Franklin County was played in 1867 between the Greencastle Kangaroos and Waynesboro First Nationals.[11] The family, however, had moved out of state by then. It does not seem that the members of the community had much opportunity to play ball locally during the Civil War, since so many major battles and skirmishes were fought there.

The Rankin children attended the Chambersburg school. The only one present at the time was the King Street School House which had been built in 1857. It was a three-story building with nine classrooms and four recitation rooms. It may have been a Latin-based education with subjects like English grammar, arithmetic, history, geography, elocution, and composition. Memorization would play a large part in the education with the recitation of verses, dates in history, spelling, mathematics and such. The school employed thirteen teachers and had 185 girls and 344 boys attending. The school kept the boys and girls separate. There were two separate primary classes for each gender; two intermediate classes for each gender; one first grammar class for boys; one second grammar for boys; and one high school for boys (perhaps what we think of as junior high school). It is difficult to trace where the girls went once they completed intermediate class, but many may have continued their studies privately or at home. The common belief was that men would pursue a career and women would keep house. However, the Rankins did encourage their girls to continue to learn. By 1877 a school would be built in town for girls to further their education, and in 1870 a women's college was established in the county. Nearly all the children in the county attended free public school. It was paid for through the tax structure. There were 177 public schools in the county with 8500 pupils.[12]

While Will and June were in their pre-teen years, the Civil War took over community life. A number of town members had been engaged in the Underground Railroad system, assisting slaves in their escape to Canada. It was illegal to harbor and aid fugitive slaves according to an Act of Congress put in place in 1850. And, some members of the community returned escaped slaves to bounty hunters, and there was a constant tension between these two forces; one side feeling slavery was evil and the other believing in just leaving things as they were. Things began to intensify after 1861 when news circulated about Fort Sumter being fired upon. At the town meeting on April 17, the focus was on the war and the need for enlistment from the community, in compliance with Lincoln's call for soldiers. Andrew Nerva Rankin was on the three-man committee ensuring that every soldier had a pocket Bible. He also printed a call to arms in his paper with the duty of Americans to maintain the Constitution and the Union, with the ending words, "READY, AIM, FIRE."[13]

Will and June had begun to learn the printing trade, on old printing presses, from their father in those early years. One might wonder what table conversations would have been like under an emotional father, incensed by the national issues around him. His printed commentary was filled with frustration; the table conversation must have carried some of the same passion. Mrs. Rankin was also known to be a person of definite opinions.[14] The Rankin women were encouraged to think, and did so freely.

In 1862 Andrew Nerva Rankin was elected justice of the peace in Greencastle and Antrim to serve for seven years while living in Chambersburg. Following the Battle of Antietam that year, Chambersburg served as a supply center and hospital for the Union Army. The army used the meeting lodge of the Odd Fellows as a hospital room and also used the school. Large numbers of wounded soldiers were shipped to Chambersburg. Their injuries were said to be awful with many maimed and suffering from gunpowder wounds. The Ladies Aid Society of the county visited the hospital each day. Those who died without family to claim them were buried in the local cemetery. Union soldiers also took area horses, saddles and bridles, and people were still complaining in 1878 that they had never been paid.[15]

Will and June could not have missed the activity and the walking wounded in a town as small as Chambersburg. Andrew Nerva Rankin often attended meetings and rallies with officers in the army. He also led prayer meetings for the Union at local churches. Their family was emotionally involved in the preservation of the Union. The town had a relay system set in place with Greencastle to watch for Confederate advances across the Mason-Dixon Line. Each early evening a rider would come back with news. The courthouse bell would ring to warn people if danger was present. The courthouse was adjacent to Andrew Nerva Rankin's newspaper.

That fall, the town suffered from a cavalry raid under CSA general J.E.B. Stuart. On October 9 General Stuart led 1800 Confederate cavalrymen, along with Major Pelgram's battery of 2 to 4 guns, and crossed the Potomac River near Clear Springs, Maryland. He raided Chambersburg. The Confederates had circumvented the Union Army under General McClellan.[16] Stuart's mission was to capture equipment for the Confederates, disrupt communication lines, take parts of the B&O Railroad at Chambersburg, and destroy parts of the C&O Canal. October 10 Stuart captured the Federal Arsenal at Chambersburg and took clothing, munitions and supplies. He cut telegraph wires and then burned the arsenal before heading back to Hagerstown, down the Old Chambersburg Pike (Route 30).

In 1863, Will was 14. He entered the Chambersburg Academy.[17] The academy was somewhat integrated with a handful of African American students. This was most likely what we would consider a high school. Andrew Nerva Rankin sold the *Repository and Transcript* that year to his friend, with the *Valley Spirit* newspaper seeming quite happy and making mention of a type of "nervous breakdown." Andrew Nerva Rankin proceeded to concentrate on being the justice of the peace, though he still wrote commentary for the paper. He also served as the president of the Mercersburg, Greencastle, and Waynesboro Turnpike Association, which had been completed in 1837. That road connected Pittsburg with Baltimore, Maryland. Pikes like this one encouraged numerous travelers carrying wares, moving west, and needing supplies and lodging. Chambersburg obliged, and news filtered through Andrew Nerva Rankin's contacts and political gatherings with Union officers. Unfortunately, the better roads also were convenient for military advances.

In June of that year, 65,000 Confederate soldiers led by General Robert E. Lee camped in Chambersburg, just prior to the battle at Gettysburg. Lee chose a local farm for his headquarters. Confederate soldiers took horses, wagons, and grain from local farms.[18] June 15 Brigadier General Albert G. Jenkins was ordered to destroy the Cumberland Valley Railroad property, resulting in the burning of their building in Chambersburg which had served to supply the Union troops in the Shenandoah Valley. He also tore up five miles of the Franklin Railroad and burned the bridge to Scotland, Pennsylvania. July 1–3, 1863, the famous Gettysburg battle was waged, just a few miles east of the town with great loss of life. The Battle of Gettysburg was the largest battle of the Civil War and reports said that the cannon fire could be heard all the way to Pittsburg. Chambersburg, much closer, also heard the constant volley. Major General George Gordon Meade led the Union Army of the Potomac with 85,000 men. General Robert Edward Lee led the Confederate Army of Northern Virginia with 75,000. There were 23,049 Union casualties and 28,000 Confederate casualties. At the conclusion of the battle, a combined group of over 7,000 men died.

Lee's retreat to Virginia began west of the town of Chambersburg and through Greencastle with an 18-mile-long train of cavalry and wagons carrying the wounded. The townspeople of Greencastle attacked the wagon train with axes and hatchets on their way, disabling wagons before the cavalry gave chase. Months later, following the battle, the family of Andrew Nerva Rankin attended Lincoln's November 19 Gettysburg Address at the inauguration of the cemetery. The family was initially disappointed that the message was so short. The battle had been an emotionally disturbing event. But later, when they read the full text in the newspaper, they conceded that it was indeed a powerful message.[19] Will was 14 and June was 12.

Andrew Nerva's next patent, published in 1863, was the Excelsior Perpetual Almanac, which was acknowledged by an Act of Congress, District Court of the United States, in and for the Eastern District of Pennsylvania.[20] It listed the days of the week for every year from January 1, 1401, to December 31, 2100, all neatly in columns on one page of printed paper. By looking at the one page chart, you could tell what day of the week an event happened in the past, or look forward into the future. This interest in printed columns is reflected in the statistics later recorded by the sons in baseball and their dedication to recording accurate numerical information. The sisters would also mention days and times when recording family births, with locations and persons present. Andrew Nerva seemed to like things under a logical type of control during this stressful time, but his house was robbed, and community life was becoming messy.

Eighteen sixty-four was a turbulent year for the entire town. William was 15 and June was 13. On January 3, the draft began in Franklin County.[21] Later in the month, a fight broke out in front of the Chambersburg Post Office among troops stationed there.[22] In February, the town was complaining about drinking and rioting among the soldiers, with many wishing they would leave.[23] A number of citizens pointed to the bad behavior of soldiers from New York.[24] By mid-February, the cavalry camp was established four miles west of Chambersburg. And in April, three snowstorms hit the town within two weeks.

By the beginning of July, rumors began circulating of a Confederate invasion.[25] Many locals took their horses up into the mountains for safekeeping. A number of persons already had some of their possessions held in Philadelphia. Some of the town leaders also left. On July 30, 1864, at 5:30 A.M., Confederate artillery fired about six rounds over the city. Then, CSA Gen. John McCausland led his cavalry unit into town, having his breakfast in a local inn. The leading citizens were arrested. He demanded an unobtainable ransom of $100,000 in gold, or $500,000 in U.S. greenbacks as repayment for the destruction done by the Union forces in the Shenandoah Valley, or the town would be burned. People tried to explain to him that the bank funds had already been removed north, and were no longer in the city. Considering the fact that the town had already suffered two raids, this was deemed a prudent move. The citizens just could not believe the Confederates would actually follow through with their threat.

The Rankin family story had Confederate men also looking for both Andrew III and Andrew IV, as spies for the North, during this event.[26] Both had been political forces in the community and served in the area as justices of the peace in Greencastle and Antrim. Both also had served as presidents of one of the turnpikes. Both knew military officers in the Union Army socially. Both campaigned for Lincoln. And then, there was Andrew Nerva Rankin's writing. Facts do show that the Confederates were rounding up the city authorities and went on a search through the town to find them, and on the Confederate list of demands for the townspeople were saddles. Andrew III was a saddler until his retirement. The Rebels also sought two printers for the paper; Andrew IV knew the printing trade and was training both boys in printing. Persons with their professions *were* being sought out. The paper in question requiring printers, which was on the Confederate list, was the *Repository and Transcript*, then the Franklin *Repository*. Andrew had sold it months prior, but was still writing commentary.

The courthouse bells were rung, summoning the citizens to the square. Barrels of kerosene were rolled out with two to three placed in the courthouse. The Confederate Army proceeded to torch the town, including the building housing the newspaper. The paper lost presses, books, type, subscription lists and accounts; nothing was saved.[27] The new editors had their residences burned with Confederates under orders to let none of their personal belongings be saved.[28] *The Valley Spirit* newspaper, however, was left unharmed. The courthouse records were lost, which proved to be very difficult for locals as they tried to prove their identity and property.

By 8 A.M., soldiers rampaged, robbed and looted homes and businesses. Furniture was smashed and piled up, and then set on fire. People in the community fled for their lives from burning buildings, carrying invalids and children, and reports were later recorded of the horrific sound of multitudes of animals being burned alive.[29] No mercy was shown. In the end, over 2,000 people were left homeless. The Confederates also torched the Chambersburg Academy, the school Will attended, simply because it educated some black students.

At the time, the town was virtually defenseless with only 100 Union soldiers, under Major General Darius N. Couch, sixteen miles away in Mercersburg with only two small cannon.[30] He had sent most of his unit to Washington to reinforce that garrison. General Averill was camped near Greencastle, but he had a large force of Confederates at his front.[31] The Confederates in Chambersburg had six cannon placed on hills looking down on the town with a citizenry who were not well armed; many locals were keeping livestock hidden, and others had enlisted in the army. It was the only Northern

Chambersburg, the hometown of Will and June Rankin, suffered three Confederate raids during the Civil War. It was the only northern town to suffer destruction during the war. This is a photograph taken by Charles E. Meyer on July 30, 1864. It was originally in the Kean Archives in Philadelphia. It shows the courthouse, built in 1843, and town hall, following General McCausland's command to burn the town. Andrew Nerva Rankin, Esq., served as justice of the peace in Greencastle and Antrim and practiced law in Chambersburg. The Rankin family left Chambersburg in March 1865 (Franklin County Historical Society–Kittochtinny Archives, used by permission).

city destroyed during the Civil War, and was done as a warning. By August 25, the 201st Pennsylvania finally arrived in town to provide border defense.[32] Later in the morning when General William W. Averell of the Union Army arrived, his unit was surprised by the devastation they witnessed. They had no idea the town had been burned. Chambersburg was under a cloud of smoke, and citizens were standing in the streets in disbelief.

Two. The Horror of the Civil War (1849–1865)

On August 31, the *Repository and Transcript* requested from the citizens donations of back issues of the paper, since their copies had been burned.[33] They ran the paper in the lecture room of the Presbyterian Church until 1866. The paper ultimately survived, but Andrew Nerva Rankin's involvement with it had ended. This was the childhood of William McDowell Rankin and Andrew Brown Rankin V. They left their hometown in ashes and rubble.

THREE

New York, New York (1865–1870)

During the Civil War, the Confederates had burned the iron works owned by Thaddeus Stevens, on June 26, 1863. Stevens (1792–1868), of Pennsylvania, was a member of the House of Representatives. He was chair of the House Ways and Means Committee and a personal friend of Andrew Nerva Rankin. Stevens was actively involved in the Underground Railroad movement. Following the war, He commissioned Andrew Nerva Rankin, Esq. (IV), to go to Brooklyn, New York, in late March 1865[1] to be the manager of an organization which sent teachers south to educate the newly freed slaves. This was part of the Reconstruction process in the South. Andrew Nerva did this for seven years, until about 1872, while also being admitted to the New York State Bar and practicing law in Spring Valley, New York. The Reconstruction Acts would be formally voted in on March 2, 1867, by Congress. Andrew was functioning in Reconstruction work two years prior to that law being passed.

Andrew Nerva Rankin's obituary states that Chief Justice Salmon Portland Chase was president of the organization, and the Rev. Lyman Abbott, D.D., of Plymouth Church in Brooklyn was general secretary. Chase was an ardent abolitionist and is the one credited with putting "In God We Trust" on our dollar bills. He had served as a member of the Senate, was the U.S. secretary of the treasury in the early years of the Civil War, and chief justice of the United States. Chase Bank is named after him. The Rev. Dr. Abbott was known for addressing social and industrial problems and calling for reform.[2]

Andrew Nerva Rankin's work may have been through either one of two organizations; both interacted with each other. The Freedmen's Aid Society was founded in 1861 and was an organization with which Thaddeus Stevens was affiliated. The society had been formed by the American Missionary Association to send northern teachers into the South. The association would then provide housing for teachers and help set up the schools for children. The educational focus in the schools was largely training in teaching, nursing and other professions which would ensure an opportunity for African Americans to have skills towards self-betterment. The A.M.A. was composed at that time of Congregationalists, Methodists and Presbyterians. Their aim was to abolish slavery, educate African Americans, and promote racial equality and Christian values.

The Freedmen's Aid Society and the A.M.A. helped to found over 500 schools and colleges for African American children and youth. Among those were Berea College, Atlanta University, Fisk University, Hampton Institute, Tougaloo College, Dillard University, Talladega College, LeMoyne-Owen College, Huston-Tillotson University, Avery Normal Institute, and Howard University. Later, in the 1870s, the leadership of these institutions was turned over to leaders in the New South.

The other option might be the American Union Commission which had the Rev. Dr. Lyman Abbott as general secretary. The Rev. Dr. James P. Thompson was president. C. Thurston Chase was heavily involved in this organization. It tended to focus on both the problems of the newly freed slaves and the suffering of loyal refugees, but it also addressed the sheer poverty in the population witnessed by its representatives with so many women and children left homeless. A number of those suffering in the South had supported the Union during the war and were called the loyal refugees. Their family members had served in the Union Army, which set them up for retaliation by Confederate troops. The American Union Commission had branches in major cities like New York, which was its headquarters; Boston; Philadelphia; Baltimore; Chicago; Nashville; and Virginia. They collected and distributed food, medicine, clothing, and garden seeds to the poor in the South regardless of color, though they did turn away Southerners complaining of loss of property, meaning slaves. They also turned away those dressed in expensive clothing with furs and jewelry, encouraging them to sell those items first. The commission was a Christian organization which made "no distinctions of caste or color," and was "not political in its aim," though it would "not restore the old order" in the South. Most of the leadership was composed of clergy and attorneys.

The commission addressed issues in education, often working with the Freedman's Society and the Free School Party of the South. Education was a large problem as the South had lost nearly all its schools. The military was encouraged to release and repair the buildings which were left. Most of those with whom the commission worked could not read or write. They gave a figure of nine out of ten as being illiterate. The American Union Commission also provided information on immigration to the North for refugees, listed jobs which were available, and pricing for land.[3] New York City had two Homes for Refugees, one in the Battery and one on West 24th Street. They reported, in 1865, on sending some 400 west, 400 north and east, and the remainder returning south after having their basic needs met. Women and children were the largest group in need. They often came hungry and nearly naked. The refugees often commented on the war as having been the "rich man's war, but the poor man's fight."

Andrew Nerva Rankin, Esq., moved his large family to Brooklyn in March 1865 to begin his work, but a few weeks later, on April 15, 1865, President Lincoln was assassinated. Andrew Nerva had campaigned tirelessly for Lincoln. He had attended rallies for him. He had put his life, and his family's, in danger protecting Union speakers. He had even been present when Lincoln gave his Gettysburg Address. The death of Lincoln was a dramatic shock to the entire family, as it was to the entire nation.

Once settled in New York, Andrew Nerva's inventions turned to the area of sanitation, and cold pack pipe storage, fixtures and tools. In 1865, he patented a deodorizer, and in 1866 he patented the first chamber vessel or urinal. The city in this post war period had many issues, sanitation being one.[4] It was a time when the nation as a whole was looking at the health of the people, especially since so many Civil War soldiers had died from disease, and because cities were increasing in size. Cleanliness and sports were being encouraged. New York City had a continual battle with diseases like cholera and yellow fever. Yet, with all the things Andrew Nerva did in his life, it is ironic that his name is often listed in funny things happening in history during March in regional newspapers. It seems that his name is usually linked to the invention of the urinal.

The United States and Europe had been successfully connected by a 2,500-mile-long telegraph cable, which was considered a miracle, in 1866. The telegraph line opened up quicker communication across the Atlantic, which had in the past taken at least 10 days by ship. Networks of wires had been strung between cities beginning in the 1840s. Prior to that, information had traveled within the continental United States largely by steam locomotives and steamships. The country had related to itself in little regional pockets. By January 1867, the American Telegraph Company put lines through to Albany on the west side of the Hudson River. The completion of this was deemed a success.[5] Individual communities within New York State would begin to relate to each other better. Telegraph transmissions also were vital to newspapers which made use of the system for gathering and dispersing information. One cannot look at the lives of Will and June without looking at information which would be front page news in a newspaper. They lived in a family of readers and writers. In fact, Will was known to weave historical events into his columns.[6] What happened in the world and was printed in the newspaper, was conversation at the dinner table.

The first baseball convention had been held on January 22, 1857, in New York City with 16 baseball clubs: Knickerbockers, Gotham, Eagle, Empire, Putnam, Baltic, Excelsior, Atlantic, Harmony, Harlem, Eckford, Bedford, Nassau, Continental, Union, and Olympic. Rules were drafted and the National Association of Base Ball Players was formed. In March 1858, the following officers were elected: William H. Van Cott from the Gothams served as president, Joseph B. Jones of the Exelsiors served as 1st vice president, Thomas S. Dakin of the Putnams served as 2nd vice president, J. Ross Postley of the first Metropolitans served as recording secretary, Theodore F. Jackson of the Putnams served as corresponding secretary and E.H. Brown of the first Metropolitans served as treasurer. Will was only nine at the time, and June was seven.

In 1860, the famous NABBP champions, the Excelsior Base Ball Club of Brooklyn, set up a baseball tour which included a number of large cities in Upstate New York, introducing many in that area to the New York style of play. The Civil War interupted this gentlemen's version of baseball and changed the direction of the game's emergence in America. During the war, a number of servicemen played baseball. This broadened the exposure to the game by members in both the Union and Confederate armies, with each group taking the game back to its individual locale. N.E. Young, a future president and secretary of the National League, wrote that baseball was unknown in his hometown in New York State prior to the Civil War. They had all been trained in cricket. The individual towns and cities in the state were not instantly connected as we are in the age of radio and television. Following the war, however, interest began to surface all over New York State. By the time of the NABBP convention on December 13, 1865, in New York City, there were 91 clubs; 48 of those were from New York State. In 1865, the Atlantic Base Ball Club of Brooklyn was the NABBP champions and they also made a tour of Upstate New York, increasing interest.

In the spring of 1866, Will, age 17, and June, age 15, discovered the sport of New York style baseball in Nyack, Rockland County, New York. The county seat was in New City. This sport would change their lives forever. Will chose the position of catcher and June vascillated between pitcher and second baseman. Protective gear had not yet been invented, which would particularly affect Will later. At that time, the ball was caught barehanded with two hands. Will worked in his father's law office in Spring Valley during the day, until August 27, 1867. On that day, William began seriously learning the printing trade, which he worked at until 1876.[7] It appears that Will made the decision not to follow in the family tradition of law. It is not clear where Will began the printing trade, but Alfred Spink mentioned that Will lived in Rockland County by 1868 and ended up working for a Nyack paper in 1870, so it may have been in that town and for that paper.

Amateur baseball flourished from 1865 to 1870, particularly in New York, and both Will and June fit into the move happening around them. The town of Nyack created two cricket clubs and two baseball clubs late in the season of 1866. The cricket clubs were the Mechanics and the Eurekas. The baseball clubs were the Liberty Base Ball Club and the Mazeppa Base Ball Club. The baseball clubs were still trying to learn how to play the New York Game. The Mazeppa Club was called the senior or heavyweights and the Liberty was called the minors or lesser weights, but the Liberty Club quickly gained ground over the Mazeppas. One game against a Brooklyn club took 5 hours and 20 minutes to play. Most took about 3½ hours. The baseball clubs played other clubs in Rockland County like the Sparkill Base Ball Club of Piermont, other New York area clubs like the Star Base Ball Club from Brooklyn, and the Riverside Base Ball Club of Fort Lee, New Jersey.[8] The big issue for the clubs seemed to have been finding a field in which to play without either hitting passers-by or having cows chew clothing left by the side of the field. The Liberty Club played on the grounds east of Oak Hill Cemetery and were the champion club of 1867. A silver ball the size of a baseball was awarded by Mr. Spencer Wood of New City, New York, following the tournament. There was also a club called the Yankee Base Ball Club in Nyack in 1866, a name that would take on its own meaning in the future. By spring of 1868 the best of the Old Liberty Base Ball Club was absorbed into the Tappan Zee Base Ball Club of Nyack. Other towns in the county also began introducing clubs.

From 1866 to 1872 Will and June played first amateur and then semi-professional baseball. In 1869, they were listed as playing for the Crescents Base Ball Club in Nanuet[9] with Will catching and Andrew "June" pitching in the beginning of the season. It is difficult, however, to find when they began on that club. Material on the brothers points to their learning the game in 1866, when the rest of the town was just beginning to learn to play the New York Game. The club captain usually was the catcher, though not always. The Crescent nine inning games apparently took over three hours to play. Each game was meticulously timed and carefully recorded.

On the team rosters were listed:

W.M. Rankin, catcher

A.B. Rankin, pitcher

Van Ruer, first base and sometimes second base (a Krender was also listed in a game as playing first base)

F. Hardy, second base (it appears his relative would umpire and score games. Springsteel is also mentioned in this position in another game)

Van Zandt, third base (but also would pitch in one game, and a Harding is listed in one game for this position)

C. Hardy, short stop (a Hutton and a Smith were listed for this position)

Kreuder, right field (a Springsteel and a Blauvelt were mentioned in this position, both playing a number of positions)

Benson, left field (perhaps Benson played center field with a typo in the paper, because two left fielders are listed. Another game listed him with d.f., meaning direct field).

Burns is also listed as left field (a Ross and a Mitchel were listed for this position in another game as well).[10]

The Crescent Base Ball Club wore the shield-front style of uniform, popular from the 1850s to the 1870s, with the jockey style cap. It was based on the firemen's uniforms of the day made popular by the Knickerbockers. It would appear that this club was an amateur club. Their uniforms might have been purchased through John H. Blauvelt's sporting store, at 45 Main Street in Nyack, which also advertized "bat-proof balls," and "a splendid variety of bats" in the *Rockland County Journal*.[11] The baseballs were made of only "two pieces of leather," making them stronger. Of course, there was virtually no protection for catchers at this time.

June was working as a stationer in the town of Ramapo, New York, beginning in 1869. Stationer implies a fixed station, or store, where a person sold stationery and did custom printing. Each brother would work at his trade and then join their club on the field. Their club played against more experienced clubs like the Continentals from Spring Valley, The Tappan Zee from Nyack, and the Sparkill Club from Piermont which had been playing long before any of Nanuet or Nyack's Clubs and was the 1868 champion club, possessing the silver ball.

In September 1869, while still working at their trades, Will and June both switched to play for the Continentals Base Ball Club in Spring Valley, which undoubtedly was a better club. The Continentals may have even been a semi-pro club. In a newspaper article in a scrapbook collected by Will

Rankin, which is in the posession of his great-grandson, Arthur, there is a letter from a Mr. Henry E. Smith to Will addressing a question on a play. The article mentions that Mr. Smith played on a club with Will and June in Rockland County. He was a right fielder, captain and manger.[12] He is listed on this club's roster with the Rankins. Will was catcher for the Continentals, and June pitched, played second base for the club, and sometimes left field. June was also assistant captain and Will corresponding secretary. Their father, an attorney and counselor at law in Spring Valley, was the solicitor for the club. William was later elected to the board of directors. The games were, again, listed as taking over three hours to play. A Mr. Frank Van Riper, "proprietor of the Fairview House in Spring Valley" gave the team ground for the club field.[13]

The club was listed in the *Rockland County Journal* as being the "Champion Club of Rockland County" in 1870.[14] It appears as though they established the club following a formula recommended in books like Henry Chadwick's 1867 *Haney's Base Ball Book of Reference*.[15] That books lists the responsibilities for electing a captain and board of directors, the role of the secretary, and so on. Or, they could have used *Beadle's Dime Base Ball Book of Reference*,[16] also edited by Henry Chadwick, which listed the rules of the game in 1860. A letter to the editor of the *Rockland County Journal* on October 1, 1870, makes mention of an issue that occurred between two baseball clubs in Haverstraw with the reference to the correct action of the umpire as per "'Chadwick,' p. 60." The *Haney's Base Ball Book* does list umpire responsibilities on page 60.[17]

Civil War hero Ulysses S. Grant (1822–1885) had become president in 1869. He would lead the country until 1877. By the summer of 1869, the IRS had gained interest in baseball. The *Rockland County Journal* printed a notice that the IRS would be taxing baseball clubs. Licenses would now cost $10 per year, and the clubs would pay 2½ percent on their gross to Uncle Sam. Treasurers also would be required to make monthly income returns.[18] The Internal Revenue Service had just been created in 1862 under President Lincoln to help pay for the expenses incurred during the Civil War. The IRS would be repealed in 1872, revived in 1894, deemed unconstutional in 1895 by the Supreme Court, and then enacted in 1913 under the 16th Amendment.[19] Had there not been a Civil War, baseball and the American public might have avoided this yearly exercise in April.

Will began writing on baseball for the *Rockland County Journal* beginning in 1870 until 1873. Reports on a number of baseball teams in Rockland County surfaced, and one game played by the Continentals drew an important comment: "The weather was fine and a large crowd of citizens witnessed the game — among them were many ladies."[20] The reference to ladies present was often added to newspaper accounts to show the growing popularity of the sport. On the team rosters for the Continentals were listed:

W.M. Rankin, catcher
A.B. Rankin, usually pitching, or second base, or left field
Smith, pitcher
Weir, first base
Milne, second base
Gardner, shortstop
Thomas, third base
H. Smith or Page, right field
Page or Beebe, center field
Van Winkle or Jennings, left field

It does appear that both Rankins made home runs. The scores were initially high (57 to 14 in one game and 63 to 9 in another), which might point to the live ball in use at the time. When hit, it traveled far. The clubs would soon switch to the dead ball, which had less spring, and playing times would drop to two hours. June had to be sure to pitch the ball properly underhand, and not throw it to the batter. It had to be delivered to the batter in such a way as to allow the batter every opportunity to hit it. Batters used a round wooden bat about 2½ inches in diameter at its thickest part.

The publisher of the *Rockland County Journal* was a baseball enthusiast who actually met with the town planning board to help promote the sport. The baseball commentary in 1870, when Will began to write for the *Rockland County Journal*, grew in detail. Will is listed as the secretary, captain, and on the board of directors for his club in one article. Secretaries often wrote commentary for the newspapers in the early days, and he signed his material. He took the minutes of the board meeting, which the article provided. In a June 28 article, there are details on the game which only a player would know. That particular article follows what Warren Goldstein, in *Playing for Keeps: A History of Early Baseball*, wrote was standard practice for the semi-pro and professional teams of that period. The clubs appear to behave like a fraternity with a constitution, by-laws, officers, a board of directors, and play schedule. There seemed to be a regular nine who were most likely the first nine, or best players, to which Will and Andrew "June" belonged, and then others seem to fill in positions, with some perhaps being the second nine. In fact, the April 9, 1870, *Rockland County Journal* does mention Will and June as members of the first nine. The challenge from the opposing team was written and accepted. They chose an umpire; in a few cases it was Mr. Alex Milne of the

Sylvan Star Club of New York City. The teams had dinner at the host's chosen hotel after the game. The hospitality of the hosting team was mentioned in great detail.[21] It was a gentlemen's game.

Another thing mentioned by Goldstein was the fact that clubs tended to revolve around skilled tradesmen, and the typographers, printers, and pressmen did have baseball clubs which would directly relate to Will and June in their daily profession. It is hard to tell what jobs were held by the other players, but one might assume they were employed in similar professions. Will does mention in the July 9, 1870, *Rockland County Journal* that several team members worked in New York City and they took a steamboat to a game in Haverstraw while the rest arrived through "private means."[22] Newspapers also often gave those involved in printing more copy space as fellows in the trade.[23]

What is interesting about the baseball commentary during these years in the *Rockland County Journal* is the fact that you begin to see a large number of clubs within that one region with their team rosters listed, as well as details on the game and final scores. Some of the baseball clubs listed during these two years were the Continentals Base Ball Club of Spring Valley, Crescents Base Ball Club of Nanuet, Spartans and Alerts Base Ball Clubs of Warren Village, Picked Nine Club of Middletown, Tappan Zee Base Ball Club of Nyack, Minnisceongo Base Ball Club of Haverstraw, Torne Base Ball Club of Ramapo, Sloatsburgh Base Ball Club and Rockland Stars of Sloatsburg, and Sparkill Base Ball Club of Piermont. All were within a short radius from New York City.[24] Also mentioned were the Spring Valleys of Cornwall; Perry Base Ball Club of New York City; Fairview Club; Chelsea Club of Williamsburgh, Long Island; Norwood Club of Norwood, New Jersey; and the Academics (who were not given a hometown by the paper). Another later 1877 issue of the Nyack *Evening Journal* also lists the Olympics of Paterson, New Jersey; Stars of Spring Valley; Nanuet Club of Nanuet; and the Pearl River Club, of Pearl River, New York.[25] The New York game was alive and well in Rockland County. Teams like the Spartans of Haverstraw would play the Atlantics of Brooklyn.[26] Will also served in the spring as an umpire for several games while playing for the Continentals.[27] It does appear that the Rockland County clubs were interacting with clubs from Brooklyn, New York City, Long Island, and New Jersey during the late 1860s. Will and June played on a winning county club against some of these clubs.

The January 21, 1871, issue of the *Rockland County Journal* mentions the Convention of Base Ball Players held in New City, New York, on January 10 which had the purpose of setting the rules of play for the county clubs. The association was to be called the Rockland County Base Ball Association and function under the National Base Ball Association, "as compiled by Chadwick." The clubs were to use the regulation dead ball.[28] The National Association of *Professional* Base Ball Players was also formed in 1871 as the first professional league in the United States, and it operated until 1875.

According to Alfred H. Spink in *The National Game* (published in 1910), William also organized the Nyack Tidal Wave Base Ball Club for which he was manager, captain and catcher for the entire three years of their existence. Spink wrote that Will did that while living in Nyack. Since Will was one of those editing Spink's book, it is likely that this is true. This was a semi-professional club. The full roster is unknown at this point, but a relative of Alexander "Sandy" Perry recently wrote that he was in the club.[29] It would seem likely that June was in the club as well. This might have been from the summer of 1871 to 1874. The Tidal Waves are mentioned in the *Rockland County Journal* in 1872 and 1873.[30]

There was a famous racing scooner named the *Tidal Wave* which had been built in Nyack in 1869. It would not be too far a stretch to link the choosing of the name to that ship, or perhaps the team even played near the shipyard. That ship belonged to William Voorhis and was built by James E. Smith of Nyack in the shipyard at the foot of Main Street.[31] When it was launched, 1,000 people were in attendance. William Voorhis appeared to have owned most of the town and was responsible for its layout. The Voorhis brothers defended and won the America's Cup. The *Rockland County Journal* mentions the Tidal Waves Base Ball Club on July 6, 1872; August 31, 1872; and September 7, 1872. William Voorhis, himself, made a presentation to the Tidal Waves Base Ball Club in August 1872 of a "beautiful ensign and two elegant foul-flags."[32] Voorhis may have actually been one of the financers for the club.

The Nyack Tidal Waves Base Ball Club won two out of three series. The series they lost was to the Sunnysides Base Ball Club of Sing Sing, which was considered a semi-professional team. The Newgate State Prison had been opened at the foot of Christopher Street in Greenwich Village in 1797 by Sing Sing Street, and then moved to Upstate New York in 1828 to Sing Sing or Ossining in Westchester County where it took on the name of the town, Sing Sing Prison.[33] Sing Sing had been the Mohegan Tribe's name for the area: Sint Sinck, meaning stone upon stone for the limestone found there. The town was named Sing Sing after the Revolutionary War and incorporated in 1813. It later changed its name to Ossining.[34] The Sunnysides came from the town as did other baseball clubs, but this was their championship club. They may have played in the vicinity of Nelson Park in Ossining by Washington Avenue and Route 9. Interestingly, the inmates at Sing Sing also played exhibition baseball games in the late 1920s against both the New York Giants and the New York Yankees. Spink notes that under Will's management in the 1870s, the Nyack Tidal Waves won forty games and lost five.[35]

Will was playing for the club, working in printing during the day, and writing on baseball for the paper. The *Rockland County Journal* in Nyack, New York, was founded in 1850 and was published until 1915. John Charleton bought the paper in 1867 and was owner during Will's time of writing. It was a weekly paper with area news and gossip. All the members of the Rankin family found their names at times in print in the *Journal* during this period, be it for baseball, legal ads, young people's gatherings, church news, or performances. Will also wrote a brief history of the Chelsea, Metropolitan and New York baseball clubs during this time.

Alfred Spink mentioned that Will met and married his wife in Nyack. Her name was Cornelia Polhemus, born about 1845. She was about four years older than he. That period appears to have been a transition point for Will as he moved from playing baseball into a concentration on reporting it, and working on the mechanics of printing. Perhaps the seriousness of a marriage made the writing field seem more dependable. His wife had a brief description in Alfred H. Spink's book, written much later, as being of "even temperament and cheerful disposition which has enabled her to bear the trials and vicissitudes of life with remarkable patience."[36] The trials he was most likely referring to in 1910 was the loss of their youngest son, William, in infancy.

Andrew Nerva Rankin, Will and June's father, was doing quite well financially at this time. The *Rockland County Journal*, in 1871, listed his 2,000 acre sale of Pennsylvania coal land for $270,000, and the subsequent purchase of a Ramapo farm in April from Peter T. Acherman with 15 acres for $7,500.[37] Peter Acherman, in an earlier story, had helped Andrew Nerva's daughter and her friend when the horse pulling their carriage was startled and ran. While trying to gain control in front of his house, the carriage was flipped and destroyed, the occupants tossed, and horse injured.[38]

The family was attending the Reformed Church in Spring Valley, perhaps the church of Mr. Acherman as well, and Andrew Nerva would go on to help the church erase its debt.[39] Andrew Nerva also lead a debate for women's sufferage against the pastor, who felt it was not proper.[40] Andrew Nerva also suggested to the editor of the *Rockland County Journal* that the town create a cranberry bog like Ocean County, New Jersey, had done for added income since the area had suitable water sources for such a venture.[41]

Andrew Nerva's daughters, the sisters of Will and June, were strong personalities. Yet for all his proclamation for women's rights, Andrew Nerva Rankin did not feel any of their suitors were worthy of them, and so they never married. The belief that they were part of the acendancy (meaning related to Archibald Acheson) blocked them from relationships with local men. They later supported themselves on Long Island with Mary, called Adela, teaching elocution or public speaking, and doing local readings and recitations, which were quite popular; Margaret, called Margie, kept house as she was deaf; Sara, called Lizzie, taught interpretive dance with scarfs and the formation of historical tableaus, and formal dances like the waltz, polka, or mazurka; and Arie, called Etta, taught classical piano and gave music lessons. They were independent, articulate, and brilliant, but they did not go against their father.

Four

Follow the Ball (1870–1879)

Eighteen seventy to 1873 were transitional years for Will and June Rankin. Will was writing for the *Rockland County Journal,* in Nyack, and managing and catching for the semi-pro Tidal Waves Base Ball Club.[1] June was a stationer, most likely playing for the same club. Eighteen seventy-one was a transitional year for baseball, too. It was the year the National Association of Professional Base Ball Players (NAPBBP or NA for short) was formed as several clubs broke free from the National Association of Base Ball Players and sought to establish themselves as professional clubs. The Cincinnati Base Ball Club, or Red Stockings, had been the first to go professional. They were managed by Harry Wright and featured players originally from the Mutuals, Excelsiors, and the Philadelphia area. The club played within the NABBP from 1867 to 1870, as they turned professional in 1869. On March 17, 1871, ten representatives from various baseball clubs met in New York City, adopted a constitution, and elected leaders for a professional league. It was considered the first professional league at the time; it lasted only until 1875.

The NAPBBP was run by players. Unfortunately, many clubs fell into such blatant gambling with a number of fixed games that baseball's future seemed to be in question. Most of the clubs were from the east, with a good representation from New York State. The NAPBBP originally included the New York Mutuals (a team with which Will would later be affiliated), Troy Unions (New York), Boston Red Stockings, Philadelphia Athletics, Washington Olympics, Chicago White Stockings, Cleveland Forest Cities, Fort Wayne Kekiongas (Indiana), and Rockford Forest Cities (Illinois). The association would later have a total of 18 clubs. Both brothers had played baseball before a professional organization existed, though they had played semi-pro, which is important to remember when looking at their later writing and their philosophy about baseball. They had a memory of a different kind of game. They played during the period when the sport was enjoyed by working gentlemen

Four. Follow the Ball (1870–1879)

as a form of recreation. Games were considered friendly competition. They played hard but enjoyed the comradeship. It wasn't about power or money; it was about the game.

With the new organization came a shift of focus from the player to the club. New bylaws were drawn up. Umpires were now professionally paid. A complete playing schedule was adopted, which clubs were expected to keep. Ticket prices were also set to maximize the best profit in large cities. The issues of fixed matches and the drunkenness of players were addressed, though not solved.[2] The problems would continue to mount. Boston dominated the National Association in the early 1870s. They won the championship in 1872, 1873, 1874, and 1875. Harry Wright had been brought over from the Cincinnati club when it folded, and he served the Boston club as both manager and player. He also brought the trademark uniform with him: red stockings.

The 1870s were the period during which public intest in baseball was growing, and newspapers adapted to this by providing more coverage. This opened positions for writers with expertise in the game.[3] However, in 1873 twenty-three-year-old Will left writing for the *Rockland County Journal* to concentrate on printing in Nyack until 1874. He was newly married, and his first son, Percy B., was on the way. Percy was born about 1874. Setting printtype was a tedious job. Each day the letters were put in place, the paper printed, and then the individual letters were returned to their appropriate boxes. It took hours, depending upon the length of the paper. All this was meticulously done by gaslight, or kerosene lamps. Will was a creative person. It was time for a change.

In 1874 when Harry Wright and Albert Spalding planned a baseball tour of England, what was considered Will's serious writing began at the *Brooklyn Daily Eagle*.[4] *Sporting Life*'s obituary on Will mentions that he did not specialize in baseball until 1875,[5] though he had been reporting it. Will wrote for the *Eagle* from about 1874 to 1883. The paper had been formed in 1841 and ran until 1955, and then returned from 1960 to 1963. It was printed initially at 34, 36, 38 Fulton; 23 to 33 Doughty; and 1 to 13 Elizabeth streets. It is now remembered at 28 Old Fulton Street, Brooklyn, New York, as the *Eagle* Warehouse. The paper had issues published in other major cities, like many of the New York papers.[6] The weekly edition had four pages, and the weekend six. It cost three cents a copy when Will began writing. Writing on baseball must have felt like a release to Will who did not follow his father into law and did not continue with the printing trade, though he did know how to set up his columns and deliver them in a timely way for those who would eventually print them.

Between the 1860s and 1870s, Brooklyn, in Kings County, was considered the third largest city in America and was dubbed the City of Churches due to the report that a church could be found on just about every block. It was independent of New York City at the time and did not become incorporated into that city until 1898. Brooklyn, or Breuckelen, had been named after a province in Utrecht, the Netherlands, during the time that the Dutch owned it. Breuckelen means broken land, most likely reflective of the many inlets and marshes surrounding it. It was formed in 1646 under the Dutch West India Company in New Netherlands. The British took New Netherlands from the Dutch in 1664 and named it New York. The name Brooklyn remains as a tie to its original European settlers in the Netherlands. Many affluent families, during the 1800s, had a winter residence in New York City, and a summer residence in the country. Brooklyn still had many country places. This was done to avoid the diseases which seemed to increase in the city in the warm weather and used to protect children and the elderly who were more fragile.

Will was a co-writer with Henry Chadwick (1824–1908) on the *Eagle*'s sporting staff.[7] He was 25 and Henry was about 46. Chadwick had been born in Exeter, England, and settled in Brooklyn, New York, with his family at age 12. He initially covered cricket in newspapers, like including the *New York Times*, but developed growing enthusiasm for baseball and became an ardent supporter of the sport. He was able to convince a number of papers to squeeze short segments on the game into their columns. Chadwick was a Wesleyan Methodist and moralist who combatted gambling and alcohol abuse within the sport. Will's name was in a short list of people Chadwick considered to be good writers; this especially included June Rankin. Will specialized at the *Eagle* on just baseball, and he was very accurate in his reporting.[8] It may be that when he later referred to "Chadwick writing on cricket while he was specializing on baseball," it related to the work the two did for the *Brooklyn Daily Eagle* at this particular time. The paper is searchable online, and baseball is under the search topic "Base Ball, Base-Ball, or Sports and Past Times." Though Henry never played for a specified club, he did seem to have things in common with Will in the area of enthusiasm for the game. He also lived in Brooklyn; had had a socially concious-activist father growing up; both men were raised in religious settings; both would lose children; and both were dedicated to the art of newspaper writing.

The baseball writing in the *Eagle* did shift during Will's period of writing, though the paper did not, like most papers, tend to always list an author. Chadwick's writing, with his name attached, had reflected his English origins and education, and articles like his February 6, 1873, "Sports and the Facilities for them in Brooklyn" points to his English bias with phrases like "The physique of Americans used to be a vulnerable point for foreigners" as he compared them to the "out-door-sport-loving Englishmen."[9] In that article Chadwick pointed to this condition now changing, thanks to the introduction of sports like baseball. He tended to be more of a philosopher in many columns, pointing to moral images in baseball and the behavior of players and managers. But, you do begin to hear the distinctive voice of Will Rankin, revealed later in the New York *Clipper*, by July 1874 in the *Brooklyn Daily Eagle*.

In the July 16 issue, for example, the writer, presumed to be Will, spent time mentioning the details involved in the play of the game. That particular issue addressed the difference in using a lively or dead ball with the writer mentioning the fact that people were making fun of those who had played with the live ball in the past. Will, of course, had played with both the live ball and the dead ball. The 1875 Ryan dead ball was the official ball used in the sport at the time of the article. The ball had less bounce than the prior live ball used by both brothers in their semi-pro years. David Quentin Voigt in *American Baseball: From the Gentleman's Sport to the Commissioner System*, mentions the fact that the 1870s dead ball was suited to the parks of that era which were smaller.[10] The idea in using a dead ball versus the live ball was to lower the number of scores within a given game. The ball simply did not travel as far since it had less bounce. The writer in the *Eagle* article commented that the play of the game had unquestionably improved since the early days, "particularly in scientific batting, but the fielding has improved very little, if any."[11] His take was that the old timers could take the younger players in that area. The focus on fielding was a major theme in Will's writing, with his repeatedly stating that fielding wins or loses games. Scientific batting related to the intentional placing of the ball in the field by the batter. Will, as a catcher, had developed a good eye for observation.

Will's coverage of baseball was unique in that it tended to encompass the entire national game in a more modern sports voice, without many flowery 1800s popular phrases. Instead of just focusing upon the New York metropolitan area, he mentioned games from coast to coast and many in-between. He covered amateur and professional teams alike, giving the reader a broader sense of what was going on. It also was a deeper coverage than other papers were printing. Quotes from other national newspapers were sprinkled throughout his text, with his own reactions to them, as were the mini-histories of the game which he dearly loved. It also appears as though he was beginning to network with other writers and managers in other cities for information, and in return covering their games. The *Brooklyn Daily Eagle* also added comments, during his period of writing, which tended to focus on the details of play. The March 15, 1875, issue, for example, focused on the art of pitching and the importance of having strategy when delivering a ball to the "batsman." It was likened to a military movement, requiring "headwork."[12]

Voigt mentions that during this early period baseball writing seemed to follow a trend with a lead paragraph recounting the highlights of the game, a longer description of the game followed by a summary and the box scores. It did not appear that individualism was necessarily encouraged.[13] Will Rankin's writing in the *Eagle*, however, did reflect creative writing and did show greater commentary on the issues of the day. Voigt also mentions the fact that the newspaper reporters helped make public heroes out of good players, and their papers became part of the entertainment industry during the Industrial Revolution.[14] Will wrote extensively on players and managers whom he felt excelled at the game. It did not matter which club they played on. If they were good, he praised them and told the readers why. If they were not, he also told them why.

Connie Mack, manager and part owner of the Philadelphia Athletics from 1901 to 1950, mentioned the fact that sportswriters were the "power behind the tremendous growth of our national game." Publicity made the difference, moving from a few lines to pages of articles. He mentioned the days when the images made the game seem very "picturesque," and the fact that in his experience "sports editors and writers" were "never silent partners in the building of the game" in his city, but he was grateful to them for their "support and cooperation."[15] Baseball writers in those early days did not make a great deal of money for their material, either, which resulted in their need to hustle their work to different papers. Andrew Schiff, in his book *The Father of Baseball: A Biography of Henry Chadwick*, states that baseball writers earned much less than other reporters on newspapers and were obviously in it for the love of the game.[16] Clever writers like Chadwick and Will saw that the money was in writing great volumes for different outlets. Both worked for a number of sources.

Meanwhile, Will and June's father, Andrew Nerva Rankin, was busy inventing again, practicing law, and serving as secretary on the Railroad Commission for Rockland County. He had always had an interest in the railroad, especially with his neighbor in Chambersburg working for the Cumberland Valley line. The Rockland County Commision was instrumental in having the Erie Railroad create an express line from Monsey, New York, to New York City and back. Andrew Nerva, at that point, invented window fasteners for sashes, and railway switches for the railroad.[17] It seemed as though his mind noticed things which could be improved by a device, especially mechanical, and he would create a design on paper to fill the need and then file a patent.

In 1873, older sister Adela was already being written up as a star in the area of recitations. She trained others in public speaking, but was best known for her own performances in local halls, churches, and residences.[18] She was 29 and continued to perfom throughout the 1870s in the New York area with a great deal of praise for her delivery. Standing errect with her brown hair on top of her head, she commanded the attention of her listeners. Recitiations were a large form of entertainment in the 1800s; these were later replaced by radio and TV. They were social gatherings where people were inspired by sprited renditions.

However, between 1874 and 1875, both of the brothers' grandparents died. Margaret Ritchey Rankin died in March 1874 followed by Andrew Brown Rankin III, Esq., in January 1875. Andrew III had been a powerful figure in the family, and the passing was not easy for them, or for the town of Greencastle, Pennsylvania, which grieved his death. Andrew III had been an important political force in Greencastle. He was credited with having had his hand on just about every municipal improvement in his town.[19] His tombstone and that of his wife are at the Cedar Hill Cemetery in Greencastle, Pennsylvania. Isaac Van Anden, founder of the *Brooklyn Daily Eagle*, also died that year, on August 4. Will was writing for the paper, and June would eventually write for the paper on baseball and golf. Both brothers lived in Brooklyn and did seem to have many close personal friends on the editorial staff at the *Eagle* because they were mentioned often in the paper; usually favorably. Later, the paper would list the wedding announcements for Will's son, and then the wedding announcements for June's son. Even the wedding of June's granddaughter was printed in the paper with reference to June's baseball and golf legacy, as he outlived Will.

June's real journalistic career began in the summer of 1875, at age 24. Up to that point, he had been a stationer. June was recommended for the sportswriter position at the New York *Sunday Mercury* newspaper by Henry Chadwick.[20] Chadwick personally named June as his sucessor when he left the paper to edit his own paper, the *American Chronicle*.[21] This was the beginning of a long friendship between June and Henry which lasted to the day of Henry's death, even while Henry and Will bickered. Chadwick had written on sports for the *Sunday Mercury* for a number of years. He had been hired to cover cricket and baseball and also covered those sports for the New York *Clipper* and *New York Times* in 1857; and the New York *Herald* in 1862.

The New York *Sunday Mercury* newspaper was printed from 1839 to 1897 at 128 Fulton Street in New York City (113 Fulton and 48 Ann in 1861). In 1897, it became part of the *Morning Telegraph*. Most of the New York papers were clustered around City Hall, across the river from Brooklyn, accessible by the Fulton Street Ferry which connected the two Fulton Streets. According to *The American Newspaper Directory and Record of the Press* for 1861, the *Sunday Mercury* was published weekly with a subscription cost of $2.00 that year.²² The paper had editions in the Eastern and Middle States as well as the city and suburbs. The *Sunday Mercury* was one of the few newspapers to print on Sunday and the first to regularly cover baseball as news, though the New York *Herald* has the distinction of printing the first material listing the word baseball in 1845. During the Civil War, the *Sunday Mercury* had published numerous stories from soldiers in the field, helping readers to get a real sense of what was happening. Will and June, of course, had their own stories to tell.

William Cauldwell (1824–1907), editor of the *Sunday Mercury* in 1850 and then owner beginning in 1853, had printed the story on the Knickerbockers versus Gothams baseball game. He is credited as being the first real American baseball reporter. Reports on games were, up to that time, submitted by the secretaries of the individual clubs with as small a description as possible.²³ Cauldwell turned them into features. June was hired to specialize in baseball writing. The main publisher for the paper during June's period of writing was William Cauldwell. His grandson, Jason Rogers, took over in 1894. June would grow to know Cauldwell very well, as would his brother. The paper, by 1875, already exceeded in circulation all other Sunday and daily papers. A number of authors like Samuel Langhorne Clemens, better known as Mark Twain, had their stories first published in this paper. Clemens (1835–1910) was originally a printer and reporter like the Rankin brothers. He also wrote for the New York *Herald* and attended baseball functions as a fan in New York City during this time.

By 1885, June would be promoted to baseball editor for the *Sunday Mercury*.²⁴ His name was listed as still writing for the newspaper in a June 15, 1896, article printed in the *Brooklyn Daily Eagle*.²⁵ That would mean that he wrote for the paper for at least 21 years. Since the paper merged into the *Morning Telegraph* the following year, in December 1897, and June was not listed as writing for that paper, he may have written for the *Sunday Mercury* up to the point of the merger, making it 22 years. The *Morning Telegraph* was mainly a theatrical and horse racing newspaper. Later it would be known for reporting on the silent film era.

There was a great deal of interplay between the Rankin brothers and Henry Chadwick during this early period, with Will working with him on the *Eagle* and June taking his place on the *Sunday Mercury*. The brothers seemed to follow Chadwick from paper to paper. Will would later follow him to the New York *Clipper*, and June would follow Chadwick to the New York *Herald*. Henry had been writing for the *Herald* since 1862. Later in life, they lived about three or four miles from each other in Brooklyn with June and Will on opposite ends and Henry somewhat in the middle, forming a triangle. They all attended the same club games, sitting in the press boxes together.

The National League replaced the National Association of Professional Base Ball Players on February 2, 1876, at a meeting at the Grand Central Hotel in New York City. They elected William Hulbert, of the Chicago White Stockings, president. The original league members included the New York Mutuals, Boston Red Caps, Chicago White Stockings, Cincinnati Red Stockings, Hartford Dark Blues, Louisville Grays, Philadelphia Athletics, and St. Louis Brown Stockings. The Cincinnati Red Stockings had been the first club to go professional. The league sought to enforce rules and conduct, set regular playing schedules, and promote the "honorable play" of baseball. They also sought to protect the interests of the clubs and players, and to make the game more profitable for club owners. Clubs were to come from cities with at least 75,000 people.[26]

Andrew Schiff, in his book on Henry Chadwick, mentions the fact that W.A. Hulbert did not like Henry Chadwick and sought to keep him out of the process. Chadwick represented the older NAPBBP, and Hulbert was forming a different organization which he hoped to control. Chadwick also did not like the clandestine process used in the organizing of the National League. Will Rankin later published W.A. Hulbert's private letter, dated September 25, 1875, from Chicago, about his desire to form an exclusive league. It mentioned his conspiracy to "carry the meeting." Hulbert only wanted "first-class clubs" for the membership. The article in which the letter was placed never mentioned how Will came to possess the letter, but it seems that Will had an interest in saving things others found of little interest. Will's comment at the time of his publication was, "Scheming is the foundation of the National League. It was put there by its builders."[27]

In addition to writing for the *Brooklyn Daily Eagle*, in the spring of 1876 Will became baseball writer for the New York *Daily Witness*,[28] a paper that only lasted from about 1871 until 1878. John Dougall (1808–1886), a manufacturer born in Paisley, Scotland, and living in Canada, founded the New York edition of the *Daily Witness* on the strict religious issue of temperance. He was a Presbyterian turned Congregationalist who created a penny paper for the working class dealing with Protestant religious issues. It had a large circulation and was located at 2 Spruce Street, in New York City, by City Hall. There is a prominent advertisement for the paper in the March 4, 1876, issue of *The Register* from Iola, Kansas. It fills the entire right column, giving great detail on the paper. In that advertisement, the *Daily Witness* is described as the only religious daily (six days a week; not Sunday) in the Union, and

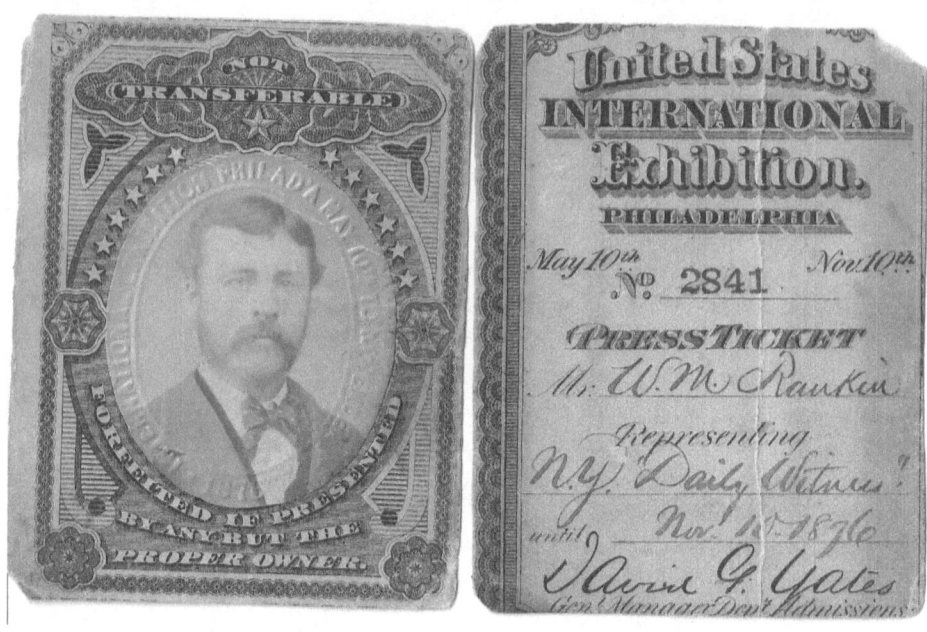

This photograph is from Will Rankin's press identification for the *Daily Witness* newspaper for the Centennial Exposition in Philadelphia. He began writing for the paper in the spring of 1876. The paper lasted only until 1878 and it is unknown how long Will worked for it since the *Weekly Witness* took over at that point and ran until 1886 (used by permission from Arthur Rankin, great-grandson of Will Rankin).

the size of the New York *Sun*. It cost $5 a year, $2.50 for six months, and $1.25 for three months. The *Daily Witness* had large coverage of the stock exchange and various markets like grain and cotton which was placed there to appeal to merchants, farmers and bankers. It had religious news on things like the Fulton Street Prayer Meeting which was formed to address drunken men who were unemployed, much like the work of the current Salvation Army; marriages; births; excerpts from morning journals; serial stories; and family oriented news. It was strongly in favor of things like "prohibition, equal human rights, sabbath obervance, missions and every good cause."[29]

When the daily paper ended, following the depression of 1878, the *Weekly Witness* took over, lasting until 1886. The *Weekly Witness* had run concurrent with the *Daily* and boasted a readership in 1875 of 100,000. It carried much of the same material as the *Daily* but in a condensed form, and it was cheaper by the year since it came out weekly instead of daily: $1.50 a year, $.75 for six months and $.40 for three months. It is unclear how long Will wrote for this paper, though he most likely focused on the healthy nature of baseball while reporting on its doings.

Will represented this paper at the International Exhibition of Arts, Manufacturers and Products of the Soil and Mine, better known as the Centennial Exposition or first World's Fair in the United States. The Centennial Exposition ran from May 10, 1876, to November 10, 1876. It was held at Fairmount Park by the Schuylkill River in Philadelphia to celebrate the 100th anniversary of the signing of the Declaration of Independence in that city. Approximately

This 1870 photograph of the New York Mutuals (Green Stockings) Base Ball Club was later used by Peck and Snyder Sporting Goods Emporium as an advertising trade card. Standing left to right: Jack Nelson, third base; Al "Phoney" Martin, right field; Marty Swandell, second base; and Dave Eggler, center field. Seated left to right: Everett Mills, first base; John Hatfield, shortstop; Charlie Mills, catcher; Rynie Wolters, pitcher; and Dan Patterson, left field (National Baseball Hall of Fame Library, Cooperstown, New York).

Will Rankin was commissioned by William Cammeyer, owner and manager of the club, to serve the 1876 New York Mutuals as the first official scorer on record. The team joined the National League that year but did not complete their playing schedule due to financial problems, and they were later expelled from the league. On the 1876 roster were pitchers Terry Larkin and Bobby Mathews; catchers Nat Hicks and Bob Valentine; infielders Bill Craver, George Fair, Davy Force, Jimmy Hallinan, John Hatfield, George Heubel, John McGuyinness, Al Nichols, George Seward, Joe Start, Pete Treacey, Billy West; and outfielders George Bechtel, Eddie Booth, John Hayes, Jim Holdsworth, John Maloney, Nealy Phelps, Jim Shanely, and Fred Treacey.

ten million people attended. Special trains ran from places like New York to Philadelphia for the event. It focused on sanitation and industry, as did the *Daily Witness*. New wonders like Alexander Graham Bell's telephone, Remington typographic machine, and the Wallace-Farmer Electric Dynamo were also on display.

On the front page in most newspapers on June 25, 1876, was General George Armstrong Custer's Last Stand. He died at the Battle of Little Big Horn while fighting a coalition of American Indians (the Sioux, Cheyenne and Crow) in the west. During the same summer, Will Rankin was appointed by President William Henry Cammeyer (1821–1898) to be the "first official scorer" on record, servicing the New York Mutual Base Ball Club in the east.[30] Cammeyer was the owner and manager of the rowdy Mutuals and had built the first enclosed ball field over his Union Skating Grounds in Williamsburg, Brooklyn, New York, which had opened on May 15, 1862. That was the first time the "Star Spangled Banner" was played before a ball game. He lived in Brooklyn, and the Mutuals played at the Union Grounds in Brooklyn which resulted in their being called the Brooklyn Mutuals, even though they were considered a New York club. Most patrons attending the games arrived in horse drawn carrages.

Keeping score had been done prior to Will being placed as official scorer, but in a less formal manner. The National League clubs assigned a scorer to a club. Henry Chadwick had improved the system of baseball box scoring in the 1863–1870 range.[31] However, Will mentioned the shorthand scoring system devised by M.J. Kelly of the New York *Herald*. It had been published in the 1868 and 1869 *DeWitt's Guides*. Kelly had used his own system for quite some time prior to that. This may have been the system Will used since he seemed to describe it in great detail in his columns, though that is not certain. He also worked with Chadwick and may have used his system. Newspapermen often served as scorers during this period on the theory that they were impartial, which in Will and June's case was generally accepted by those around them. A scorer would be appointed to a local club and cover all of their home matches.

In the early days of baseball, the scorers sat in chairs along the first-base line and were chosen for a particular game. Later, they sat in the press box.[32] The press box was seen as less contaminated from influence by the team, its managers and the like. Scorers, according to the 1864 rules, were expected to be gentlemen whose conduct rendered them "acceptable to all who are liable to make inquiries of him relative to the score of the game." They were to "fully understand every point of the game" and "note down correctly the details of every inning of the game." No person was to speak to the scorer during the game, unless it was in reference to a play needing to be correctly recorded. Scoring of baseball games became a fad with the general public as well, with many stadiums giving out scorecards to be used during the game.

The new system of scoring told more than just players, outs and runs.[33] Through the system of scoring, one could pick up patterns in players and reconstruct the events of the game, inning by inning.[34] This naturally led to statistics in baseball. Professional scorers could reconstruct a game with great accuracy from their shorthand symbols on the score sheet. No two scorers used exactly the same symbols in their recording; each tailored the system to his own personal liking. Even Henry Chadwick, in his early writing, gave options for scoring. They turned their scores in to the league at the end of a game. They also, on occasion, made judgment calls on plays. Newspapermen also contributed copy to their own, and other, papers. The *Brooklyn Daily Eagle* carried a number of columns on the Mutual Base Ball Club during this year.[35]

The Mutuals had been originally formed in 1857, named after the Mutual Hook and Ladder Company Number 1. Their first club president was the corrupt William Marcy "Boss" Tweed from 1860 to 1871. Tweed was a Tammany Hall politician known for his shady deals. In the winter of 1871, the Mutuals joined the National Association of Professional Ball Players and remained in the league until it ended in 1875. That was the period of their questionable behavior. Eighteen seventy-six, the year Will scored for them, was the Mutuals' only season in the newly formed National League. William A. Hulbert, of the Chicago White Stockings, formed the National League, which became the second professional league, replacing the NAPBP. The National League was to hold to a higher standard. The Mutuals ended the season in sixth place. The Chicago White Stockings were in first place. However, the Mutuals failed to complete their playing schedule and they were expelled from the league.[36] The club was suffering financially and could not afford trips to the Midwest which were on their playing schedule.

Will Rankin wrote in 1908 that there was no suspicion of crookedness in the 1876 Mutuals at that time. Mr. Cammeyer simply told him that there was "more money in playing exhibition games at Brooklyn and this vicinity than there was in going West, and he, with the Athletics, refused to fulfull their agreements as per schedule." They forfeited their membership in the league after careful thought.[37] Playing for the Mutuals in 1876 were pitchers Terry Larkin and Robert "Bobby" Mathews; catchers Nat Hicks and Bob Valentine; infielders Bill Craver, George Fair, Davy Force, Jimmy Hallinan, John Hatfield, George Heubel, John McGuinness, Al Nichols, George Seward, Joe Start, Pete Treacey, and Billy West; and outfielders George Bechtel, Eddie

Booth, John Hayes, Jim Holdsworth, John Maloney, Nealy Phelps, Jim Shanely and Fred Treacey.[38] They wore new uniforms with white and red leggings instead of the old green or brown leggings. It may have been an attempt to present a clean, new image.

Terry Larkin and Bobby Mathews were both prominent pitchers. Mathews, in particular, had joined the Mutuals to take Arthur Cumming's place. He developed his skill during four seasons with the club. The New York *Clipper* reported that much of the success the club had was due to his "very effective pitching." Nat Hicks caught for Mathews. He had begun catching with the Eagle Club and joined the Mutuals in 1872. Both Mathews and Hicks joined the Cincinnati club when the Mutuals were expelled from the National League in 1877.[39]

On May 10, 1879, David Force received the New York *Clipper* prize as a shortstop. He was said to be a very good infielder and batsman. First baseman Joe Start was nicknamed "Old Reliable" due to his integrity and skill on the field. He began with the old Atlantic and Enterprise clubs in Brooklyn and joined the Mutuals in 1871. He left the club in 1877, joining Hartford and then the Chicago and Providence clubs.[40] He would receive the *Clipper* prize on June 28, 1879.[41]

Before the club's expulsion, however, in an October 5, 1876, article in the *Brooklyn Daily Eagle*, a comment was made on the disbanding of a crooked club, the Alaska Nine of New York. They had allowed the Olympics of Paterson to win due to betting. It is particularly interesting to see strong comments against the players, and the mention that Mr. Cammeyer would not allow the "crooked team" to play on the Union Grounds again! The Mutuals, of course, had had years of crooked play in their past, and it appears as though a real effort was being made at that time to try to rout gambling out and to try to live up to the ideals of the newly formed league.[42] When the Mutuals did not complete their playing schedule, they were expelled, along with the Philadelphia Athletics. The Mutuals attempted to form a League Alliance with the Philadelphia Athletics, but the club fell apart shortly after that. This also left the National League of Professional Base Ball Clubs without a club in New York.

Even though Alexander Graham Bell patented the telephone in 1876, it was not in use yet. Sports communication was generally done through teletype, beginning in the 1870s. Most machines used only capital letters in three rows and transmitted material through telegraph wires to the desired location. There were telegraph centers throughout the city.[43] Both brothers made use of this system to report on baseball, and Will used it on November 16, 1876, to comment upon Dicky Pearce, of the St. Louis nine who he felt was the one of the best managers of players on the field and in winning matches.[44]

Brooklyn had been considered baseball's heart in those early days, with many of the orginial New York and Brooklyn players living there.[45] It was the perfect location to get the inside story from those on the field. That summer, Will also began writing for the New York *Tribune*, *New York Times* and *New York World*. He would continue writing special pieces for those papers throughout his life. Will also provided statistics over time for a number of papers beyond those already listed: he was the New York correspondent for the *Boston Herald* and *Boston Globe*; did work for the *Brooklyn Citizen*, which was a daily paper in circulation from 1886 until 1947; *Baltimore American*, a paper in circulation between 1883 and 1945; New York *Evening Sun*, a paper published between 1833 and 1950 with an evening version introduced between 1887 and 1916; many weekly and monthly papers; *Free Press* of Detroit, which began publication in 1831 with offices at 23 Park Row in New York and is currently in print; *Evening Journal* of Detroit; *The Sporting News*; *The United*; the *New England*, *North Western* and *Associated* presses; and the New York Press Association.[46]

The National League club owners had a tight control on the game in the 1870s and tried repeatedly to form a monopoly. Hulbert ran the league and had seen to it that league clubs were placed in large cities with high revenues. Rules were enforced: baseball would not be played on Sunday, no beer would be served, entrance admission would be 50 cents and the clubs would play by a regular set schedule. This, for the most part, resulted in knocking out patrons from the lower economic strata. Clubs from smaller cities would be pushed out as well. Those excluded cities, and expelled clubs, tried repeatedly to form their own associations and leagues, which often resulted in the raiding of clubs for players. Over time there would be repeated wars for dominance.

Albert Goodwill Spalding not only pitched for the Chicago White Stockings in the National League and managed the club to winning the championship in 1876, but he also had an interest in the club. He also had a very shrewd business sense, formed a sporting goods company first with his brother J. Walter Spalding in 1876, and later added his brother-in-law William Thayer Brown. The company would be called A.G. Spalding & Brothers. Spalding worked closely with Hulbert, promoting National League interests. He proposed a League Alliance in 1876, which was put in place in 1877, as a tripartite agreement between the National League, the American Association, and the Northwestern League. The idea was to have independent clubs affiliate with the National League, and for the National League to honor their contracts. Affiliates would honor territorial rights, player contracts, and the National

League's blacklist of players who were not acceptable. The National League would then offer them protection along with their $10 membership fee, but also had the condition that the clubs in the League Alliance would have to have goals which were consistent with the objectives of the National League. Clubs in the League Alliance included Alaskas, Albany M.N. Nolan, Auburn, Binghamton Cricket, Brooklyn Chelsea, Buffalo, Chicago Fairbanks, Elizabeth Resolute, Erie, Evansville Red, Hornellsville Hornells, Indianapolis Blues, Janesville Mutual, Livingston, Lowell, Ludlow, Memphis Reds, Milwaukee, Minneapolis Browns, Philadelphia, Philadelphia Athletics, Philadelphia Defiance, Springfield Champion City, St. Paul Red Caps, Syracuse Star, Troy Haymakers, Wheeling Standard, and Winona Clipper. The National Agreement would ultimately replace the League Alliance. Albert Spaulding would supply the official baseballs to the clubs and have the rights to publish the official National League organ.

During the spring of 1876, along with writing for the New York *Sunday Mercury*, June began writing on baseball for the New York *Herald*.[47] He would eventually become their baseball editor from 1885 to 1889, and then cover other sports for them until about 1898, a total of about 22 years.[48] Herald Square in New York City is named after the New York *Herald*. The paper was located on the corner of Broadway and Ann Street, not far from the *Mercury* and close to City Hall. Scottish-born James Gordon Bennett, Sr., was the original owner of the *Herald*. He died in 1872. Bennett had prided himself on getting scoops on the news before other papers and even had ships in the harbor interviewing people before they got to port. Yet, he was best known for what he was against.

The paper was founded as a Democratic, pro–South paper, which was the polar opposite political side to June's father. The paper tended to carry a minstrel view of African Americans which was demeaning. In 1864, however, Bennett Sr. had shifted to a more neutral position on the Civil War. Some feel Abraham Lincoln made overtures to him. According to James Crouthamel in *Bennett's New York Herald and the Rise of the Popular Press*, the paper had the largest circulation in Europe of any American paper and was read by politicians across the United States, with many editions in major cities.[49] It had both Paris and London editions. Bennett's employees also were said to be among the best paid in the field and used the best equipment.[50] James Senior also owned the Polo Field at 110th Street and 5th Avenue upon which baseball games would later be played. James Junior had introduced the United States to polo and played the sport there.

June began working for the paper when Bennett's son, James Gordon Bennett, Jr., was editor. In 1866, twenty-five-year-old James Jr. took over.

Many felt that James Jr. would not take control of the paper since he seemed disinterested, but they were wrong. James Jr. wanted the paper. However, he was not as decisive as his father. Crouthamel called James Jr.'s leadership style "eccentric and absentee," which ultimately led to the paper being "sensational and erratic," losing "much of its focus on news as news."[51] Don Seitz in *The James Gordon Bennetts, Father and Son: Proprietors of the New York Herald*, published in 1928, went much further, painting a picture of James Jr. as completely unstable. James had been raised in France because his father was deeply disliked by the New York public, which had largely supported the Union during the Civil War. His family feared for their safety after the war, and James Jr. was tutored privately abroad. Junior seemed to have difficulty following in his father's footsteps and was not as good of a writer. James spent his time with a fast group in New York who spent much time at Delmonico's restaurant and The Union Club.[52] When he was handed the paper, it had the highest circulation in America but began to lose ground. Ultimately, the paper merged with its rival, the New York *Tribune*.

Seitz quotes James Jr. as telling his executive staff that he was the "only reader" of the paper and the "only one to please." If he wanted text printed "upside down" that would be what they would do. He would also "pick the features." Added to this was eccentric behavior in the office, with Seitz writing that when he was sober he was "the coldest and most calculating of men," and when drunk he was "a madman." It appeared to take only two drinks to set him off. He had a fondness for small dogs and always had a small pack of them around him. James Jr. was also known to demote people without explanation and cut their pay. He would call people "indispensible" but then claim that nobody should be indespensible and therefore they should go. He would write "strange things" into articles on the proof sheets, which usually were caught by his staff. He expected a certain "form of approach" from those employed by him. The editors called him the "Commodore" due to his three terms in command of the New York Yacht Club, where he spent most of his time aboard the *Henrietta*.[53] And, if he was served a meal he did not enjoy, he would blast the restaurant in his newspaper.

The *Herald* had been the first paper to join forces with others to save money on telegraph usuage. In 1849 a partnership was formed called the New York Associated Press. Members initially of the *Associated Press* were the New York *Herald, Sun, Tribune, Courier and Enquirer, Journal of Commerce*, and *Express*. They shared a lease on the telegraph line with "the same news delivered to six member papers the same day."[54] Their information was then relayed to others for a fee. Bennett had correspondents around the globe, so the paper was able to provide details others simply could not.[55] It is important to note that some of the stories on baseball carried in papers across the country which list "written by *The Associated Press*" or *AP* for short, sometimes had their origins in people like Will and June Rankin. Both of them wrote for The *Associated Press*, and June had complete control of baseball coverage for the *Herald*, which was the first member of The *Associated Press*, until 1889. One-third of all dailies printed reports written by The *Associated Press* in 1880.[56]

According to the *American Newspaper Directory* of 1861, the *Herald* daily subscription rate was $7.00, and the weekly was $3.00, with the European weekly costing $3.00, and the California large monthly costing $1.50.[57] In the 1900 directory, the *Herald* was listed as publishing a morning paper which was 8 to 16 pages in length, and 16 by 23 inches in size. The Sunday edition was 16 to 40 pages in length. A subscription to the daily paper in 1900 cost $8.00 and the Sunday subscription cost $2.00.[58]

In the September 16, 1876, edition of the New York *Herald*, when June began to write for the paper, the "Base Ball" article focused on the seventh game of the series at the Union Grounds between the Cincinnati and Mutual baseball clubs; with the comment that they were "two of the weakest in the league."[59] The Mutuals came in 6th place. It was obvious that Will and the writer, most likely June, were at the same game with one scoring and writing his own articles, and the other simply writing copy. This happened often since they were covering the same general area. Most New York and Brooklyn baseball games occurred in the afternoon, about 3:30 P.M., when there was light. This enabled patrons time to make it home for dinner. It is difficult to clock the brothers' writing hours, however. Some of the material may have been written ahead and given to the typesetters at their various papers, with the events of the particular game added later. Those setting type worked very long hours. Crouthamel lists those at the *Herald* as working, from 10 A.M. to 1 or 2 A.M. with three hour breaks for meals. The brothers, as writers, would have finished their articles long before this, however, perhaps by dinner time or early evening. But, they wrote for multiple papers, making the distribution of their material a bit of a challenge.

On February 20, 1877, June was a delegate to the newly formed International Association of Professional Base Ball Players which met in Pennsylvania. It was a combined league of Canadian and American clubs including the London Tecumsehs (London, Ontario, Canada); Guelph Maple Leafs (Guelph, Ontario, Canada); Pittsburgh Alleghenies (Pittsburgh, Pennsylvania); The Rochesters (Rochester, New York); The Manchesters (Manchester, New Hampshire); Columbus Buckeyes (Columbus, Ohio); and the Lynn Live Oaks (Lynn, Massachusetts). The league operated from 1877 to 1880 and 1888 to 1890. William A. "Candy" Cummings, pitcher for the Lynn Live Oaks, was the first president. Harry Gorman of London, Ontario, was vice president, and James A. "Jimmy" Williams, of Columbus, Ohio, was the league's first treasurer, secretary and chief administrative officer. Clubs paid an admission fee of $10 to join the association, and if they wished to enter a pennant race they paid an additional fee of $15.

There were actually two separate versions of the Canadian-American leagues with the same name. This one lasted until 1880, and the second one existed from 1888 to 1890. The league was considered a minor league, though they played against major league clubs as well. The distinction between major and minor was not really formalized. The National League tended to see itself as the only major league. Admission to the International League games was only a quarter for championship games, with visiting clubs splitting the receipts with their hosts. The first championship was won by the Canadian London Club, using players from the United States. Initially, the International League was derided and called the Colored League because of its relative tolerance of African American players.[60] In the 1870s and 1880s, there were a number of African Americans playing for clubs. This would change, however, in the near future as racial segregation in the South spread throughout the nation. The second version of the International would made a drastic decision in this regard.

June served on the Judiciary Committee for the International Association. The Judiciary Committee was composed of H.D. McKnight of Pittsburg; L.E. Waite of St. Louis; N.P. Pond of Rochester, New York; A.B. Rankin of Brooklyn, New York; and George Siceman of Guelph, Ontario.[61] The *Brooklyn Daily Eagle*, where Will was writing, printed an article on the formation of the International Association, stating that the addition of more clubs would be good for baseball and be an added "protection" for "honest clubs and players which the limited membership of the League does not admit of." It went on to address the opposition to the association by the league which the writer felt "was not at all consistent with their profession of acting solely for the welfare of the professional clubs."[62]

By 1878, Hulbert and the National League began discussions on limiting salaries for players, and attaching certain salaries to certain positions. *The Sunday Mercury*, on which June Rankin was writing, reponded by telling players that they should form a league of their own.[63] June, in particular, had a problem with what he saw developing within the National League structure as a small group sought control over all of the players. He used his writing platform to comment on injustices he saw occuring within the organized game. Both Will and June were set in their career path as baseball writers by the mid–1870s with their short cropped hair and full mustaches. They would continue to observe and comment on the development of the sport during these struggles.

Eighteen seventy-six also was a time of success for the Rankin sisters. They were teaching on a daily basis. Mary Adella, "Adda," performed *Readings, Recitations and Music* at the Association Hall in Nyack. Etta may have been part of the the music performance. The story on Adda was covered by the *Rockland County Journal* on July 22 and then on December 2, 1876. The writer flowed with many flowery details about her recitation techniques, her distinct pronunciation, and her graceful manner with eyes "bright and clear," which "sparkle and flash continually."[64] It is hard to truly appreciate the role of recitations in the lives of those living in the 1800s. Memory work and repetition of long passages was encouraged as part of school and church curriculum as well. It was a major form of entertainment with large groups gathering to hear a live performance. All lighting for performances was done via gas lamps, kerosene lamps or candles. The electric light would first be used in Brooklyn's Loeser's store on Fulton Street on December 14, 1878.[65] Most streets, houses and public buildings were fitted with interior gas lamps, which would affect June later in life in a devistating way. Adda, at this point, appeared to be a local star.

February 14, 1877, Will's second son, Sydney Irvine, was born.[66] The family was growing and living in Brooklyn. Most of Will's time was spent on the ball field or in the newspaper office. Hours tended to run late covering stories, with writing and editing information in time to submit them for publication deadlines. Daily papers required great discipline on the part of writers and editors. Both brothers were very disciplined and serious about their careers, but their families rarely saw them, which was a common complaint by many during the Industrial Revolution with its long work hours. America was moving from a purely agrarian society to one reliant upon industry and cheap labor. The cities felt this shift more dramatically than the rural areas.

Baseball players were not paid very much, but young men who were white and athletic had doors opened to them. Things were often, however, a challenge to persons of color in this post–Civil War period. The August 1879 edition of the *Brooklyn Daily Eagle* mentions an incident of racism involving James Randolph Jackson, a black pitcher for the Live Oak Club of Herkimer. It seems that a Mr. John Steele, owner of the Central Hotel at Richfield Springs, had blocked James from sitting with his team members at the same table. In the article, the issue came before a United States commissioner, and the hotel keeper had to acquiesce. This paragraph on Jackson was included within notes about the national game with the last line stating, "The hotel keeper had to succumb."⁶⁷ The *Eagle* reported on a wide variety of teams and issues. This one was included for a reason. It was sympathetic to the player.

The managers of the second International Association, however, would block African Americans from entrance into their league within eight years. Many New York newspapers, including the *Herald*, would use minstrel images for African Americans, and include affected and artificial Negro dialogue into stories which tended to project an image of African Americans as less competent. The press set impressions before the public which would not fully be addressed until the civil rights movement. Even though New Yorkers generally had fought on the side of the North during the Civil War, there was little understanding of equality for persons of color. The African American population in the city was still relatively small at this point, and the press tended to cater to their white clients and their biases. It would take three generations for June's family to be fully integrated.

When it came to the elements of the game of baseball, however, both brothers were purists. Will would often interject his expertise in the form of correction. An example of the type of correction Will often wrote about can be found in a *Brooklyn Daily Eagle* article from 1879. It criticized the league code rules of that year in the area of "Collisions in Base Running." Section 15 of rule 5 was considered the worst, which had the fielder, after touching a runner with a caught ball, required to hold the ball in order to consitute an out. The writer felt that it would encourage the runner to "collide with the base player," forcing the base player to drop the ball and thereby remain safe.⁶⁸ Both brothers commented when they saw a technical error in the game, and when they felt something was handled improperly. Will would also correct others who were inaccurate in their reporting, and chastise teams for taking their personal issues to the field or for failing to perform up to standard. June would raise a complaint when he saw the national game being stifled by a "clique." Also, in 1879, the *Sunday Mercury* printed a complaint that the sport was becoming "fourth rate entertainment" which had a focus on "gate money."⁶⁹ Neither sat quietly by simply as spectators; they tended to be emotionally involved in the game itself. As a mater of fact, the fraternal view of the game of baseball, which was developed in them when they played ball in the late 1860s into the early 1870s, never left either brother. Will tried to keep the concept alive in the mind of the reader by re-telling the history of the old game. June painted emotional word-pictures about the brotherhood found in the game, though the *Herald* was exclusive when it came to interpreting brotherhood for all.

FIVE

Rising to the Top (1880–1884)

The 1880s were all about westward expansion of the country with settlers traveling in wagon trains filled with their worldly goods. Everyone looked to the newly established states and territories as places of possibility with their stories of abundant land, tumbling rivers and the potential for great wealth. Western dime novels were the rage, especially for those living in the industrial north who dreamed about life on the prairie. They outsold newspapers. The novels carried exciting stories about real men like Wild Bill Hickok, Kit Carson and Buffalo Bill Cody. Cowboys were idealized and American Indians marginalized as the frontier was tamed by heroes who maintained honor and saved women from unthinkable harm. When Will and June were born, there were only 30 or 31 states in the Union. By the end of the decade, North and South Dakota, Montana, Washington state, Idaho, Wyoming and Utah would be added. Six other states would join in the next century, completing what we know as the United States. Newspapers responded to the public interest in this expansion by added stories in their columns about the west, as they tried to compete with publishers of the dime novels like Beadle and Adams who had a large fan base in both America and England.

In the 1880 census, June was living at 197 Halsey Street, Brooklyn, with his mother and sisters. This was two blocks north of Fulton Street. He was listed as the 29-year-old "head of household," and a reporter. He would continue to live in Brooklyn and commute to New York City using horse-drawn trolleys, and the Fulton Street Ferry. The ferry carried about 40 percent of Brooklyn's work force to Manhattan, and in turn, Manhattan sent vacationers to Brooklyn to stroll along Coney Island, Brighton Beach, Bath Beach and Manhattan Beach with parasols, straw hats and canes. On the census, next to his mother's name was a very large pronounced captial "D" by the marital status column. This was never discussed, but it implies a divorce happened prior to 1880 between Elizabeth McDowell and Andrew Nerva Rankin. It

Five. Rising to the Top (1880–1884)

appears as though William stayed in close contact with his father, and June became increasingly protective of his mother and sisters.

The divorce helps to explains numerous family properties, separate burials and family secrets. It is difficult to say what caused the divorce, which was very shameful in those days. Perhaps living through the Civil War, under constant stress with Andrew Nerva Rankin's continual political causes, left the marriage shaky. He had placed his family in danger. Perhaps the fact that he forbade his daughters to marry, due to his belief that they were from the ascendancy and needed husbands of a high station, was difficult for Elizabeth to accept. She was not related to the Achesons. Nerva's non-stop inventing may have been frustrating. The stress of many moves, the blocks in the daughters' marriages, the chasing after new inventions, the drive for public expression, and legal wrangling, ultimately took a toll on the marriage. Perhaps the cause was sheer exhaution. Andrew Nerva Rankin stayed in Rockland County.

June was not only covering baseball for the Sunday New York *Mercury* newspaper and the New York *Herald*, but also was assigned to be official scorer for the New York Metropolitans Base Ball Club from their inception in 1880 until their close in 1883.[1] The September 1880 New York *Herald* reported on the formation of the club, made up mostly of schoolteachers.[2] John B. Day (1847–1925) and James J. Mutrie (1851–1938) were owners of the club, with Jim as manager. Day was a tobacconist who had formed a club in Orange, New Jersey. He thought of himself as a pitcher but soon discovered he was better suited elsewhere. James Mutrie was an adventurer who had managed a troubled club in Massachusetts and played shortstop. The story had him traveling from Bedford, Massachusetts, to New York on bicycle to try to form a club. He met Day and

Andrew Brown "June" Rankin V, baseball editor for the New York *Herald* and the New York *Sunday Mercury* newspapers. In the 1880s, he was considered a celebrity in baseball circles (used by permission, Rankin Family Archives).

Pictured above is the 1882 New York Metropolitans Base Ball Club. Standing left to right: Jack Lynch, Charlie Reipschlager, Tip O'Neill, Ed Kennedy, John Clapp, John Doyle, Frank Hankinson, and Steve Brady. Seated left to right: Tom Mansell, Terry Larkin, Candy Nelson, and John Reilly (National Baseball Hall of Fame Library, Cooperstown, New York).

June Rankin served the club as official scorer from its inception in 1880 until its close in 1883. He initially connected manager James Mutrie to owner John B. Day. Playing for the club in 1880 were pitchers Tim Keefe and Jack Lynch; catchers Bill Holbert and Charlie Reipschlager; infielders Steve Brady, Sam Crane, Dude Esterbrook, Candy Nelson and Dave Orr; and outfielders Ed Kennedy, John O'Rourke, and Chief Roseman.

together they formed the Metropolitan Exhibition Company. Day's club in Orange, New Jersey, was playing against a local Brooklyn club on the day of their meeting. The new club formed, the Metropolitans or Mets for short, was made of players taken from the Brooklyn Unions and from the Rochester Hop Bitters Base Ball Clubs and run as an independent professional club. The Hop Bitters had been sponsored in 1879 by the manufacturing company by that name which produced an alcohol-based cure-all medicine advertising powers over many internal diseases, including drunkenness.

Will Rankin mentioned in a 1904 *Sporting News* article, and in a 1905 history of the Metropolitans Base Ball Club, something interesting about June's involvement at the formative time of the Metropolitans. He wrote that James Mutrie, when he arrived in New York, was having trouble finding financial backing to form a New York club. Most people looked at him as though he were crazy, believing that he, from Massachusetts, could create a club in New York. In desperation, he called on June Rankin who was working at the New York *Herald*, and from him learned that "Mr. Day would pitch for a team on the next afternoon at the Old Union Grounds, in Brooklyn." Mutrie met Day through June. Jim arrived at the grounds "as Mr. Day was leaving the field." That was when Mutrie introduced himself to Day and laid out his plan for a New York club. The next morning, Mutrie and Day met in Day's office on Maiden Lane and formalized the plan.[3] June Rankin and James Mutrie were the same age. John Day was a few years older. June then became the official scorer at the team's inception. Will wrote that June was the connecting tissue between Mutrie and Day at that very first meeting. Had Mutrie not learned about Mr. Day from June, the Metropolitans might not have materialized, at least not in the partnership of Mutrie and Day.

The Metropolitans took their name from an earlier New York club now long gone. They initially played exhibition games in 1880 as an independent club, and were formally organized in 1881. However, the 1880 season against amateur clubs did end with 12 wins and only 1 loss. They were successful from the start. In the fall of 1880, the club began playing against National League clubs and did well. The Metropolitans played in New Jersey and then at the Union Grounds and Capitoline Grounds in Brooklyn before moving to Polo Grounds I,[4] 110th Street and Sixth Avenue in Manhattan, which was owned by James Gordon Bennett, Jr., June's publisher. One story had a shoeshine boy pointing Day towards usage of the Polo field.[5] June would have also known about the field. However it happened, John B. Day approached the Manhattan Polo Association in 1881 asking for permission to play on the field. He then leased the Polo Grounds for his club for a number of years with an option of renewal. He would eventually build two ball fields there, which would be separated by a canvas fence. In the future, there would be three more consecutive Polo Grounds, each located at a different location. This one, however, was the only one which had been used for polo. The name Polo Grounds became deeply associated in the minds of the public with New York baseball. This also was the first professional field within the New York City limits. The New York Mutuals had played in Brooklyn.

June Rankin, in his book on the club, wrote that it was through Jim Mutrie's "untiring exertion" that the club was established in New York. June continued to write that Mutrie stuck with "his first love [Metropolitans] until they won the Championship of the American Association in 1884." He also stated that the New York public were "great baseball admirers, and they thoroughly appreciate good ball playing."[6]

On the 1880 first nine roster for the Metropolitans were pitcher John Daly; catcher Pat Deasley; first baseman Walker; captain and second baseman Steve Brady; third baseman Joe Farrell; Shortstop Jack "Candy" Nelson; left field Ed Kennedy; center fielder Pike; and right fielder Bill Hawes. Will Rankin mentioned that Brady, Farrell, Hawes, Deasley, Kennedy and Daly all came from the Rochester Club, and Dude Esterbrook and Walker came from the Buffalo National League Club. He also listed Jack Nelson on that beginning roster. In addition, Will mentioned frequent displays of fireworks at the Polo Grounds, given by the Metropolitan Exhibition Company, which made it a very festive place.

Playing for the club in 1881 would be Steve Brady, Fatty Briody, Jim Clinton, Hugh Daily, Jerry Dorgan, John Doyle, Denny Driscoll, Dude Esterbrook, John Farrow, John Hayes, John Kelly, Ed Kennedy, Jack Leary, Tom Mansell, Mike Muldoon, Jack Neagle, Tom Poorman, Phil Powers, Chief Roseman, Lou Say, Dan Sullivan, Sleeper Sullivan, Rooney Sweeney, and Billy Taylor. In 1882, Jack Lynch, Charlie Reipschlager, Tip O'Neill, Ed Kennedy, John Clapp, John Doyle, Frank Hankinson, Steve Brady, Tom Mansell, Terry Larkin, Candy Nelson, and John Reilly were on the roster. The last year of June's scoring, 1883, had the following roster: pitchers Tim Keefe and Jack Lynch; catchers Bill Holbert and Charlie Reipschlager; infielders Steve Brady, Sam Crane, Thomas "Dude" Esterbrook, Candy Nelson and Dave Orr; and outfielders Ed Kennedy, John O'Rourke and Chief Roseman. The Metropolitans played 151 games in 1881, which was "the greatest number of matches played by one club against professional nines in one season up until then."[7] Games generally ran from spring until autumn; 60 of the games were against league clubs, and gate receipts for the season were over $30,000.[8]

Timothy Keefe, nicknamed "Sir Timothy," would become the dominant pitcher of the century, earning himself an induction into the Baseball Hall of Fame in 1964. Known for his gentlemanly behavior, he began pitching at the 45 foot distance and graduated into the 60 foot, 6 inches modern distance. Pitching was now done from a distance of 50 feet instead of 45 feet. Keefe pitched for the Troy Tojans in 1880, where he set all time records. He joined the Metropolitans and soon became their star. When he went on to the New York Giants, he became a living legend. William "Buck" Ewing would be paired with him later and the two would become a formidable team. Buck was called, by the New York *Clipper*, a model player who had "no superior," and "few equals." He could play "any position" and was a "swift and accurate thrower, hard-hitting batsman, and clever base-runner."[9] William H. Holbert and Charlie Reipschlager, on the club in 1883, were also able to catch the pitches sent by Keefe. Holbert was a "swift and accurate" thrower and was called "good-humored and reliable."[10]

John "Candy" Nelson was a Brooklyn boy who played for a number of clubs prior to joining the Metropolitans. He was a left-handed batter who was called "swift and accurate" in throwing and displayed "much coolness in critical emergencies."[11] David Orr was a New York City boy who had filled in for an injured O'Rourke. He ended up leading the Metropolitans with his "hard hitting." He was reported to have "hit the ball over the left-field fence into the river for a home-run" at the May 22, 1884, home game.[12] Edward Kennedy played most of the Metropolitans' games in left field. He was a favorite of the fans due to his quiet nature, and he was close to James Mutrie, staying with the club until 1886. Kennedy was said to be able to complete very difficult plays, including one where he did a somersault but still held the ball.[13]

In 1882, the American Association was formed by clubs which had been cast aside by the National League. Cincinnati, Louisville, Philadelphia, and St. Louis joined with Baltimore and Pittsburgh in the association. The Metropolitans were invited to join the American Association, but at first the club remained independent, joining a League Alliance with Philadelphia with only two clubs. The National League was without a New York City club, and many felt the Metropolitans might join that league, especially because Day often spoke in public about the fact that New York City and Philadelphia should be in the National League.[14] Worcester and Troy then stepped out of the National League, opening a spot for New York and Philadelphia. Day applied to the league for the spot but then surprised everyone by having the Metropolitans join the American Association (AA) and announcing the formation of an entirely new club for the National League spot.

The American Association of Base Ball Clubs had organized in 1882 to compete directly with the National League. H. D. McKnight served as the first president. The cities initially in the association were the Baltimore Orioles, Cincinnati Red Stockings, Louisville Colonels, Philadelphia Athletics, Pittsburg Alleghenys or Pirates, and the St. Louis Brown Stockings or Browns. The association, which lasted until 1891, offered cheaper gate tickets to the public (25 cents instead of 50 cents), Sunday baseball, and served beer to patrons. The association was nicknamed the Beer and Whiskey League, because many manufacturers of liquor supported teams, particularly in the Midwest. It generally drew a rougher crowd than the National League, due to the alcohol served and lower ticket prices. David Voigt makes mention of a number of contributions made by the American Association to the game of baseball. On his list were bringing games into urban areas not served prior to this; giving young players a place to improve their skills, giving a form of recreation to those working a six-day work week who could watch games on Sundays but were not available on Saturdays, and the general promotion of baseball for the young. Yet, because of the association's lower prices and less competent management, it eventually suffered.[15] The association would eventually be absorbed into the National League.

David Nemec in *The Beer and Whiskey League* begins his book by mentioning the fact that this period in baseball, 1882–1891, was "the most vibrant and freewheeling time" as the American Association tried to exist with the National League.[16] June was in the middle of the new association's beginnings in the New York area. The Metropolitans joined the American Association in 1883. June had scored for the club and recorded the games up to that point. But in 1883, June was switched to score for the management's new club. The Metropolitans did go on to win a pennant in 1884, but in December 1885 they were sold to Erastus Wiman's Staten Island Amusement Company for $25,000.[17]

Will, who loved playing the game of baseball, was mentioned in papers as often practicing with the Metropolitans in his free time and was reported to have frequently taken players aside to give them extra help.[18] It appears June practiced with them as well. However, the March 29, 1913, *Brooklyn Daily Eagle* obituary on William mentions the fact that Will frequently practiced with the Metropolitan*s*, as a *pitcher*. The article had Andrew *catching*, which is a reversal of their original positions. This may show the problems which had surfaced in Will's hands. Another later newspaper article on Will does mention a plaster cast of June's "catcher's foot,"[19] which also may reinforce the reversal of positions at this time. The article in the *Eagle* did say something interesting about William and Andrew; together they "kept the heavy hitters of the time guessing." It also mentioned Will's "twisted fingers and disjointed knuckles" which he had "received through stopping hot liners with the bare hand."[20] One family photo of June also reveals what appear to be badly damaged hands, though no mention of them was ever made. The Metropolitans finished with a 54 to 42 record and placed 4th in the American Association.

The issue of protective gear began to surface early in the game. Injuries were common for catchers, particularly broken fingers and the loss of fingernails, bruises on the face, kneecap injuries, as well as the danger of being in close proximity to the batter.[21] In the 1870s the only players wearing protective gear were pitchers and catchers. The protection usually consisted of leather gloves with the fingers cut out.[22] Balls had changed their size to the more common 9–9½ inch, 5–5¾ ounce ball known now, and the balance between a live and dead ball was addressed so the ball had the right amount of spring, without too much or too little.²³ In the 1880s the official league ball was accepted. The ball was thrown underhand at first by pitchers, though pitchers were beginning to make their throws more difficult to hit. However, even back in 1872 the overhand pitch had begun to be used by some.²⁴ Catchers often caught the ball with two hands before the glove came into use.²⁵ Catching, in particular, was a very dangerous position because the catcher had to move up close to the batter in order to be in position to throw out runners trying to steal base. Some catchers wore a rubber mouthpiece, but the mask was not introduced until 1878, after Frederick Winthrop Thayer, captain of the Harvard University Base Ball Club, sold the rights to patent it to Albert Spalding. Thayer had based his 1875 version on the fencing masks used at Harvard.²⁶

It is important to realize all of this when looking especially at Will Rankin. Beginning in 1866, he had not used gloves for catching. June, too, in pitching had little protection. Both later often practiced with the Metropolitans Base Ball Club, which was a professional club with heavy hitters. Over time, Will had severely damaged his hands. He caught line drives without gloves and as an adult suffered from "twisted fingers and swollen knuckles" of which he apparently was "quite proud."²⁷ Actually, most professional players shunned gloves until the early 1890s.²⁸ However, as early as August 24, 1879, the *Brooklyn Daily Eagle*, the paper for which Will wrote, advocated the wearing of the catcher's mask for protection.²⁹ This was something that Henry Chadwick, in particular, thought was wise.

It is difficult to imagine how William and June, with such badly damaged hands, were able to write volumes of commentary at all. Manual typewriters began to surface in the 1880s and 1890s; they were often difficult to use and required a great amount of hand strength. Reporting mostly made use of teletype machines up to that point. The only way one with badly damaged hands would be able to use any of these mechanical machines would have been by using something like two index fingers hunting and pecking. It must have been painful.

The production of protective gear greatly helped players and made sporting companies, like that of Albert Spalding, quite rich. Even Spalding commented on how his left hand had been badly bruised by catching without a glove.³⁰ He first witnessed a player from Boston, Charles C. Waite, wearing a glove in 1875 and then began using one himself in 1877, much to his embarrassment at the time.³¹ Gloves and catcher's masks based on fencing masks were being slowly introduced in the late 1800s. Guards for shins and the chest would come later and help players be able to have longer careers in the game.

Will's third son, Harold Emerson Rankin, was born on October 17, 1881.

During this period, Will wrote a brief history on the national game, and one on the Metropolitan, Brooklyn and Chelsea baseball clubs. But 1883 was the last year Will was on staff for the *Brooklyn Daily Eagle*; it was also the year the Brooklyn Bridge was completed and became a major tourist attraction. The bridge connected Brooklyn newspaper writers with New York City writers at Newspaper Row. The Fulton Street Ferry was no longer needed to get to Manhattan. Both areas grew as a result of that bridge, and access to games was made much easier as well. Will seemed to follow the opening of the bridge to New York City.

During the early 1880s, Andrew Nerva Rankin, father of Will and June, launched a number of corporations to help produce his inventions. On June 5, 1880, the *Rockland County Journal* listed the Great American Egg Company, which produced a chemical meant to preserve eggs with a ten million dollar capital startup. The egg company was mentioned in a number of New York newspapers that year, with June and Will listed as trustees with their father, along with Henry M. Haigh and John Van Boekorck. Wickey's soluble chemical compound, for which they had exclusive rights, was to be manufactured at the factory, and it was to be mechanically applied to eggs. Andrew Nerva was a mechanical genius, not a chemist. So, he may have figured out a delivery system for the chemical as well. The funds would largely go towards the purchase of a property at Hunters Point, New York. Papers listed the amount of the secured capital differently, anywhere from one million to one hundred and ten million dollars. However, the *Rockland County Journal* had strong connections with the family, so its figure may be the most accurate.

In 1881, Andrew Nerva Rankin also formed the Nerva Pipe Protecting Company in Camden, New Jersey, and the Continental Conduit Company of Hunter's Point, Long Island.[32] The latter may have used the same location as the Great American Egg Company. The pipe and conduit companies most likely used his cold pack pipe fixture patents. It was a process for protecting pipes from freezing by lining pipes with pipes. Andrew Nerva seemed to be ever creating and expanding his ideas. Adela, too, continued to perform recitations and even traveled within regions of Pennsylvania.[33]

June was busy writing and scoring, and during this period of serving on the Judiciary Committee for the International Association of Professional Base Ball Players, he expressed his anger at the National League. He felt that they were acting to "control the baseball fraternity" and felt they were a "clique, or ring." He also felt that the League Alliance was nothing more than a ploy intended to destroy the International. There was nothing in it which served the interest of that group. He called for those outside the National League to "stand by each other" in order to create a "grand organization."[34] The International began to disintegrate, losing Canadian clubs, and ended in 1880. The National Association expired in 1880, and then the League Alliance was abolished in 1883 by the National League, having served its purpose.

Later in 1887, however, the directors of the newly reorganized International League would make their own mistakes with a terrible decision prohibiting black players from signing contracts within their league, allowing racism to block talented athletes from the game simply due to the uncomfortable feeling some of the white players experienced with them present. They did let those with existing contracts keep them, but that ban would stand until 1946. Cap Anson, manager of the White Sox, was the one who was openly intolerant, pushing for segregation. The second International Association would only last until 1890.

From 1883 to 1884 Will became the official scorer for both the Brooklyn Base Ball Club, and the Inter-state Association, a member of the American Alliance.[35] The Brooklyn Base Ball Club, formed in 1883, according to most reports was the brainchild of George Taylor, city editor of the New York *Herald*. He drew together his friend Charles H. Byrne with brother-in-law and businessman Joseph J. Doyle and Ferdinand A. Abell to form a club. Byrne was a baseball fan and had made a lot of money in real estate. Abell was the owner of a society club which most likely provided gambling.[36] Byrne became the club president.

However, in a 1906 article for *Sporting News*, Will Rankin told another story. In that article he mentioned that June, working on the *Herald*, was the one who suggested to George J. Taylor of the same paper, in the winter of 1882 and 1883, the advantages of having a club in Brooklyn. Taylor wholeheartedly agreed with him but could not see where they would be able to play ball. Will and June then met with Charles H. Byrne and his brother-in-law, in late February or early March 1883, at the "location of the ground on which future base ball history was to be made by the Brooklyn Club." The Third and Fifth Avenue, and Third and Fifth Street location, unfortunately, was under water at the time and did not look very promising. However, after Taylor saw the grounds, he sought the financial backing for the club, and then the partnership was formed.[37] Will became official scorer for the club at its inception. The article placed both Will and June in the story of the formation period for what would become the Brooklyn Dodgers. Had June not pressed the city editor of the New York *Herald* with the idea of a Brooklyn club and met with the real estate man who later funded the process, it might have been a while before that city would have seen a championship club. June had served as the catalyst once again.

Brooklyn had had a long history of playing baseball beginning with teams

The 1889 Brooklyn Bridegroom Base Ball Club (later called Dodgers). Top row left to right: Geroge J. "Germany" Smith, shortstop: John "Pop" Corkhill, center field; William H. "Adonis" Terry, pitcher; David Luther Foutz, first base; William D. "Darby" O'Brien, left field; Albert John "Doc" Bushong, substitute; American Indian Joseph Paul Visner/Vezina, catcher. Bottom row left: George Burton Pinkney, third base; Robert Lee "Parisian Bob" Caruthers, pitcher; Hubert B. "Hub" Collins, second base; William Henry McGunnigle, manager; Thomas P. "Oyster" Burns, right field; Robert H. Clark, catcher; Tomas Joseph Lovett, pitcher. Front on ground: Michael J. "Mickey" Hughes, pitcher (courtesy New York Public Library).

In 1882 and 1883 June Rankin approached George Taylor, editor of the New York *Herald*, with the idea of forming a Brooklyn baseball club. June and Will Rankin then visited the potential field with Charles H. Byrne and Joseph J. Doyle in 1883. In 1883 and 1884, Will Rankin served as official scorer for the newly formed club at its inception as the Brooklyn Grays in 1883 and then named the Brooklyn Atlantics in 1884. On the team in 1883 were Barnes, Maurice Bresnanhan, Burns, John Campana, Jack Corcoran, Tom Dolan, John Doyle, Jim Egan, John Farrow, Frank Fennelly, John Firth, Billy Geer, Bill Greenwood, Charlie Householder, Sam Kimber, Henry Luff, Tim Manning, John McCabe, M. McManus, Mellon, Bill Morgan, Miah Murray, Dave Oldfield, Bill Schenck, Edgar Smith, Tony Suck, Adonis Terry, Charles Tuttle, Oscar Walker, West, and Wash Williams. George Taylor served as manager.

like the Atlantic, Excelsior, Putnam and Eckford clubs in the 1840s. The Atlantics had joined the National Association of Baseball Players in 1857. They were national champions in 1864 and 1866. In 1870, they even beat the famous Cincinnati Red Stockings, the first professional club. The Atlantics largely played on the Capitoline Grounds in Brooklyn. They remained amateurs. The Mutuals had played in Brooklyn, too, but were considered a New York club. This new Brooklyn club, formed in 1883, was that city's first professional club.

In a November 1906 article in *Sporting News*, Will mentioned the fact that the Brooklyn club was incorporated under the laws of New Jersey. They held their annual meetings in Jersey City. Each year they filed their annual report with the secretary of the state of New Jersey as part of the incorporation process.[38] Byrne obtained a spot in the Inter-state Association. The club was initially called the Brooklyn Base Ball Club or Brooklyn Grays, and then called the Brooklyn Atlantics in 1884, when they sold their franchise in the Inter-state and joined the American Association. The old Atlantics had been a successful minor league club in the early days of baseball in the city.

The other names for the club in the future would be a whirlwind established mainly by the press: Brooklyn Bridegrooms (1890–1910), after a number of members married; City Nine and Church City Nine, since Brooklyn was called the city of churches with the report that a church could be found on every block; Brooklyn Kings, since Brooklyn is in Kings County; and the Brooklyn Superbas (1899–1910), when Harry Von de Horst and Ned Hanlon purchased half interest in the club with Hanlon managing. There was a Vaudeville group named Hanlon's Superbas. The name Brooklyn Trolley Dodgers (1891–1912) was given because a number of trolley tracks criss-crossed in their playing area and one had to dodge the trolleys to see the game. Most people from Brooklyn, however, were called trolley dodgers by New Yorkers because of the city's network of rails. Next, they were called the Brooklyn Robins (1914–1931), named after new manager "Uncle" Wilbert Robinson; Brooklyn Dodgers (1832–1957), as the shortened nickname became the formal name; and now Los Angeles Dodgers (1958–present), when the club moved to California. The formal name of the club was, however, The Brooklyn Base Ball Club and they needed permission, initially, from the Metropolitans in New York to play at Washington Park in Brooklyn since the field was only five miles from the Polo Grounds. The National Agreement rules listed a ten mile perimeter between clubs.

Many of the original members had come from the Merritts Base Ball Club of Camden, New Jersey. On the team in 1883 were pitchers John Doyle, Jim Egan, John Firth, Sam Kimber, John McCabe and Adonis Terry; catchers

Jack Corcoran, John Farrow, Charlie Householder, Tim Manning, Bill Morgan, Miah Murray, Dave Oldfield, Tony Suck, Charles Tuttle and Wash Williams; first basemen Egan, Farrow, Householder, Morgan, Terry and Oscar Walker; second basemen Frank Fennelly, Bill Greenwood, Manning, and Walker; third baseman Bill Schenck; shortstop Billy Geer; right field Tom Dolan, Corcoran, Greenwood, Sam Kimberly, M. McManus, Terry, Tuttle, and Walker; center field Barnes, Henry Luff, Tuttle, Walker, and West; left field Egan, Henry Luff, Edgar Smith, and Terry; and outfielders Doyle, Morgan and Farrow.[39] George Taylor left his editorial position at the New York *Herald* and served as manager in 1883. They won the Inter-state Association Championship that year with the *Clipper* reporting that the club was run on "business principles," and Taylor was liked by managers and players alike. He only had one year's experience yet his "executive ability" made the difference that year.[40]

The Brooklyn Club played their first game on May 12, 1883, to a crowd of about 6,000. They developed an excellent reputation as ballplayers, playing mainly at Washington Park which had been named after George Washington's Continental Army; it had fought the Battle of Long Island in that vicinity.[41] The ballpark featured a grandstand and bleachers. There would be three Washington Parks over the years. The first one on Third and Fifth streets and Fourth and Fifth avenues was used during Will's time as scorer. The second park was diagonally opposite the first park and used in 1889 by the club. It was on First and Third streets and Third and Fourth avenues. The third park was in the same location as number two but rebuilt with steel and concrete stands. At that time a Federal League club, the Brooklyn Tip-Tops or Brook-Feds, used it while the Brooklyn National League club moved into its new home at Ebbets Field.

Charles Hercules Ebbets, Sr. (1859–1925), would work his way up for this club from bookkeeper in 1883 to share holder in 1890, team manager and president in 1898, and owner. An 1892 biography on Charles Ebbets in the New York *Clipper* mentioned the fact that he was a master at mathematical scheduling of championship games. He drafted schedules by making a skeleton and then filling in the dates; he calculated the mileage to equalize time and expenses with holidays considered, and then the clubs were placed in a regular order. Both the American Association and National League passed resolutions thanking him for this. Ebbets mentioned 1892 being his most difficult scheduling of twelve clubs. The 1884 list was of no use to him at that time since that twelve club schedule played fewer games.[42] But in 1883 he was just beginning his long legacy with the club and in baseball.

The Inter-state Association of Base Ball Clubs was initially composed of seven clubs: the Brooklyn Grays, Brooklyn, New York (who switched to the American Association in 1884); Camden Merritts, Camden, New Jersey (who eventually sent players to the Grays); Harrisburg, Harrisburg, Pennsylvania; Pottsville Anthracites, Pottsville, Pennsylvania; Reading Actives, Reading, Pennsylvania; Trenton, New Jersey; and the Willington Quicksteps, Willington, Delaware. By 1884 Will was an American Association club scorer. He seemed to have followed the Brooklyn club into that association. The American Association was the rival to the National League from 1882 to 1891. The Inter-state Association folded by 1885.

In 1883, another league attempted to compete with the National League. The Union Association of Base Ball Clubs was made up of the following clubs: Altoona Mountain City, Baltimore Monumentals, Boston Reds, Chicago Browns, Cincinnati Outlaw Reds, Kansas City Cowboys, Milwaukee Brewers, Philadelphia Keystones, Pittsburgh Stogies, St. Louis Maroons, St. Paul Saints, Washington Nationals, and Wilmington Quicksteps. Henry Lucas, a millionaire from St. Louis, was the president; Thomas Pratt of the Philadelphia club was vice president; and Warren W. White of the Washington club was secretary. It was quickly branded by both the National League and American Association as "wild cats," and both leagues attempted to boycott them. The Union Association attacked the National League's reserve clause, reserving a certain number of players to a club. The Union lasted only one season and died in 1884, coming under the harsh treatment of the National League which was denounced by the New York *Clipper.*

Charles Endler managed the Brooklyn Base Ball Club, under the title Brooklyn Atlantics, in 1884. The name Atlantics paid homage to the earlier Atlantics Base Ball Club of Brooklyn. On the roster that year were pitchers John Holzberger and Stoltz; catcher Arthur Thompson; first baseman McGurk; second baseman Dooley; third baseman Bonney; shortstop Simmons Steiner; right fielders John Holzberger; Kerwin, and Stoltz; center fielder Kelly; and left fielders Higgins and Jones. The club had won the Inter-state Association championship and was then invited to join the American Association in 1884.

June Rankin left scoring for the American Association in 1883, and Will Rankin began scoring for it in 1884. The American Association at that time was made up of the Baltimore Orioles, Brooklyn Grays, Cincinnati Red Stockings, Columbus Colts, Indianapolis Blues, Louisville Colonels, New York Metropolitans, Philadelphia Athletics, Pittsburgh Alleghenys, Richmond Virginias, St. Louis Browns, Toledo Blue Stockings, and Washington Nationals. Byrne, who had managed the club initially, had turned management over to William H. McGunnigle. The club remained in the American Association for six seasons, until 1889, when they were called the Bridegrooms after six players married. The club would later enter the National League in 1890. The Brooklyn club would belong to three different affiliations during its rich history.

Will was present during the early formative years of the club, recording scores and on occasion making calls on play, particularly in the area of errors. Scorers needed to be able to untangle complex plays so as to record them correctly, deciphering if a play was merely an accident which had happened or an error attributed to a particular player. Records point only to Will scoring for the club in 1883 and 1884 while writing for the *Brooklyn Daily Eagle*. He would move to a New York paper in 1885, and that might have been the reason he no longer scored for a Brooklyn club. In Will's later years, he would often be handed a confusing play and asked to comment on it. Also, it appears that both brothers developed friendships over time with players on this particular club. In fact, Will mentions at the turn of the century in his *Sporting News* articles taking members of this club to New York games with him on days when they were not playing in Brooklyn.

While the brothers were experiencing success, December 1883 was particularly difficult for the sisters of Will and June. Lizzie, their younger sister, had been teaching dance. She was thirty. She mentioned it as recreation, not really a financial necessity. She also taught Sunday school at the Reformed Church. The superintendent of the Sunday school apparently confronted Lizzie in public about teaching dance with the fear that she might possibly teach children the sinful art. She assured him that she did not, but he told her to stop teaching dance all together or leave the Sunday school. The pastor sided with the superintendent's actions resulting in Lizzie leaving that church and joining the Presbyterian Church in Jamaica, to which Etta already belonged. The new church had no problem with Lizzie teaching dance. It is difficult to understand how the seemingly harmless forms of dance taught by Lizzie could arouse such chastisement, but in fact, a number of denominations strictly prohibited all forms of dancing during this period, so the Reformed Church was not alone. An unmarried woman teaching dance would have been a bit scandalous, even if the dance was the waltz. Lizzie, to her credit, continued teaching dance and even taught kindergarten Sunday school for the Presbyterian Church.

The dramatic story was covered in the *Brooklyn Daily Eagle* with dialogue perhaps furnished by Will, who was completing his last year writing on baseball for the *Eagle*. The verbal assault by the superintendent was reported by the writer as an embarrassment and brutal, leaving Lizzie very shaken.[43] The article also made mention of one of the sisters suffering from malaria, but did not list which one: Margaret or Arie. It is difficult to image malaria being a

Five. Rising to the Top (1880–1884)

The 1888 New York Base Ball Club (Giants) with manager James Mutrie (center). Photograph by Joseph Hall taken at the Polo Grounds in Manhattan, New York. June Rankin served as official scorer for the club from 1883 to 1889 (National Baseball Hall of Fame Library, Cooperstown, New York).

threat in New York, but it was. Malaria in various places within the United States was not controlled until the mid–1950s, and even today New York still has a few cases, mostly due to international travel. John J. McGraw, later of the New York Giants, would be diagnosed with the disease in 1895.[44]

The National League had been looking for a club to be located in New York City. John Day applied for that spot, and then stunned everyone by not entering the Metropolitans as expected, but rather a new club developed from scratch. June Rankin ended his scoring for the Metropolitans in 1883 and became official scorer for the newly formed New York Gothams Base Ball Club, or Green Stockings, from 1883 to 1889. The Gothams paid homage to an earlier club name as well. The new club was also owned by John B. Day under the Metropolitan Exhibition Company, which owned clubs in both the National League (The Gothams or Green Stockings Base Ball Club) and the American Association (The Metropolitan Base Ball Club). This was not illegal at the time. Many of the Gotham players lived at the Grand Central Hotel.[45]

The Gothams also played at Polo Grounds I. The club took the Metropolitans' field while another, cheaper one was to be built for the Metropolitans next to it, separated by a ten foot canvas fence. The Metropolitans played, for a time, at Metropolitan Park by the East River. It had been the site of the old city dump and unfortunately the park took on the nickname "The Dump" by the public, not only because of its past history but because the factories surrounding the field sent out awful fumes. This ultimately forced the Metropolitans to avoid its usage when at all possible. Originally, the Metropolitans and Gothams were to alternate their games at Polo Grounds I, but soon both fields were being used, and it was said that persons sitting in the top bleachers could see two games for the price of one by looking over the canvas fence.[46] The Gothams or Green Stockings, however, had the owner's best players slowly transferred onto the roster.[47]

The Metropolitans played on the Western 6th Avenue side of the Polo Grounds, with cheaper tickets, no frills, and many drunks. It appealed to the working classes. The Giants played on the Eastern 5th Avenue side with a fine grandstand, appealing to the middle and upper classes. It appears as though John B. Day felt that the American Association would not have the staying power of the National League. He played the Metropolitans on a shoestring with limited equipment, transferring his best players to the Gothams. When the Metropolitan Club was eventually sold, the Gothams took over both baseball fields. The new club was called many names: the Gothams, the Green Stockings, the New Yorks, the New York Nationals, and eventually nicknamed the Giants. It existed in New York from 1883 to 1957.

The manager of the Gothams in 1883 was John Edgar Clapp (1851–1904), nicknamed "Honest John," who had been a veteran catcher and outfielder for a number of clubs including the Philadelphia Athletics, St. Louis, Indianapolis, Cincinnati, and Cleveland. He had managed a club in Buffalo as well. He was called a great batter and base runner by the New York *Clipper* in 1881.[48] On the roster in 1883 were: pitchers Myron Allen, James "Tip" O'Neill, and "Smiling Mickey" Welch; catchers John Clapp, Buck Ewing and John Humphries; infielders Ed Caskin, Roger Connor, Frank Hankinson, John "Dasher" Troy; and outfielders Dick Cramer, Mike Dorgan, Pete Gillespie, Dave Orr, Gracie Pierce and John Montgomery Ward. Ewing, Connor, Gillespie and Welch had all come from the Troy Club when it disbanded. Frank Hankinson and John Clapp were moved over from the Metropolitans. Ward was brought in from Providence. Troy came from Detroit. Dorgan had played for the National League. O'Neill was a local player. Many of these players also lived at the Harlem House hotel at 115th Street and 3rd Avenue. The club played their first game on May 1, 1883, against Boston. There were 12,000 persons watching, General Grant being one.

Five. Rising to the Top (1880–1884)

The New York press also felt a shift in 1883. The New York *Herald*, in particular, had been very profitable from 1873 to 1883. That decade was the period in which the paper functioned the best under James Gordon Bennett, Jr. However, Joseph Pulitzer had taken the helm at the New York *World* and had successfully turned that paper around. As a result, papers like the *Herald* had marked decreases in their sales. Coupled with this was James Jr.'s extravagant lifestyle. He needed cash to support his properties. The move of June to the Giants, on a field still owned by Bennett, may have been one discussed by both the owners of the Metropolitan Club and the editor of the *Herald* to maximize profits.

By 1884, John Clapp managed the club for part of the season and then John M. Ward managed for the rest of the season. On the roster in 1884 were pitchers Ed Begley, Jim Brown, and Mickey Welch; catchers Buck Ewing, John Humphries, Bill Loughran, Charlie Manlove and Henry Oxley; first baseman Alex McKinnon; second baseman Roger Connor, third baseman Frank Hankinson; shortstop Ed Caskin; and outfielders Mike Dorgan, Pete Gillespie, Sandy Griffin, Danny Richardson, and John Ward.

James Mutrie was transferred to the New York Club in 1884 and began to manage it in 1885 when it formally took on the Giants name. James Mutrie seldom sat in the dugout. He left most of the managing to Buck Ewing, the club captain. James preferred working the crowd. As a matter of fact, the nickname Giants was said to have been given to the club by James Mutrie when he yelled, "My big fellows! My Giants!" from the stands.[49] April 14, 1885, is a date referred to for the name Giants being used as per the New York *World*.[50] That was the year their official name changed to The New York Giants Base Ball Club. Mutrie also coined the phrase "We are the people" for his club, leading a chant: "Who are the people? We are the people." Mutrie wore formalwear, tall hat and tails, to each game.[51] On the roster in 1885 were pitchers Larry Corcoran, Tim Keefe, and Mickey Welch; catchers Pat Deasley and Buck Ewing; first baseman Roger Connor; second baseman Joe Gerhardt; third baseman Dude Esterbrook; shortstop John Ward; and outfielders Mike Dorgan, Pete Gillespie, Jim O'Rourke, and Danny Richardson.

The 1886 season would add Jim Devlin as a pitcher. Eighteen eighty-seven would add Bill George, Mike Mattimore, John Roach, Bill Swarback, Cannonball Titcomb and Stump Wiedman to the pitching staff. A number of players would be listed for third base: Buck Becannon, Buck Ewing, Joe Gerhardt, Gil Hatfield, Candy Nelson, and John Rainey. By 1888 Ed Crane and Cannonball Titcomb would pitch with Tim Keefe and Mickey Welch and Stump Wiedman. Willard Brown would join Buck Ewing and Pat Murphy catching. The infielders would be Elmer Cleveland, Roger Connor, Gil

Hatfield, Danny Richardson, John Ward and Art Whitney, and the outfielders would be Elmer Foster, Bill George, George Gore, Jim O'Rourke, Mike Slattery, and Mike Tiernan.

Meanwhile, the Metropolitans Base Ball Club was purchased by Erasmus Wiman in 1885. He owned an amusement company which featured assorted animals. He also owned the Staten Island Ferry. Noel Hynd, in *The Giants of the Polo Grounds: The Glorious Times of Baseball's New York Giants*, wrote that the Baltimore and Ohio Railroad had expressed an interest in his property for a New York terminal. He was paid for use of his ferries and terminal based upon the number of persons using them. A baseball team on Staten Island was seen as a means to bring more patrons on the ferry to Staten Island, thus increasing the revenue he received.[52] The Metropolitans were purchased to be a money maker for him, not only due to gate receipts, but also due to the combination with ferry fees and their value.

The Giants played at Polo Grounds I until the Board of Aldermen of the city moved them out to make a housing development. The city had warned them for years that the enclosed 111th Street would have to be opened as a public street.[53] Eventually they landed at 155th and 157th Street in 1889, in the southern part of Coogan's Hollow, and called that park Polo Grounds II. At the time June was scorer for the club; until 1889, the Giants were members of the National League. June's period of scoring coincided with their membership in the National League, and their playing at Polo Grounds I. The club's first game at Polo Grounds 1 was on March 1, 1883, and their last game there was on October 13, 1888. The Giants won pennants in 1888 and 1889.

June would later write a history on the New York club in 1887 and 1888 and publish it in book form. The New York *Clipper*, when Will was baseball editor, would also do a history of the club members on April 28, 1894. June was still writing for the New York *Herald* and the *Sunday Mercury*, and also provided baseball information for the *News*, a paper published every evening, except Sunday, which also had a special weekly Wednesday and Sunday issue. It ran 4 pages in length weekly and 8 pages on Sunday, and was sized 19 by 31 inches daily, and 16 by 19 inches on Sunday. That paper was published on Park Row in New York.

In 1884, Richard K. Fox of the *National Police Gazette*, dubbed the "Bible of the Barbershop" for its sensational writing, advertised that the public could send in questions on any sport and it would be answered by an expert in the field. Fox was a boxing journalist who was inducted into the International Boxing Hall of Fame in Canastota, New York, in 1997. He also had a separate publishing company, which June would use later. The Fox Building, in lower Manhattan on Dover and Pearl Street by the Brooklyn Bridge, known as

Franklin Square, was considered the sporting center of the world according to Edward Van Every in *Sins of New York as "Exposed" by the Police Gazette*.[54] As a matter of fact, locals set their watches to the large clock on the Fox Building. On the list of those answering questions for that paper in 1884 was June Rankin. In a little play on words, Rankin also means kin of, or related to, the fox (rand).

The editor, Fox, held letters from the public for June on his desk, and published in nearly every issue that year the need for June Rankin, and others, to pick up their letters. June was not on staff, but served as one of the specialists, most likely on baseball. Among the others was John L. Sullivan, the boxing marvel. June answered his letters one by one. It is unknown if there was a fee involved for June's services, though it is probable. Also printed in the section on this service in the *Gazette* would be the name of a particular person with instructions for them to contact June Rankin directly at the New York *Clipper*. What is interesting about that was that June wrote for the *News*, *Herald* and *Sunday Mercury*, and not the New York *Clipper*, as far as records show. Will Rankin did not begin writing for the *Clipper* until 1885, but Henry Chadwick was there. So, the *Clipper* also held letters for June Rankin, which he appeared to keep separate from his regular place of work.[55] This actually was not unusual for sportswriters in that day who seemed to be writing for many papers at the same time in order to make a living.

Six

Celebrities in Baseball (1885–1889)

In 1885, the National Agreement was newly adopted between the American Association and the National League. That year Will began writing for the New York *Clipper*. He would stay with the paper, and eventually become baseball editor, for a total of twenty-eight years of the paper's seventy years of existence. Henry Chadwick had also been writing on cricket and baseball for that paper beginning in 1857 or '58, ending about 1889 with a small break in the middle. The two worked together again for a period of about four years as writers for the New York *Clipper*. Will was now 36 and Henry was 61. Writing for the New York *Clipper* appears to have been a life-long dream for Will, who always admired the *Clipper*'s presentation of baseball and was a big fan of Frank Queen. Will mentioned in a 1905 article for *The Sporting News* that Queen was very important in his own development as a sportswriter, even though Frank's brothers and heirs controlled the paper during Will's time there. Frank Queen had died on October 18, 1882, and Will came on staff in 1885. However, he knew Queen from his writing circles. Will wrote that he had begun reading the *Clipper* in the summer of 1865. That would have been when he first moved to New York as a youth. He found Frank Queen to be "thoroughly posted on all base ball matters." In fact, Will mentioned that everyone, Henry Chadwick included, followed the rules set in place by Frank Queen. Queen was a "stickler for rules," and Will gave him, alone, the credit for making the *Clipper* what it became. Will also mentioned the *Clipper* suffering when Queen was no longer the publisher.[1]

Will worked closely with baseball editor Alfred L. Hector Wright (1842–1905) on baseball and would eventually replace him. Wright had been born in New Jersey and played on the Manhattan Cricket Club. His father, a journalist and book seller, had branches of his business in other cities, one being

Six. Celebrities in Baseball (1885–1889)

William McDowell Rankin's press identification for the New York *Clipper*. Will wrote articles on baseball for the paper from 1885 to 1901, contributing biographies on players, managers and umpires until 1903. He served as assistant to baseball editor Al Wright beginning in 1888 and then succeeded him as baseball editor in 1893. Will remained on staff after the paper discontinued coverage of baseball until his death in 1913, serving the paper for a total of twenty-eight years (1885–1913) (used by permission from Arthur Rankin, great-grandson of W.M. Rankin).

Philadelphia. Wright began writing on cricket and baseball for the Philadelphia *Sunday Mercury* from 1868 to 1879. While there, he helped organize and became the official scorer for the Philadelphia Athletics for eleven years, using his own system for tabulation. He wrote a history of the club as well. The Athletics were members of the American Association and played against the Brooklyn Grays-Atlantics and New York Metropolitans, clubs both Rankin brothers had served as official scorers. They had much in common.

Wright also was the first one to compile a National League average showing the greatest percentage of victories in games played and suggested awarding the championship based upon those percentages. This was adopted by the American Association and later by the National League. He had toured England in 1874 with the Philadelphia Athletics and managed the club in 1876 when Will was official scorer for the New York Mutuals. Wright had replaced Henry Chadwick as cricket and baseball editor of the New York *Clipper* from 1879 to 1894. Chadwick continued to supply stories to the paper, but Will was working under Wright. Wright was another man Will adopted as a hero.

Will meticulously cut out past and present baseball sections from the paper and saved them in scrapbooks. He used the clippings as the authority on club scores and important events in the sport. These scrapbooks became one of his references for writing articles, and the basis for disputing claims made by others who had no statistical proof to back them. The scrapbooks also became part of his library, used for research by people like Henry Chadwick, and later John Montgomery Ward.

The New York *Clipper* had been initially formed in 1853 by Harrison Fulton Trent and then sold to its editor, Frank Queen (1823–1882), in 1855. It was designed with an entertainment focus and was initially located at 150 Fulton Street. Then, it moved to Ann Street, next Nassau Street, Spruce Street, and finally arrived, in 1869, to a 5-story building at 88 and 90 Centre Street on the corner of Leonard Street, close to newspaper Park Row.[2] The spot also was close to where Frank Queen had first started his own business career. The slogan of the *Clipper* at the time was "The Oldest American Sporting and Theatrical Journal," and sports played a large part in its popularity. It was published, according to the *American Newspaper Directory* of 1900, on Saturdays and featured sports and drama. It usually ran about 16 pages in length, and was 13 by 19 inches in size. A yearly subscription in 1861 cost $2 and by 1900 it was $4. It was in publication from 1853 to 1924, and reporting on baseball was an important part of its success in circulation in the middle years before it was absorbed into *Variety*.[3] Concise wording resonated with the public, an example of which is found in the August 1, 1885, issue as related to the Brooklyns in their victory over the Metropolitans in a July 25 game held in Brooklyn. The writer, perhaps Will, recorded that "they outhatted the Mets, punishing Lynch's pitching for six earned runs off seventeen made hits."[4] In the simple phrase you can not only see the game but also hear the bat hitting the ball in the staccato of the word choice.

The *Clipper* had begun using woodcut portraits of players, managers, and others in the 1880s which became very popular with the public, though some writers thought they made players look rather sinister. The portraits included a contemporary biography, giving the public a sense of the contributions made by the person being covered while viewing their picture. About 800 baseball biographies were printed in total.[5] The weekly *Clipper* also printed detailed box scores of games played across the country. Some of these box scores were collected and pasted into Will's scrapbooks, though he did not list the papers.[6] The preservation of baseball scores was the goal and not necessarily acknowledgment to journals or journalists.

The *Clipper Annual* during this period presented a one line per-event summary of a given sport, like baseball, by the week of the month on about two pages of double column copy. Baseball usually preceded reports on billiards. The *Annual* gave the reader a clear view of the progression happening within a given sport, with the major events of the year covered.[7] It was a short and easy guide to follow, set in place by Frank Queen. The Annuals, in particular, are collected in a number of public and private libraries.

While Will Rankin and Henry Chadwick were writing articles for the *Clipper*, with both also writing for other papers, Henry later mentioned June's scoring in an 1887 issue of *Sporting Life*. He wrote about June being one of the early scorers prior to 1882; of course, Will had been the first official scorer, but he was not mentioned in the article. Chadwick called June "very fair and impartial in his work."[8] June was scoring for the New York Giants at the time of the article. By all accounts, both June and Will appeared to have scored and reported honestly, which seemed to be an increasing challenge for June serving as both a baseball reporter and the official scorer for the New York Giants Base Ball Club in the mid-1880s.

The *Brooklyn Daily Eagle*, on October 25, 1885, had mentioned that the Metropolitan Company, owners of the New Yorks or Giants, was at that time seeking to control the press. Pressure was being felt by many reporters to write prejudicial material in favor of the company and against the Brooklyn club, a member of the American Association. The *Eagle* usually covered the Brooklyn club. The writer mentioned that the company seemed to want to "secure a monopoly of the professional business in the whole metropolitan district ... controlling influence over the press writers on the game, especially on the New York papers."[9] The newly adopted National Agreement was briefly mentioned in the text, but the issue of the Metropolitan Company exerting control would continue to build for June, in particular. He tried to branch out into self-publishing of independent material just prior to the breaking story.

But first, June was moved up to the sports editor position on the New York *Herald* in 1885, succeeding Mr. Kelly.[10] Michael J. Kelly had been the first editor of *DeWitt's Guide* and baseball editor for the *Herald*. Kelly was the one, according to Will Rankin, who introduced the shorthand system of scoring and the box scores.[11] The *Brooklyn Daily Eagle* mentions June as the baseball editor for both the *Herald* and *Sunday Mercury* at the same time in 1885.[12] The *Sunday Mercury* also was the paper which printed dissatisfaction over the control of baseball by a small group of men in the National League, a common theme in June's writing.

In addition to all the things June was doing at this point, the *Brooklyn Daily Eagle* mentioned that June also was writing independently for a paper called the *Base Ball Record*.[13] Added to his writing, scoring, baseball editing of two major newspapers, was this other paper. The February 17, 1886, issue of *Sporting Life* publicly thanked June Rankin of the *Herald* "for a bound volume of the *Official Record*," "the interesting little sporting daily which he published last summer." June apparently delivered a bound copy of his "daily newspaper on baseball" to the editor of that paper, which he had published during the summer of 1885.[14]

The two references to the paper for which June was writing and pub-

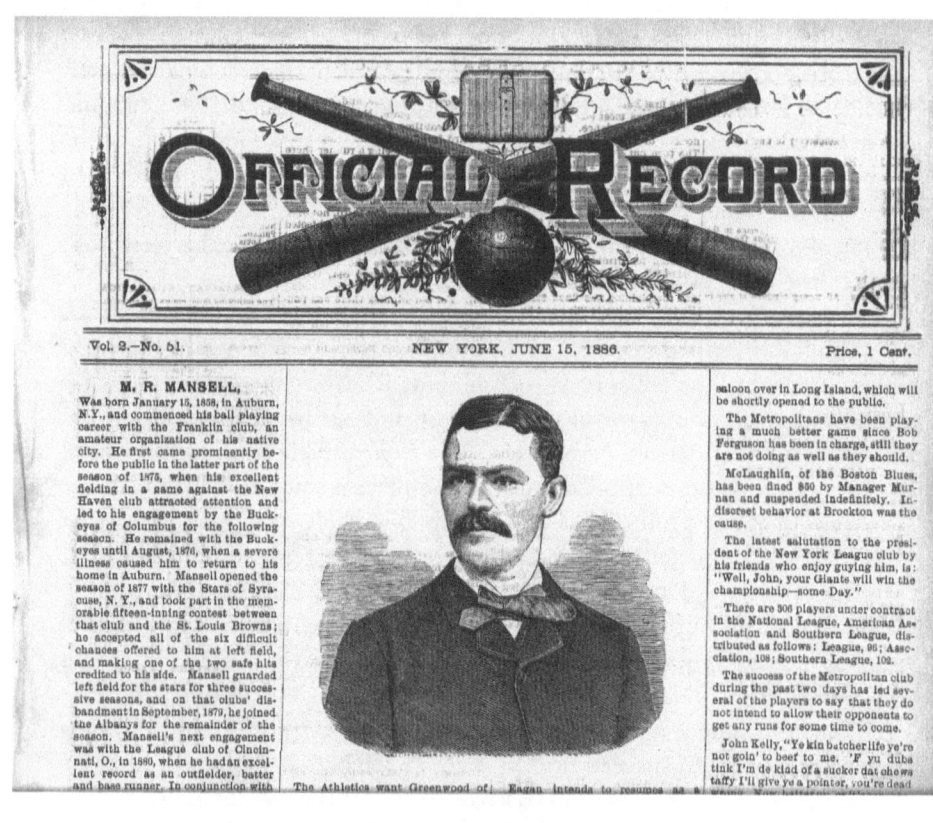

June Rankin published *Official Record*, a baseball daily, between 1885 and 1886. Pictured is the June 15, 1886, issue which profiled M.R. Mansell, outfielder first for the Stars of Syracuse, then the Cincinnati and Allegheny clubs. He was considered the "fastest sprint runner in the country" by the writer. The paper generally covered many of the games played at the Polo Grounds, where June served as official scorer and added chatty comments on the national game (used by permission, Rankin Family Archives).

lishing may be leading to the daily (six weekdays, and not Sunday) *Official Record*, also called *Official Baseball Record* on the inside pages (2 to 4), which was published by the Official Record Publishing Company, without a list of editorial names, P.O. Box 2013, New York City. It is important to remember that June was first trained to be a stationer, most likely doing customized printing. We are fortunate to have the entire run of that daily on microfilm in places like the Hesburgh Libraries at Notre Dame. There are also hard copies still floating around.

The *Official Record* or *Official Baseball Record* was printed on both sides of one sheet and folded in half to make four pages. It measured 10⅛ inches in width by 13⅛ inches in height when complete. It was run during the baseball season, offered at local newsstands, and cost a penny per issue, or $1.00 for the season. It promised portraits of players and managers in each issue as well as a wide coverage of the national game from across the country. The last two pages usually consisted of purchased advertisements, much like the New York *Herald*.[15]

One of the advertisements on page three in a number of the October 1886 issues was for a bound copy of the *Official Record*, which was available for the public following each season, costing $2.00. This correlates well to the bound copy given to *Sporting Life* of the *Official Record* by June Rankin in 1886, which was a daily baseball paper he printed the summer before.[16] The volume is described in an October 9, 1886, issue as containing summaries on the national game with "tables, portraits, percentages, biographical sketches, anecdotes, etc." It was 600 pages in length and "handsomely bound in cloth" with an "elegant gold stamp."[17] This rare newspaper was actually said to be the very first daily sports newspaper "dedicated exclusively to baseball," as it promised. The engraved title is superimposed on two crossed bats with a baseball beneath and a canvas base above. Each cover usually had an engraving of the person being highlighted. Timothy Hughes, of Timothy Hughes Rare and Early Newspapers, describes the paper as having lasted for less than 15 months from July 15, 1885, to October 9, 1886. The first volume had 63 issues and the second 150 for a total of 213 issues. The first volume (1885) was printed on high-quality rag paper and the second (1886) on more acidic newsprint making it more fragile.[18]

The initial volume, printed in 1885, does not list a publication location or individual persons associated with the paper. The first issue of the second volume, printed in 1886, does mention the first of two locations. The first location noted may have been used for the 1885 first volume as well, though that is uncertain, especially with the use of different qualities of paper for each year. The address 340 Pearl Street is printed on page two from April 17 until July 7. On July 8 the address changes to 26, 28 and 30 Frankfort Street with the announcement that the paper is now available in the morning, with that being the first issue of the A.M. edition. Both locations are near each other in the publishing district by the Brooklyn Bridge and close to both the New York *Herald* and the *Sunday Mercury*.

The building at 340 Pearl Street was owned by Richard K. Fox (1846–1922), rough and ready publisher of *The National Police Gazette*. *Official Record* most likely leased the presses from Fox since the current managers of the *Police Gazette* have found no record of ownership of this paper by the *Gazette*. The *Police Gazette* is mentioned only once in *Official Record* in a report on their baseball team playing against the Harper Brothers Publishing House of Franklin Square. The *Police Gazette Nines* won 20 to 7, though both were reported to have done "bad fielding," something June was very good at. June had answered sports questions for the public through the *National Police Gazette* in 1884. Also, Fox's publishing company would later publish June Rankin's two baseball books in 1888. So, a relationship between June and Richard Fox was definitely there.

The second location of publication for *Official Record*, Frankfort Street, was a few blocks over from the first location and was the center of the publication of German and some other ethnic newspapers. The street also had the old Sun Printing and Publishing Association which did some publishing for the New York *Herald* and the New York *Sun*. The street housed manufacturers of printing ink, and the famous engraver Charles Magnus ran a business out of 12 Frankfort Street. The engravings on *Official Record* became larger and more detailed during this year, often placed in the center of the first page, again without acknowledgement as to the artist.

What is interesting about the paper is that it largely focused on games played at the Polo Grounds, where June was busy keeping score; and listed the upcoming New York and Brooklyn games. It mentioned the games he would have witnessed by clubs like the New Yorks (Giants).[19] James Mutrie and John Day, along with their teams, were sprinkled into the chatty text with some praise and some very pointed ridicule. The way the club "handled the ash" (bat) was praised in one game, as they made Kansas City "look kind of tired."[20] The Metropolitan Base Ball Club, on the other hand, was called a "sad wreck of the old 'champs' of 1884."[21] John B. Day was teased with, "Well, John, your Giants will win the Championship — some Day."[22] And then the writer quelled the rumor of Jim Mutrie being released as a manager at that time, mentioning that he was safe at the moment, and that there were "many worse fellows" in the profession.[23] Also, Mutrie's staffing decision was rebuked with, "Had the New York Club not agreed to refrain from strengthening its team in the spring, Manager Mutrie would have had Denny, Hines and Shaw and the pennant would fly from the Polo Grounds."[24] None of those phrases would sit well with a company reportedly wishing to control the press in New York.

The taking of a photograph of the New Yorks on the ball field, on the Thursday prior to the Monday, May 3, 1886, edition, was mentioned with comments about "Truthful Jim" in the center with his "high hat and a little silver headed cane."[25] The photo is now quite famous, and the moment was captured in the paper with a date. The writer was most likely present. Henry Chadwick was the one who actually gave Mutrie the mocking nickname of "Truthful James" in the *Brooklyn Daily Eagle* in 1885. He railed into him often in columns.

The Brooklyn club was praised in one issue for its "even set of batters" which the author believed to all be "good hard hitters and there is not a weakling among them." They were said to give opposing clubs problems due to the fact that pitchers usually have a few opponents which allow them to rest between the hard hitters, but the Brooklyn club at that time did not give pitchers any place to rest.[26] They were all good.

A joke titled "Prizes for Baseball Players," in the April 24, 1886, issue lists awards for things like broken fingers, etc., suffered by players, and also lists "for killing a scorer, $1,000 United States Bonds!"[27] June was scorer for the Giants, or New Yorks as he called them. Scorers were usually the invisible men who worked for newspapers. *Official Record* also mentioned the Players Union briefly the next month. The writer related that the union was seeking to do away with the reserve and limit rules "or else bankrupt the associations by a counter organization." It also mentioned the union originators' "confidence in its success."[28] In 1885, Pennsylvanian John Montgomery Ward, a shortstop for the New York Giants and practicing lawyer, had organized players into a union called the National Brotherhood of Base Ball Players. Ward had played on an International Association team earlier, while June had serve on the Judiciary Committee of the International Association. June was official scorer for the Giants from 1883 to 1889, during the period Ward organized the Brotherhood, or Players Union. Roger Connor, Buck Ewing and Tim Keefe, also from the Giants, joined the union as it attempted to confront management on issues like the reserve clause, limits set on salaries, arbitrary fines given out, and the blacklisting of players.[29]

Another article in September 3, 1885, of the *Official Record* related to June, though again without his name. It is about the game that was to be played between the reporters and the Metropolitans, which had been canceled. In the article, the reason for cancellation was given as fear on the part of the

Metropolitans that the reporters would actually win which might "cast a slur" upon the whole American Association.[30] June actually played for the New York Reporters Base Ball Club with other celebrity writers. This will be covered in greater detail later, but the Reporters Club usually played benefit games.

Also, an August 16, 1886, issue defends Henry Chadwick's article on scientific pitching. The author, most likely June, goes into the skill of pitching in a straight line that diverges with a curve at the end to deceive a batter. The technique was said to be something comparatively few at the time had mastered but which all would like to learn. June had learned pitching in its earliest forms in the mid–1860s. The article shows an appreciation for how the position had progressed to that point.[31]

The advertisements are telling as well. About the time Will began writing for the New York *Clipper*, the *Clipper* began to advertise in *Official Record*. Brogan and Sullivan, caterers at the Polo Grounds, had an advertisement throughout the entire run of the paper as do businesses across from the field. Brogan and Sullivan would also place an advertisement in June Rankin's book. The games of the Metropolitans and Giants are listed in a prominent manner. DeWitt's publications and guides are listed. Kelly had been the baseball editor of the *Herald* prior to June, and he had edited the *DeWitt Guides* as did Henry Chadwick. The Staten Island Amusements Company had a full page spread on the back cover in many 1886 issues, followed by a half page spread. They had purchased, in December 1885, the Metropolitan Base Ball Club, for which June had scored. As a point of interest, an advertisement for Buffalo Bill's Wild West Show ran for several months in 1886, adding a wonderful graphic of Buffalo Bill and Miss Lillian Smith, "The California Girl and Champion Rifle Shot," to page three. Buffalo Bill was being sponsored by Erasmus' Staten Island Amusements Company.[32]

In terms of availability, beyond subscriptions, it does give a very detailed list of where it could be purchased in the August 4, 1885, issue.[33] It was placed throughout the city including in the Bennett Building news stand. From City Hall and the Brooklyn Bridge, to Cortlandt and Greenwich and many points along Fulton Street, the paper was placed in a number of newsstands by hotels, elevated rails, steamboats and the ferry.

Another possible tie between June and this particular paper lies in the fact that June would later, in 1906, be editor and publisher of a journal on golf called *The Official Golf Record*.[34] The Official Record Publishing Company was used for the first paper and The Official Golf Record Publishing Company would be used for the other. June was listed as editor in the golf journal and it would be published in close proximity to the *Official Record*. The names are similar, the publication location within blocks, and both have newspaper articles linking them to June Rankin.

June seemed to have been trying to establish himself as a sports publisher, and he made at least three attempts during his life to become independent, while serving as writer or editor for major newspapers. He appeared to be seeking his own voice in sports and control in writing about sports the way he wanted. The publication of an independent newspaper would have been a step towards that, but the paper did not last long, and conflicts with power structures in baseball for June would ultimately climax in 1889.

June understood the full process of publication from the ground up. Also, his father was an attorney in New York State with his own multiple incorporated businesses, manufacturing things based upon his inventions, and had published his own newspaper.[35] Andrew Nerva's inventions of pipe joints and cold-packed pipe joints were being written up in places like the *Official Gazette of the United States Patent Office* and *The American Engineer: An Illustrated Weekly Journal*.[36] Forming a publishing company for June would have been easy, if only serving as a reference person.

Within the larger Rankin family, younger sister Etta began to find her voice. She was now thirty. She was the musician in the family, and she joined in an interdenominational gathering through the Presbyterian Church in Jamaica in the spring of 1886. Her sisters were most likely present as well. The gathering was to form the Woman's Christian Temperance Union. The parent organization had been founded in 1874, and this was a New York chapter. Etta was elected to serve as corresponding secretary. The position of secretary seemed to be one that all the Rankins enjoyed as they made sure the minutes or resolutions were correctly recorded.[37] It does seem ironic, though, that both of Etta's brothers had served as scorers for the American Association, dubbed the Beer and Whiskey League, which also played on Sunday. Organizations like the Woman's Christian Temperance Union would eventually push for Prohibition, and succeed.

Will and June, while covering sporting events, kept detailed statistics and histories during their careers. In 1886, 37-year-old Will published "Our National Game" or "Early History of Baseball," which was syndicated in just about all of the major newspapers around the country. He was the first to publicly counter Henry Chadwick's theory on baseball's roots coming from the English game of rounders, or town ball. Will believed it originated with the Knickerbockers Base Ball Club, a belief he would defend for the remainder of his life, though adding the possibility of it "springing up" in Manhattan over time. His history was published while he and Henry Chadwick were both writing for the New York *Clipper*. Chadwick did not end his writing for that paper until 1889. A full chapter will be devoted to this controversy.

The cry for baseball being an American invention did resonate with many Americans, most of whom had grandparents who had fought the English in the War of 1812. The nation also had passed its first centennial celebrating its independence from England a few years prior to the publication of that article. The "no rounders" chant, which occurred at a later dinner in New York where Abraham G. Mills was speaking while celebrating the return of the All American Team from a world tour under Albert Spalding in 1889, may have actually originated with Will's history on the game at this time, which many in the country had read and affirmed. Mills, himself, initially agreed with Will's belief that baseball began with the Knickerbockers, but later supported the Doubleday myth.

In the late 1880s baseball clubs were increasing all over the country, and the public interest in the sport was really catching on. Will's columns were in a number of papers including the *Sporting World*.[38] Henry Chadwick actually mentioned him being sporting *editor* of *Sporting World* in a *Brooklyn Daily Eagle* article. Gossipy stories about baseball captured the imagination of the nation, and it is hard to believe that while these reports and debates on baseball, and its origin, were occurring around the country, on the front pages of the newspapers in the 1880s were also stories of the 1881 killing of Billy the Kid; the 1882 killing of Jesse James; and the funeral for the 18th president, Ulysses S. Grant. Grant's body came to rest in what is known as Grant's Tomb in Riverside Park, New York City. On October 19, 1886, the Statue of Liberty was dedicated in New York, and in 1888 the public devoured the newspaper pages for stories on Jack the Ripper. All of these worlds seem miles apart, but all of these things were happening within this narrow period of time and were printed in newspapers with Americans avidly reading.

In addition to playing and recording baseball, June seemed to enjoy winter sports. Henry Chadwick, in a small article for the *Brooklyn Daily Eagle* mentioned the formation of a New York Press Tobogganing Club. Tobogganing was the new rage in New York, and George Taylor was to be the president, June Rankin the secretary, and Henry Chadwick the treasurer. They were in the process of designing "a rich and attractive uniform," and the toboggan was being built. It was to be named "Little Johnny Green." The club even had a motto, "More Space!" This undoubtedly shows the sense of humor of the trio. Tobogganing was done at Washington Park and listed in the area papers. Dangerous spills off of toboggans with their resulting injuries were also listed as the consequence of the wonderful sport.

Also, David A. Curtis in a later article on ice skating, in the New York

Weekly News and Democrat, mentioned that June Rankin was an excellent ice skater. June used the Old Capitoline Grounds in Brooklyn for ice skating and was able to do fancy figures, but according to June, he could only do the figure 8 with the little loops attached at either end.[39] The fancy designs printed in the article were apparently beyond him. Since both Will and June grew up in areas surrounded by streams, they may have learned to skate as children. Brooklyn still had many rural qualities to it with its streams and woods.

June's life, during this latter part of the 1880s, was about to change. He married Annie F. Mitchel in 1887. She had been born in September 1861 in New York. He was 36 but she was only 26. Annie's mother had been born in New York and her father in England. They were Irish-Catholics. Upon notice of the engagement, her family declared her dead for marrying a Protestant. They literally had a funeral service for her, cutting her off entirely. June's family felt that he was marrying someone of a lower class than he, especially with the sisters forbidden to marry local New York men for the very same reason. Annie's family had come to America during the potato famine in Ireland and had been very poor. June's sisters felt that their family was part of the Acheson ascendancy. So, there was conflict in the family over the marriage in the very beginning. Even though both families originated in Ireland, there was a rift of class, ethnicity (Scottish versus Irish), and religion (Presbyterian-Reformed and Roman Catholic). They never saw her family again, even though she raised her children to be good Catholics.

Shortly after the marriage of June and Annie, tragedy struck the family of Will. His fourth son, William M. Rankin, died in infancy in early July 1887. Will was 38 and his wife 43. The tragic event was briefly mentioned in *Sporting Life*, a paper which seemed to write a number of pieces about the brothers.[40] No mention was made of the cause, just Will's affection for the child, his namesake. Little William was buried at Green-Wood Cemetery in lot 21072, section 4. The cemetery has his date of internment as July 3, 1887. Also, Will's son Harold became blind at an early age.[41]

Will was writing for the *Clipper* and *Sporting World* at the time.[42] He added writing for the *Mail and Express* between 1887 and 1888. It was printed at 23 Park Row.[43] The *Mail and Express* had been established in 1836 and published every evening, except Sunday, and had a weekly Thursday edition. It was a Republican paper which supported temperance. The daily was 4 pages in length and measured 26 by 40 inches in size, and the Saturday and Thursday issues were 8 pages measuring 18 by 26. Each issue cost $.03 with the year's subscription costing $1.00. Will actually wrote and published a number of baseball poems in the *Mail and Express*. They were thoughtful, humorous and clever with a Longfellow flavor. Two were published on April

27 and 29, 1887. This was a period of deep reflection for him as he negotiated through his family crisis. The fact that he was writing for a second paper dedicated to temperance suggests that he most likely supported that issue.

By 1886 June was writing and editing for the Sunday New York *Mercury*, the New York *Herald* and the *Official Record–Official Base Ball Record*.[44] There were only a handful of baseball writers in New York at this time with the expertise necessary for the sophisticated papers located there, which explains why people like Will, June and Henry wrote for so many papers. Many of the New York papers had affiliates across the nation and overseas, and the demand was great for writers who really understood the complexity of the game.[45] There was also quite a bit of competition for information on baseball. The *Clipper*, *Sporting Life*, and *Sporting News* were on the top in the 1880s. David Voigt mentions the fact that the *Clipper* was the leader for a time, specifically because of the "imaginative" editorial leadership of Will, setting up "baseball centers" and blanketing "the major-league world."[46]

Even with the competition for information between the papers, there appeared to be a bond between the writers. They often attended the same games, sitting closely together. The April 27, 1887, issue of *Sporting Life*, published in Philadelphia, mentioned the fact that Will, June and Henry Chadwick continually sat together in the tiny press boxes during this period.[47] Will's history of baseball was already in the public's hands, but the three of them continued to interact and work together on projects as they watched the games. The major-league writers also decided to gather and form their own association on December 12, 1887, in Cincinnati. The National Base Ball Reporters Association voted in George Munson as president, Henry Chadwick as vice-president, George E. Stackhouse as secretary, and John Mandigo as treasurer. The motive was to improve game coverage and to promote official scoring. Will and June did not seem to take any offices in this association, but all of their friends did.[48] The board of directors for the National Base Ball Reporter's Association was Joseph Pritchard, Ren Mulford, Jr., Frank H. Bunnell, and Francis Richter.

Both brothers also befriended players. John Ward's letter to June Rankin of 1887 was published in the *Brooklyn Daily Eagle*. In that letter, he thanked June for his "fair and impartial" coverage in the *Herald* of the baseball game. He commented on "wading through the personal abuse" which was printed in other papers. He appreciated June's work adding, "I owe you my thanks."[49] Later in the *Eagle*, the letter was mentioned a second time, with the comment by the writer that the New Yorks had been receiving abuse which they did not deserve. The writer placed the "blunder work" as "emanating from the management."

Six. Celebrities in Baseball (1885–1889)   91

Pictured are the two books written by Andrew B. "June" Rankin between 1887 and 1888. They were published by Richard K. Fox Publishing Company. Left: *The New York and Brooklyn Base Ball Clubs: Brief and Authentic Sketches of the Clubs with Portraits of the Managers and Individual Players*. Right: *The New York Base Ball Club: A Brief and Authentic Sketch of the Club, with Portraits of the Managers and Individual Players*. The portrait is of James Mutrie, manager of the New York Giants Base Ball Club. June was official scorer for the New York club from its inception and through this period. Will had been official scorer for the Brooklyn club at its inception and for its first two years (National Baseball Hall of Fame Library Cooperstown, New York).

In 1887 and 1888, June Rankin wrote and published two books on baseball history: *The New York and Brooklyn Base Ball Clubs: Brief and Authentic Sketches of the Clubs with Portraits of the Managers and Individual Players* and *The New York Baseball Club: A Brief and Authentic Sketch of the Club, with Portraits of the Managers and Individual Players*. He was serving as scorer for the New York club (Giants) at the time, and had access to their historical data. He witnessed their beginings. Also, a number of the club members lived in Brooklyn, making them easy to interview. Interestingly, the New York *Herald* had been the paper which published the original November 11, 1845, account of the first New York clubs' second anniversary game at Elysian Fields. The second New York club took its name from that club and now had a scorer from the New York *Herald*. Will had served as scorer for the Brooklyn Club (Dodgers) at their beginning. June had also been present during their formation. Both brothers also lived in Brooklyn, and it appears as though they befriended a number of players particularly on that club. Will would also record histories on these two clubs. They were able to speak to New York and Brooklyn players firsthand because they were basically neighbors. June's two short books, which are pamphlet size, were published in New York by Richard K. Fox, owner of *The National Police Gazette*. Copies of each of these books are in the Baseball Hall of Fame Museum's Abner Library. The New York Public Library has the first one in its Spalding Baseball Collection of Pamphlets. The publishing location for June's books was close to the prior location for the *Official Record*. It had been printed, at least for a few months, in a building owned by Richard K. Fox.

The book on the New York and Brooklyn clubs is particularly interesting. First, it gives a ten page history of the national game. In it, June speaks about the origin of baseball. It first was played with a variety of rules by school boys prior to 1845, and then the Knickerbockers became the "nucleus" from which "the succeeding clubs derived their rules of playing."[50] He then gives a brief history on the New York and Brooklyn clubs, followed by a page dedicated to each player for each club. A woodcut portrait is at the top of the page and a brief biography at the bottom. For the New York club, it includes nice biographies on James Mutrie, John Ward, Timothy J. Keefer, Michael Welch, William Ewing, James O'Rorke, Roger Connor, George Gore, Daniel Richardson, Michael Tienan, William Brown, Emer E. Foster, William George, Gilbert Hatfield, M.J. Slattery, Elmer E. Cleveland, George E. Weidman, Edward Crane, Patsey Murphy, and Lidell Titcomb. The biographies for the Brooklyn club are on William H. McGonnigle, David Orr, William H. Holbert, A.J. Bushong, Paul Radford, Edward Silch, M.F. Hughes, Robert Caruthers, W.D. O'Brien, Robert H. Clark, David L. Foutz, William H. McClellan, Al Mays, James E. Peeples, George B. Pinkney, George J. Smith, and W.H. Terry. The book closes with ten pages of advertisements including a prominent one by A.G. Spalding & Brothers, the caterers at the Polo Grounds, the New York *Clipper*, the New York *Sporting Times*, and others. The complete schedule for both clubs is also posted as are their home games.

The *Brooklyn Daily Eagle* did a short review of *The New York and Brooklyn Base Ball Clubs*. It stated that the book had sketches on players preceded by a chapter of baseball history. It was called "an interesting base ball book."[51] In that same column in the *Eagle* is an announcement about

President A.G. Spalding "now fully decided upon the trip to Australia this winter." National League planning during that tour would impact June in the near future.

In 1888, Will was moved up to assistant baseball editor by Alfred Wright on the *Clipper*. Will Rankin credited Al with being the one who introduced the checkerboard arrangement showing the standing of clubs with percentage of victories and defeats adopted by the American Association and later the National League.[52] Eventually, Will would be promoted to baseball editor for the paper. In many ways, the *Clipper* would become associated with baseball because it simply had a better system of reporting. This was all due to the networking done by Will. The baseball biographies of players, managers, owners and others, complete with woodcut portraits, were also a steady presence in the *Clipper*. They presented contemporary biographies which are still widely referenced today for details on individuals. Some of them were quite detailed. Of the 800 biographies published beginning in 1869 and ending in 1903, 652 were written after Will began writing on baseball for the paper (1885). He did play a part in their publication.[53] In fact, he may have been the one who wrote most, if not all, of those later pieces. Many area papers, like the *Brooklyn Daily Eagle*, attributed player biographies to Will in the *Clipper*.[54]

June's functions at the *Herald* often encompassed more than just baseball. He was said to have had his hand in many sporting events happening in New York. For example, June and John P. Eckhardt managed a fundraising event sponsored by several newspapermen on February 18, 1888, at Madison Square Garden. It was for the widow of Billy Dempsey who had died during a contest with Swipes the Newsboy. Mrs. Dempsey was living in Brooklyn and was destitute. Barnum and Bailey gave the use of the Garden for free. Among those sparring were to be Johnny Reagan, Mike Donavan, Dominick McCaffrey, Billy Dacey, Jimmy Ryan, Jack Delancey, Jack Fallon, Denny Kelleher, Tommy Danforth, Steve Brody, and Jack Kenny. Swipes the Newsboy would end the evening with a match with Eugen Hornbacker. Jack Dempsey, with Billy Madden, would appear if able. Also wrestling would be Gus Hill and Mike Dempsey.[55] Boxing would take on a greater role in June's life in the near future.

During this time, June was playing on the New York Reporters Base Ball Club with a number of reporters. The *New York Times*, September 8, 1888, covered a comedic benefit game for Carl Rankin (no relation) between the Reporters club and the Actor's Athletic Association. Fifteen hundred people attended the game. The reporters wore New York Giants uniforms, probably secured by June, and the Actors performed in full costume: ballet, boxing, swimming, a tramp, schoolboy, and such, complete with gags and stunts. Listed at that time for the Reporters club were:

    J.C. Kennedy, captain and first base (*New York Times*)
    L.M. Smith, catcher (New York *World*)
    Glen McDonough, pitcher (New York *World*)
    John Mandigo, right field (New York *Sun*)
    George Stackhouse, right field (New York *Tribune*)
    M.J. Lane, second base (New York *Star*)
    June Rankin, left field (New York *Herald, Sunday Mercury*)
    William O'Brien, center field (*Sporting Times*)
    W.I. Harris, right shortstop (New York *Press*)
    John MacDonough, third base (New York *Star*)

Photograph by Joseph Hall of the N.Y. Press-Gang v. The Elite of the "Pro-fesh," August 15, 1889, at the New Polo Grounds (II). Occasion: Benefit game between the New York Reporters Base Ball Club and the New York Actors Amateur Athletic Association of America Nine (5 A's or New York City Nine). The reporters are wearing New York Gothams (Giants) uniforms because June Rankin was scorer for that club at the time. Notice the muddy new field.

    Pictured are: 1. Mandago; 2. Eschevege; 3. Rudolph; 4. Smith; 5. Harris; 6. Doc. McDonough; 7. Dickerson; 8. Austin; 9. June Rankin (center seated); 10. Metcalf; 11. Engle; 12. Stackhouse; 13. J. Kelly; Umpire; 14. Adams; 15. "Luckey" DeHolf; and 16. Hopper (National Baseball Hall of Fame Library, Cooperstown, New York).

An actor who refused to return to base was playfully shot dead by the umpire, and later one of the actors had to be driven back to the field at bayonet point. The game ended in a tie with an exhausted audience and raised $1,200.[56]

James C. Kennedy, baseball writer for the *New York Times*, left that position in 1888 and formed the New York *Sporting Times* with John B. Day, James Mutrie, and P.J. Donahue. Kennedy served as the editor for the paper for the first two years. He went on to promote boxing and 6-day bicycle races at Madison Square Garden. Bicycling was gaining the interest of the public.

The Actors' Amateur Athletic Association of America had an Actors' Nine which played a number of groups over the years and was often written up in the newspapers. People like Maurice Barrymore (1847–1905) played for the club, and he was considered one of the founding members. The overarching organization was nicknamed the A.A.A.A.A. for short, or the 5A's. Later, in 1890, the Actor's nines would play against a newly formed club in the Players League called the Ward's Wonders, a Brooklyn club managed and captained by John Montgomery Ward, formerly of the New York Giants, and lose.[57]

On August 15, 1889, the *Brooklyn Daily Eagle* covered a return match between the Actor's Athletic Association and the New York Reporters Base Ball Club. The game was played at the New Polo Grounds (II) with more than 1,200 people watching. The admission was $.50 and the money went to the two clubs, presumably for their own charities and expenses. The writer of the article in the *Brooklyn Daily Eagle* mentioned the bad condition of the field with new sod in the infield and mud in the outfield. The Reporters did well, but the Actors ultimately won even though June Rankin made "the outfield catch of the game" and made a "two bagger," bringing in "two runs and giving his side the lead" for a time when at bat.[58] The roster of the New York Reporters Base Ball Club at that time was listed as:

Dickenson, first base (New York *World*)
Rudoph, pitcher (New York *Star*)
McDonough, third base (New York *World*)
Stackhouse, shortstop (New York *Tribune*)
Mandigo, first base (New York *Sun*)
Metcalfe, second base
A.B. Rankin, left field (New York *Herald* and *Mercury*)
Harris, right field (New York *Press*)
Smith, catcher (New York *Herald*)

The Hudson *Evening Register*, July 10, 1889, had recorded the Giants' feelings about the difficulty in hitting a ball over the center field fence in the new Polo Grounds II. June Rankin had made a bet that Roger Connor (1857–1931) would do it before the season's end, and he did. Roger Connor was a terrific athlete, tall and strong. Apparently that ball was returned to Roger Connor by a policeman and presented to DeWolf Hopper who had it gilded and inscribed. It hung in the clubhouse of the Actor's Amateur Athletic Association thereafter.[59]

In 1889, the scorers gathered to develop their own association. The Scorer's League was formed to try to bring some standardization to the process of keeping score using symbols, letters and numbers for bases, players, and plays. Newspaper reporters had generally served as scorers, and most reports went through the telegraph. By 1890, they would begin using *The Orr-Edwards Code for Reporting Baseball*,[60] which used symbols for a number of things to make it easier. The interest in preserving statistics and baseball seemed to go hand in hand.

Baseball went through a series of revisions in the style of play but two issues kept resurfacing: gambling and drunkenness at baseball games. They had been continual problems beginning with the organization of professional play and probably during the amateur period as well. Some players even played while drunk. The Giants had a bar on the right side of the field which was finally closed in 1893 with references to the problems it had caused to ladies needing to pass it.[61] That club was not unusual in this regard. Henry Chadwick continually spoke out against gambling and drinking in his writing. He used the issues as a platform for a moral discourse on the game of baseball. In an 1887 *Sporting Life* article, Chadwick referred to an article written by June which stressed the signing of a pledge by James Mutrie to keep his players on the straight path. Chadwick seemed to want more from the pledge. He used the article to comment on the drinking habits of some of the managers who were "drunk as owls,"[62] meaning Mutrie. Mutrie was notorious for drinking binges with his team members, apparently feeling that if they drank with him, he could keep a better eye on them. June was reporting on a pledge not to drink while serving as scorer for the Giants. Day was owner of the Giants, and Mutrie was their manager. Chadwick seemed to feel that the managers must also make a commitment and set an example in their personal behavior.[63] Back in an 1885 *Brooklyn Daily Eagle* article, Chadwick had referred to Mutrie in a mocking phrase, "Truthful James," and then blasted him again in 1886. The phrase took on a life of its own and became "Truthful Jeems" by others in the press. By 1891, even Albert Spalding would push for Mutrie's dismissal.

June's first son, Andrew Brown Rankin VI, or Drew for short, was born on June 28, 1889. Later in life, Drew commented that as a child he could not go anywhere without someone asking him if he was related to June and Will

Rankin. They were widely followed and people treated them like celebrities because they knew all of the players and were deeply involved in the goings on in Brooklyn and New York. They were very well liked by the public, the players, and the press.[64] Even distant press knew the Rankin brothers from New York. As late as August 1889, papers like the *Boston Daily Globe* referred to scorers like June as "base ball experts," "unbiased and intelligent" in their opinions on the individual clubs.[65]

June served as scorer for the New York Giants from 1883 to 1889 and it is interesting to note that a number of the players during that period ended up being inducted into the Baseball Hall of Fame. In 1939, Buck Ewing was inducted; 1945, Jim O'Rourke; 1964, brothers-in-law Tim Keefe and John Ward; 1973, Mickey Welch; 1976, Roger Conner; and 1977, Amos Rusie. June was present when these men were setting their records, which are still referenced today. He was the one recording their statistics. His last year, 1889, the roster for the New York Giants was pitchers Ed Crane, Tim Keefe, Hank O'Day, Cannonball Titcomb, and Mickey Welch; catchers Willard Brown, Buck Ewing, and Pat Murphy; infielders Roger Connor, Gil Hatfield, Danny Richardson, John Ward, and Art Whitney; and outfielders Elmer Foster, Bill George, George Gore, Harry Lyons, Jim O'Rourke, Mike Slattery and Mike Tiernan. June was the official scorer for the club from their beginning in 1883, but he also knew some of the older players who had played for the Metropolitan Club. It was a powerhouse lineup, which would also cause the National League some major problems that year.

June also had complete control over the New York *Herald*'s baseball coverage from the spring of 1876 until the fall of 1889. He was one of the best known New York reporters with his hands in many sporting events. Then, a sudden shifting happened within the editorial department of the *Herald*. James Gorden Bennett, Jr., decided to restructure June out as editor of baseball in the fall of 1889, and June furnished scores and local news for the paper thereafter[66]; perhaps until 1898. He may have still functioned as a general sporting editor, but no longer in baseball. Writers across the country were stunned.

June stepped out of baseball scoring that year too, and seemed to drop direct coverage of baseball altogether after the fall of 1889. He had a new child and went from celebrity baseball editor on the New York *Herald* and New York *Sunday Mercury*, publishing his own baseball daily, writing two books on baseball history, and serving as a scorer for the National League, to being shuffled out of baseball reporting and seeming to leave the entire game. Why would the paper do that to their famous celebrity baseball editor? What may have been happening in the life of June, who was only 38 in 1889, to make him want to drop out of baseball coverage?

According to his brother, who wrote the baseball writers' biographies in Alfred Spink's *The National Game,* June simply "retired from baseball to focus more on golf," becoming an "expert on the sport."[67] Yet, that did not officially happen until 1894. June covered sports like boxing in the interim. Then in the mid–'90s he devoted himself to golf for a number of papers like the *Brooklyn Daily Eagle,* and the New York *World,* and even organized golf tournaments.

Eighteen eighty-nine and 1890 were difficult years not only for June, but for the entire world of baseball. The very structure of the game was threatened and would not stabilize for a decade.[68] The New York area was directly affected by the power struggles. The American Association and the National League had been competing all along, and then the Brotherhood of Players (Brotherhood, or Players Union) began to really organize and flex their muscle. They made a fierce assault in New York. The National League reciprocated. The New York Giants were in the center of the controversy, where June served as scorer. The Brotherhood had been formed initially on October 22, 1885, by Giants shortstop John Montgomery Ward, who was the president of the Union. Ward was a charismatic leader and considered a heartthrob by the ladies. Buck Ewing, Roger Connor and Tim Keefe, also of the Giants, were in the Union as were Gerhardt, Welch, Dorgan, Richardson, and O'Rourke. Keefe served the organization as secretary. Ward had graduated from Columbia Law School, and in 1889 the Players Union began to seriously organize to address the National League's classification system with its limits on salaries; the reserve clause, which restricted the movement of players; and the selling of players to other teams. Ward, himself, was in danger of being sold to Washington when he really wanted to go to Boston.

In 1887, they had opposed the reserve clauses in their contracts, but according to Frank Graham in *The New York Giants: An Informal History of a Great Baseball Club,* the "cause of the rupture was the classification rule adopted by the club owners in 1888 as a dodge to avoid impending trouble over a salary limit of $2,800 they had set in 1887." The owners had set a graded limit and were to decide the value of each player without the players having a right to individually bargain. Players would fall into a scale from A to E and be arbitrarily graded according to ability, performance, morality, and off-field deportment. The owners could circumvent their own scales at will. This forced the players to work together to have a voice.[69] The conflicts would have happened in 1888, but Ward of the Giants and president of the Players Union was sent on a world tour playing baseball with 35 Professional National League Base Ball Players until March 1889, while members of the National League developed a War Committee under Albert Spalding to address the problem. The tour went from Hawaii, to the South Pacific, New Zealand and Australia — as far from New York as possible. Ward played shortstop and was captain of the All-Americans, made up of a number of National League clubs. Ward, however, came home early and in July 1889, called the members of the Brotherhood together in New York to see if they could obtain capital in their own cities to form a Players League which would directly complete with the National League.

Chapters of the Brotherhood were in New York, Detroit, Philadelphia, Boston, Chicago, Washington and Kansas City with most of the local stars signing up.[70] Albert G. Spalding listed Boston as having 3 members in the Brotherhood, Brooklyn 7, Buffalo 9, Chicago 14, Cleveland 4, New York 12, Pittsburgh 10, and Philadelphia 14.[71] In December 1889, the Brotherhood met and expelled those members who had signed with either the National League or American Association, and the next week the Giants took Ward to court to block him from playing for another team in 1890. According to Mark Rucker in *150 Years of Baseball*, "Most of the National League personnel and many of the American Association players had joined the Players' League; some came over as whole teams."[72] It was a major assault on the very structure of the National League. In the end, Spaulding branded the Brotherhood as union strikers, and they lost favor with the public. The fear of unions by management was very real in the United States. Workers had struggled under poor conditions, low pay and long hours for many years. The organization of labor to address the injustices was being felt in major cities all over the country. To label the Players Union as one of those groups, was sure to have a negative response from managers who feared loss of profits. Spalding had dubbed the Brotherhood anarchists.

Coupled with this were other issues within the Giants organization. Day needed the players from his club in order to win the 1889 pennant. They had just won the 1888 pennant. Day also was losing his playing field at Polo Grounds I, located at 110th Street and 5th Avenue, as the board of aldermen of the city of New York planned to use the field for more housing. Daniel M. Pearson in his book, *Baseball in 1889: Players vs. Owners*, suggests that some of the city officials may have been seeking payoffs from the Giants to keep their field, but Day had financial problems.[73] As a result, Day had to move his club to Oakland Park in Jersey City, New Jersey, for a few games which resulted in poor attendance and low revenue. Then he used Metropolitans owner Erastus Witman's St. George Park on Staten Island for a few weeks, which also resulted in loss of revenue.[74] Both fields were unsatisfactory. Many reporters at the time of the potential loss of Polo Grounds I had mentioned the need for a ball field in New York City. The New York *Clipper* even printed that the public felt the national game was a necessity. "The day has come when the public will not do without their game."[75]

James J. Coogan's Polo Grounds II, 155th Street and 8th Avenue, was not open until July 8, 1889, and it was not an idyllic field due to its propensity to flood. Day had to pour funds into the preparation of the meadow to be used as a ball field. It also featured a rocky cliff overlooking the area called Coogan's Bluff. Day had built a wooden horseshoe-shaped grandstand with 15,000 seats which cost a great deal of money. Coogan then threw Day a curve by announcing that he would grant the Brotherhood a two block plot adjacent to Polo Grounds II, just north of the field. Then, after the Giants' two year lease was up, he would grant Polo Grounds II to the Brotherhood. Ward had secured financial backing in eight cities. Ward also tried to keep the American Association neutral during this period by promising not to raid their clubs. However, the association was leery about the issue of labor and management and fought both the Players League and the National League. This resulted in their clubs being raided by the Players League, and the National League took in Cincinnati and Brooklyn after dumping Washington and Indianapolis.[76]

The Brotherhood games in Brotherhood Park brought in more crowds than the Giants, and the latter could see their competitor's success.[77] Both sides tried to inflate their ticket numbers when giving reports to the press. The Brotherhood were said to have deliberately scheduled games to compete with the National League in the same time slot. July 14, 1889, Spaulding also published his plan for reorganization of the National League in the New York *Times*, which the New York *Clipper* called a "baseball trust," using the minor leagues as a training ground for the major leagues with limits on salaries, a plan they always wanted. The public did not like the idea of trusts.[78]

The National League's War Committee was led by Albert Spalding with John I. Rogers and John B. Day, owner of the Giants. Daniel M. Pearson, in *Baseball in 1889: Players vs. Owners*, mentioned the fact that Albert Spalding was a "master of using the newspapers." He realized early on that reporters could increase attendance at games and by "manipulating the news" he could eliminate his competition, which he did.[79] The National League bribed players to entice them to leave the Players League, used propaganda against the Brotherhood, financially harassed unfavorable newspapers by getting advertisers to drop their advertisements, gave free tickets to the public, withheld the playing schedule until after the Players League schedule was published, and generally led a massive campaign to destroy their competitors. The Players League tried similar tactics, but with less capital.

Spalding's book, *America's National Game*, paints an entirely different

Six. Celebrities in Baseball (1885–1889)

picture of events. The National League was honest and beneficial to players and even sought to offer advice and protection to minor leagues from 1876 to 1899. The players, on the other hand, were shown to be scheming, rebellious and out of control. They bred dissatisfaction. He had a quote from Henry Chadwick stating that they "secured the services" of journalists in each league club city. It was done to "influence capitalists among the wealthier class of patrons ... eager to join them." He went on to state that the Players League wanted the press to "denounce players" as "scabs or deserters" who didn't play for them.[80] His accounts of the rebels made them sound like a combination of little children needing adult supervision and subversive, ungrateful employees. Yet, Spalding also wrote that "the League was determined to win if it took every dollar that had been made and saved."[81] Ultimately, he called a peace meeting at the Fifth Avenue Hotel in New York City. Those to attend were only to be the owners of the National League and American Association, and the financers of the Players League — not the players. He successfully separated the players from their backers.

Eighteen eighty-nine is an interesting year to look at when watching June move from baseball editor to more general coverage of sports and specific coverage of golf. You have to go back earlier to find a possible reason for the shift that particular year. Beginning in 1877, June had been a delegate to the International Association, serving on the Judiciary Committee. The International received constant pressure from the National League with June raising comments against "a small clique" which he felt was trying to take over the entire game and "control the baseball fraternity."[82] He also witnessed the same pressure on the American Association while serving as scorer there. In 1880, the New York *Mercury* had recommended players "rise up in their man hood and rebel" against some of the perceived abuse being imposed upon them by a small group seeking to control the game.[83] June had been writing on baseball for the *Sunday Mercury* beginning in 1875 and became the baseball editor of that paper in 1885 while also serving as baseball editor on the *Herald*. The two papers were physically close to each other, making this possible.

June's writing continually opposed the control of the game by a small group. He had criticized the National League directly while on the Judiciary Committee of the International Association for being a clique. He also was scorer for the Giants when the Players Union was formed with key members of the Giants. June continually supported the players in their efforts to form a fraternity of players, based upon his own warm feelings about the game when he was young, before there was a National League. He seemed to want players to be able to chart their own destiny without a choke hold over them both financially and in terms of reserve rules.

National newspapers were reporting on the Players Union in different ways. Some had felt that the salaries for ballplayers were already good, considering their short season of work and short hours[84]; still others supported the players. Chadwick, for one, supported the National League during this battle. He was aging and employed by them to edit their official organ. Will was the *Clipper*'s assistant baseball editor at this point, and the paper seemed to try to present both sides, giving copy space to those involved. Voigt mentions that the *Clipper* and *The Sporting News* "neither criticized the organization [Players Union] nor failed to applaud its leaders."[85] *Sporting Life*, however, backed the players all the way and would later hold up June as a hero.

The *Eagle*'s story on the Metropolitan Company's attempts to control sportswriters appears to have been true. Day was under a great deal of pressure and was taking action. He needed money. Albert Spalding not only ran the White Sox Base Ball Club, but intentionally bought an interest in the New York Giants Base Ball Club to help him out. John Brush, owner of the Cincinnati Base Ball Club, also had stock in the New York Giants. Ned Hanlon of the Baltimore Orioles Base Ball Club partly owned the Brooklyn Superbas (Dodgers) Base Ball Club.[86] People like Spalding sought to break up the brotherhood through infiltration into the clubs and the movement of team members. The National League was taking control.

June had written that he felt strongly that the sport of baseball was being controlled by a clique within the league, and he supported the striking players during the time when the National League was on the attack against them. If the Metropolitan Company was seeking control of the press, then this might have set him up for a fall. By 1890, June had been moved out of a power position on the *Herald* and out of baseball scoring.

In fact, the person who helps clarify what happened is J.H. McDonough in his scathing article, called "The Centre of the War: Some Facts About the Scoring in New York," published in the *Sporting Life* on June 7, 1890. He explained exactly what he felt had happened in New York. He began by mentioning the fact that in the spring of 1890, the baseball editors of the *Star, Sun, Tribune, Journal, Herald* and *Times* did not even attend the Players League games at all, but instead got the scores from two sources which McDonough felt were unfair. The two men agreed with each other at every point and one was employed by John B. Day. That man, Joe Vila, at the time had never scored a professional game before and knew little about the intricacies of base hits and errors, according to McDonough.

McDonough went on to mention his own experience when pressure was put on him to step down from writing for the *Star* after John B. Day went to his publisher and said the Brotherhood would hurt capitalism. He was told to support the league or get out, so he left and wrote for another paper. Then he mentioned what happened to June Rankin. In a move he felt was astonishing, he accused Oliver Perry "Ollie" Caylor of printing something in a National League organ meant to injure "Honest June" Rankin. Caylor had managed the Cincinnati Red Stockings, in the American Association, in 1885 and 1886, but was let go due to his combative nature. He wrote on baseball initially for the *Cincinnati Enquirer* and *Cincinnati Commercial*. He was hired to be manager of the New York Metropolitans in 1887 by Erastus Wiman but then was fired. He went to write for *Sporting Life* in Philadelphia before coming back to New York. Spalding also bought the New York *Sporting Times and Theatrical News* in 1890, and placed Caylor as editor. McDonough wrote that the material written by Caylor resulted in June's dismissal and the replacement of him by Vila and Caylor on the *Herald*. Vila took June's position as scorer for the Giants. Caylor would function as scorer for the club as well. David Nemec, in *The Beer & Whiskey League*, mentions Caylor's "pen" which "continued to scorch" in New York. He was well known for his caustic writing in the Midwest.[87] McDonough accused Vila of being on John Day's payroll. His article seemed to point to James Bennett, Jr.'s, ignorance of what was happening on his paper as members of the National League took over the columns.[88]

Oddly enough, *Official Record–Official Baseball Record* had done a biography on O.P. Caylor August 16, 1886. In that article, complete with woodcut portrait, Caylor's writing for the *Cincinnati Enquirer* was called "thoroughly independent ... full of humor," and the writer, most likely June, commented on the fact that the "baseball fraternity" looked at his accounts of "their games" as "particularly readable." The article commented on the fact that at that time, 1886, Caylor had stepped out of writing for the *Enquirer* in 1881, and was working in his law business.

Noel Hynd, in his book *The Giants of the Polo Grounds: The Glorious Times of Baseball's New York Giants*, mentions why New York was so important to the National League. The War Committee of the league, made up of Rogers, Spalding and Day, saw New York was a key arena, because the money was there. Hynd states that "if the Brotherhood could be defeated in the largest market area, the league would crumble," which is why the attack was so brutally calculated there. The public was attending the Players League games in much larger numbers than those of the National League. Day's franchise was taking a large hit, and he worked as hard as possible to stop it.[89] The leaders of the Brotherhood were in New York.

McDonough's article presented the possibility that Bennett might somehow have been unaware of the infiltration into his paper, which seems unlikely.

Bennett had told his editors to write the paper to his own liking. He was an avid sportsman and owner of the original polo fields upon which baseball had been played. June, his baseball editor, scored for, and covered, the New York Gothams (Giants). Vila was now given that assignment. The changes on Bennett's staff would have been fully known and endorsed by him, particularly in a period when the city was moving the team from Polo Grounds I to what would be called Polo Grounds II. Bennett was most likely paid for his land by the city. He was not a man easily manipulated. He also was known to not like the idea that any of his employees were indispensable. If the possibility of advertisers pulling their ads from his paper existed, he would not protect an employee. He needed money to support his extravagant lifestyle. It would be seen as merely a good business decision.

It appears as though June was shuffled to silence him. Perhaps he, too, decided he had had enough of the power plays and stepped into general coverage of boxing championships and other sports which were less stressful to him. The paper restructured the baseball department, and it seems other papers did as well, at the very moment of the Baseball Wars. There was a successful power play, and June and others lost. He did not, however, seem to put up a fight, nor did he discuss the details of what happened. He quietly moved over.

The scorer sent to replace June was then being accused by McDonough of "enlarging the error column and reducing the base hits" against Players League games. He suggested that Vila was changing the actual scores intentionally against the Players League before forwarding them to the press, who were looking the other way as they printed Vila's account. Whether or not this is true is hard to say. The totality of what actually happened is still unknown. McDonough was protective of June and also angry at the system which had invaded his own life.

The closest we get to hearing Will's feelings on the matter are a brief comment written in a 1905 article titled "Rivals Relations: National Magnates Selfish and Shrewd," related to their treatment of the Highlanders Base Ball Club: "The Old Magnates were always noted for their shrewdness and cleverness in working out ways and means for throwing down a rival, even if it required time to turn the trick."[90] Also, William Rankin wrote and published several baseball poems during his life. One, called "The Baseball Slaves," specifically mentions John M. Ward and the "baseball giants held in bondage" who were "in the magnates' power."[91] For the most part, though, Will seemed to be protective of his brother during this period, and did not comment on the matter, probably because he was trying to save June from embarrassment. People in the late 1880s generally did not speak about difficult private issues in public.

Six. Celebrities in Baseball (1885–1889)

In a 1904 article for *Sporting Life*, Rem Mulford, Jr., wrote that a number of baseball writers left the game during the Baseball Wars and chose entirely different sports to cover, but at that time Will and Henry Chadwick were the remaining members of the "Old Guard."[92] It seemed as though the wars had spilled over into the press, changing the occupational focus of a number of writers. Sam Crane, in a December 5, 1914, article on a local ballplayer, took time to mention June and "Doc" McDonough in a list of "Press Gang Heroes," which might very well also refer to their sacrifice made in reporting during that early period.[93] They were not forgotten by their fellow pressmen. In fact June's reputation seemed to remain strong, and he would continually be referred to as "having attained celebrity status while writing for the *Herald*."

Seven

A Decade of Change (1890–1899)

While Ellis Island was being built in New York Harbor in 1890, baseball was experiencing a disastrous year. The public stayed away from the games due to the arguments within the clubs and began finding enjoyment in other sports like bicycling, basketball, volleyball, and college football. The Players League had franchises in New York, Brooklyn, Buffalo, Boston, Philadelphia, Chicago, Cleveland and Pittsburgh. Of the original New York Giants, only Welch, Tiernan and Murphy had stayed. Connor, Richardson, Whitney, Hatfield, Keefe, Crane and O'Day all left the Giants. Ewing was managing the New York Players League Base Ball Club with many of the ex–Giants as members, including Crane. The New York Players League regular nine members were Keefe, pitcher; Ewing, catcher; Connor, first base; Richardson, second base; Whitney, third base; Hatfield, shortstop; Slattery, right field; Gore, center field; and O'Rourke, left field. Ward was managing the Brooklyn Players League club, called Ward's Wonders. The Brooklyn Players League Club members were Van Haltren, pitcher; Daly, catcher; Orr, first base; Bauer, second base; Joyce, third base; McGeary right field; Andrews, center field; and Seery, left field. The New York *Clipper* did biographies on most of the Brooklyn Players League members between 1890 and 1891 and a number of the New York Players League members from 1896 to 1900. Each player was highlighted, showing his abilities, and no negative comments were made about his choice. The players were never called rebels.

John B. Day had been without a ballpark in 1889, and then sunk money into Polo Grounds II to ready it for play, which did not happen until July. In 1890, he had only three players and had lost a great deal of money during the Baseball War. When John T. Brush, a share owner in the Giants, turned in his Indianapolis franchise, Day bought his players, including Charlie Bassett,

Harry Boyle, Dick Buckley, Jerry Denny, Jack Glasscock, Amos Rusie, and Jack Sommers. But, as a result of selling shares in the Giants to others in order to gain capital, he ultimately lost financial control of the club. There was a major power shift. He had borrowed money from Arthur Soden of the Boston club and sold stock to Edward B. Talcott. Talcott, according to the New York *Clipper*, was a good businessman who was very well liked.[1] Talcott gradually acquired more shares in the club. He ultimately demanded the removal of James Mutrie, who was let go by 1892. His excessive drinking had not helped. Day would resign by 1893 but returned for a short and unsuccessful attempt at managing the club. Both Mutrie and Day tumbled into poverty in their declining years as the Giants developed into a great club without them.

The Boston Players League Club was the only winner in 1890. That was the only pennant for the new league. It collapsed at the end of the season thanks to Spalding's engineering of public opinion against the "striking union" and due to its own financial woes. The 1890 National League Brooklyn Bridegrooms (Dodgers) had played against a Players League club, winning the pennant. The Players League club had been completely "outplayed" on the field. This resulted in loss of confidence in the new league's ability to compete against the National League, and financing was pulled from the Players League by people like George Chauncey, which contributed greatly to the folding of the league.[2] Spalding had made sure that the financers saw that the Players League would not last. In a 1905 article on the club, which also included a nice biography on James Mutrie, Will Rankin wrote that the men of the National League "favored the war policy to the death."[3]

Peace ultimately was declared between the Players League and National League as the "rebellious players" returned to their original clubs. Ward, however, went to manage the Brooklyn National League club, but by 1893 he would resign and turn to the practice of law. He continued to interact with baseball players, however, assisting them legally. Meanwhile, the Giants took over Brotherhood Park at the insistence of Edward B. Talcott. Day had just renovated Polo Grounds II, but Brotherhood Park was larger. Talcott named the Players League field Polo Grounds III. Polo Grounds II was renamed Manhattan Field and used for things like track meets and horse racing.

By 1891, the leagues had merged. The National League had absorbed four American Association clubs in December: Baltimore Orioles, St. Louis Browns, Louisville Colonels and the Washington Senators. It became a 12-club league: the National League and the American Association of Base Ball Clubs. But, by 1900 it would drop the long title in favor of the National League, also called the Senior Circuit, and by 1901 the American League would be called the Junior Circuit. The national game was monopolized by the National League as they slashed players' salaries, and clubs tried to financially restructure. The war with the Brotherhood eventually resulted in the league trying to make contracts more equitable for the players, but they did not have to do that right away. They held all the cards.

The September issue of *Sporting Life* mentioned that June Rankin also lost money in 1890 on another paper called *Sporting Critic*. The journal seemed to have had a short and difficult life, and it did not succeed.[4] It was June's second attempt at launching a sports paper. It is not clear exactly what it covered, since copies are not available. Yet, the name seems to be reflective of the role he felt reporters should have when covering games. The paper is mentioned in a few newspapers, one being *Sporting Life*. In May 1890, the *National Police Gazette* mentioned that the new business manager of June Rankin's "bright little paper, *The Sporting Critic*," was to be William H. Germaine, "prominent in the Sullivan-Kilrain match." Germaine was called a "hustler" by the *Gazette*, probably in the best sense of the word. The match between John Lawrence Sullivan (1858–1918) and Jake Kilrain (1859–1937) had been fought under the London Prize Ring Rules featuring bare-knuckle boxing on July 8, 1889, in Richburg, Mississippi. Sullivan was the victor. June and Sullivan had a connection through the *National Police Gazette* and through June's work at the New York *Herald*, which is most likely how June came to be acquainted with Germaine.

The London Prize Ring Rules of 1838 were based upon an early set used by Jack Broughton in 1743 to govern English prizefights using bare knuckles. Among them were items such as the ring size, surrounded by ropes, which was usually made of turf; aggressive acts like biting, head-butting, kicking, and blows below the belt were not allowed; rules were set dealing with betting; certain spiked shoes were allowable; an assistant held the water bottle for the boxer; handkerchiefs were used for the boxer's colors; and two umpires were used to call time.

The Rochester *Democrat Chronicle* mentions *Sporting Critic* as a weekly, making its debut Thursday, April 3, 1890, in New York City. It was under the editorial supervision of A.B. Rankin, "better known in the baseball world as June Rankin."[5] The New York *Evening Telegram* listed it as being published weekly on Thursdays and "dealing with all sorts of sport." It was a "singularly handsome publication" with between three to five "cuts by eminent artists" per page. June liked graphics. It was said to have a "staff of writers" from "every branch of sport," which were deemed by the writer to be "the most capable critics that can be secured."[6] June put a great deal of money into this venture in order to produce a first rate publication.

There is, also, a small sketch of the paper recorded in *The Newsdealer: The Organ of the Trade,* which was published in San Francisco, California, in 1890. *Sporting Critic* appears in that journal for the first time in June of that year as a weekly that was published in New York. The yearly subscription rate was $3.50, and unsold copies were initially returnable, but that was dropped by August. It was listed in a column with *Sporting Life, Sporting News, Sporting Review, Sporting Times, Sporting World* and *Sportsman* in the June, July, August, and September editions of *The Newsdealer,* but in the October edition the editor stated: "The deaths since last issue are *Santa Claus, Chicago Figaro, Sporting Critic, Saturday Library,* and *Woman's Cycle*" (bicycle).[7] It would appear that *Sporting Critic* ran from April 3, 1890, to late September of the same year. *The Newsdealer* had readership in the Midwest and California, so June might have been attempting to advertise the paper beyond New York, but it failed. The New York *Herald* published a California edition. June would have had contacts through that paper in that state.

Francis Richter mentioned in his chapter on the press and sports in *Athletic Sports in America, England and Australia* that the sporting pages of local newspapers really challenged individual sports journals. Papers solely dedicated to sports were able to amplify what was happening, but the major papers carried large sections on things like baseball and horse racing, making it a challenge for smaller sports-focused papers. The dedicated sports papers were able to provide specialists on sports who helped educate the public,[8] but the public often chose what would give them the largest selection of news at the best price. There was a national depression going on in 1890, as well, which was agriculturally based. A number of banks would fail by 1893 and unemployment would surge.[9] It was bad timing for a new sports journal.

Another blow came to the brothers that year: William, now 41, and June, 39, lost their father on October 3, 1890. Andrew Nerva Rankin, Esq., died in Philadelphia of apoplexy and was buried in Green-Wood Cemetery in Brooklyn. Green-Wood Cemetery was set on land used during the Revolutionary War for the Battle of Brooklyn, in 1776. Henry Pierrepont had incorporated the cemetery in 1838. Richard Upjohn created the gothic gates and installed them in 1863. It was a lovely sculpted cemetery, which was also a tourist spot with its historic burials, especially of the beloved Knickerbockers and other early baseball team members. There are close to 200 baseball players and writers buried there. It is still a tourist spot. June's paper and father seemed to have come to an end at about the same time.

But by December 17, 1891, the *Brooklyn Daily Eagle* had a detailed account of a boxing match between New Jersey's Pat Cahill and Brooklyn's Jim Butler.[10] Amid the dramatic retelling of each round, with chaotic blood-spilled fighting and audience yelling, the author mentions the people at the event, including June who most likely was covering the match for the New York *Herald, Associated Press*, or perhaps the *Sunday Mercury*. What is interesting about the article, in which the fight ended in a draw, was the fact that June was listed in a section filled with baseball players, retired players and umpires. Having been removed as baseball editor of the New York *Herald* at some point in the fall of 1889, June was as popular as ever with baseball players in 1891, particularly members of the Brooklyn club. He was still providing scores for the paper, but he no longer wrote feature articles on baseball.

Prizefights were generally held outside New York State with many boxing matches in state called exhibitions or demonstrations instead of prizefights to avoid legal ramifications in a state where the sport was unlawful. Prizefights fought without regulation protection were controversial in America, with 21 states, beginning in 1890, having laws pertaining to them.[11] Louisiana had the most stringent list of statutes. Boxing fell into the area of laws pertaining to assault, injury or harm, and the concept of "beating each other" was a constant problem addressed in the press and from pulpits.[12] There weren't a large number of fights each year for a given boxer because he needed time to recover, and medicine was not as advanced as it is today. Prizefights even came before the Supreme Court. New York did not legalize prizefighting until the 1920s with the passing of the Walker Law. James John Walker, called Jimmy Walker or "Beau James," had been a member of the New York State Assembly from 1910 to 1914, then a member of the New York State Senate from 1914 to 1925 when he sponsored the Walker Law to legalize boxing in the state. The legislation established rules to govern the sport and restrict some of the more aggressive acts. At that time the world heavyweight champion, Jack Dempsey, held the title from 1919 to 1926. Walker would go on to be mayor of New York City from 1926 to 1932, until scandals and corruption charges drove him from office.

Edward James printed a book at the New York Clipper Building titled *Boxing and Wrestling; with Full and Simple Instructions on Acquiring these Useful, Invigorating, and Health-giving Arts* in 1878 which gives a clear picture of the style of boxing done at this time. The book was designed to help boxers lessen their injuries, detailing how to protect the thumb and arms from damage; how to throw one's weight properly; and sparring in a well-ventilated room or outside "in pleasant weather" was encouraged. The boxer was to wear "a short-sleeved undershirt; pantaloons or knee tights; long white stockings; high laced shoes with low heels; and have a handkerchief or belt worn around the waist. In that edition, medium sized gloves were mentioned though the boxer was encouraged not to use "pillows."[13]

Seven. A Decade of Change (1890–1899)

In New York, Ellis Island was officially opened on January 1, 1892, bringing with its opening thousands of immigrants which eventually changed the dynamics of New York and Brooklyn dramatically with the sudden population bursts. Within a decade, with the addition of the opening of the subway in 1904, New York would absorb close to one million immigrants. Prior to that, places like Brooklyn had been seen as a village, suburbs, or even the country with a number of farms. During all of these shifts in 1892, in the sixth month of that year, June's second son Herbert, called Hub, was born. June was 41 and his wife 31.

The following fall, September 7, 1892, June was the correspondent in New Orleans covering the Corbett and Sullivan Boxing Championship for the *Associated Press*[14]; the bout was called "The Battle of New Orleans." This was most likely through the New York *Herald*. John L. Sullivan had been the heavyweight champion for ten years, using bare-knuckle boxing. His nickname was "Boston Strong Boy." He weighed about 212 pounds. James J. Corbett from San Francisco was called "Gentleman Jim." James boxed with gloves and is considered the father of modern boxing, changing the game from a brawling match into a gentlemen's game using the Marquess of Queensberry Rules. The Queensberry Rules were named after John Douglas, 9th Marquess of Queensberry, but written by Welshman John Graham Chambers and published in London in 1865 and 1867. Those rules listed such things as ring dimensions, prohibition against hugging or wrestling, round duration, use of gloves, and such. The fighters were to wear five ounce gloves.[15] We get our expression of treating someone with kid gloves from this transition in boxing. There were 10,000 people present at the fight. James weighed 25 pounds less than Sullivan but knocked him out. Representing the *Associated Press* for this bout was a great honor, and June's report was then franchised out to other papers. Modern boxing was beginning, and June was there, just as he had been for baseball.

Both Sullivan and Corbett also played baseball. Sullivan pitched for a semi-pro baseball club, as a type of promotional event, on May 28, 1883, at the Polo Grounds I. June was scorer for the Giants at that field at that time. Corbett later played first base for a minor league club, also as a type of promotion, in 1895. His younger brother, Joe, was a pitcher for the Baltimore Orioles. Corbett became a fan of the New York Giants, attending many of their games for the remainder of his life.[16]

June generally covered a myriad of sports for the *Herald* during the close to the century, especially boxing, with general coverage of gun clubs, yacht races, and water polo. The big sports in the 1890s were horseracing, boxing, baseball, and bicycling; with lawn tennis, croquet and archery enjoyed by the general public. The 1892 Los Angeles *Herald* carried June's coverage of sports as "News from New York." In that particular article, they also listed his comments on the new popular sport of football, which had surfaced on college campuses beginning in the late 1880s. The games he witnessed in the city and Brooklyn were well attended with people noisily enjoying it "no matter whether they understand the game and are enjoying themselves or not."[17] The song sung most often at sporting events of the day, like football, was "Ta-ra-ra-boom-de-aye."

Will wrote exclusively on baseball, and 1892 was a split season in that sport, but the following year many changes happened which affected his reporting. For one thing, in 1893, the pitching distance increased to 60 feet, 6 inches which changed the game dramatically with quicker and more powerful pitching required. The distance, in the 1860s, had been only 45 feet from home base to the pitcher's mound, which also used the underhand throw. July 25, 1893, amid all the changes in the style of play and pace of baseball, 44-year-old Will succeeded Al Wright as senior baseball editor of the New York *Clipper*. Though many times the baseball articles were unsigned by authors, generally the editorial staff wrote copy. This is especially true of the Rankin brothers and is important to remember when reading the papers during their period of leadership.

The New York *Clipper Annual* for the year 1893 was particularly reflective of Will. In addition to giving the weekly, monthly, and year's baseball news with information on the leagues, baseball legislation, wins, and play in places like the United States, Canada and Cuba, that particular issue gave an overview of the entire national game from the year 1833 to 1893, sixty years. It was as though Will wanted to make sure the history of the game was chronicled in print, and it was his moment to do it. Within fifteen double column tightly organized pages, in smaller print than used during the 1880s, one could see the major events in baseball for each month within a given year leading up to the current year (1893) of Will's position as editor.[18] Each following *Annual* recorded the events of that particular year in greater detail. The *Annual*, in particular, was a gift to baseball, and baseball historians looking for dates and broad coverage of events. In general, the *Clipper* was helpful when looking for stories and descriptions of games both professional and amateur and for finding scores and team rosters. It was factual and very easy to follow. Metropolitan newspapers often used Will's *Clipper* columns in their columns, sometimes quoting large sections. In particular, his reports on players were used.[19] Will seemed to track individual players and could often recite their particular histories. This was helpful when they were newly hired to play for a local club.

Seven. A Decade of Change (1890–1899)

Eighteen ninety-three was the year of the financial panic in America, with many struggling. Pasteurized milk was given out to children at milk stations in New York City for the first time in an attempt to lower childhood mortality rates, blamed largely on unpasteurized milk. There was a station by City Hall in the newspaper district. Another loss happened for the Rankin family that year; Elizabeth McDowell, the mother of Will and June, died July 25, 1893, at age 71 in Jamaica, Long Island, after a bout of dysentery. She had been living with the sisters of Will and June. Elizabeth was buried at Springfield Cemetery in Queens in a numbered plot without a headstone. The family often sited headstones as vanity. She had been a powerful influence on her family and her passing left a void, particularly with the sisters who seemed somewhat lost without her.

On August 22, 1894, a daughter named Elizabeth, "Betty," was born to June and Annie, but tragedy struck his family somewhere between 1893 and 1895 (perhaps closer to 1893) when June's wife, Annie, fell down a flight of stairs. This was witnessed by her son, Drew. After the fall, she was deemed "never quite right." She developed a blood clot in her brain. She would have good and bad days. She was able to walk and talk, but did so on "good days." On bad days, she was unresponsive, "like a store window dummy," or somewhat violent.[20] She needed supervised care and June was always traveling. Son Drew was sent to live with his aunts in Lynbrook, Long Island, and Annie later became dependent upon her young daughter, Betty, for care. Betty dressed her mother in the best clothing, and tried her best to help. The stress on the family was enormous with a wife incapacitated, a husband often traveling and trying to re-establish his writing career, the eldest son living with aunts. Hub and Betty remained with their troubled mother. Annie's fall would have lasting consequences.

In October 1894, the Sandusky *Register* in Ohio mentioned June's presence at a meeting at the New York *Herald* between boxers James J. Corbett, the American world heavyweight champion, and Robert James Fitzsimmons, known as "Bob," "Ruby Robert," and "The Freckled Wonder" from Great Britain, a three time division world champion. They, with their managers, met to set up a prizefight for the two with a few members of the press as witnesses. June was not only covering the gathering for the *United Press*, according to the account, but the boxers were to sign their agreement and then forward it to the sporting editor of the New York *Herald*. June was the only representative from the *Herald* listed. The Corbett-Fitzsimmons match became "The Fight of the Century," on March 17, 1897, in Carson City, Nevada, and was filmed by the Edison Picture Company (Edison Kinetoscope). The documentary, filmed by Enoch J. Rector, originally ran over 100 minutes in length which made it the longest film at the time. Three cameras filled with nitrate film were used. Wyatt Earp covered the fight for the New York *World* and Bat Masterson was present in the audience. Fitzsimmons won the $15,000 purse; $10,000 of Corbett's stake money; and $13,000 from the Edison Picture Company.

June was also increasingly absorbed in golf, eventually organizing tournaments. H.B. Martin, in his book *Fifty Years of American Golf*, published in 1936, mentions the fact that June was in the first small group of New York reporters covering American golf. Hugh L. Fitzpatrick was given first place as golf scribe in New York in 1894. June was placed in the second place group in 1895 while writing for the New York *Herald*.[21] The first official amateur USGA Championship happened that year in Newport, Rhode Island, during October. The New York *Herald* reported on the 100 spectators with women in "silks" and men in their "red golfing coats" as C.B. MacDonald was set against Laurence Curtis. MacDonald was viewed as the one most likely to win due to his "low short drive" compared to Curtis' "directed drive."[22] H.L. Fitzpatrick mentioned the fact that most of the amateurs playing at that first championship were "doctors, lawyers, clergymen, and men of business prominence, but the college player had not yet developed into championship form."[23]

The use of red coats was a tradition dating back to Scotland. Initially, clubs like the St. Andrews Golf Club in Yonkers, just dressed in regular attire. But, when other clubs from Shinnecock Hills in Southampton, Long Island, and Newport, Rhode Island, showed up in the traditional red coats, the Yonkers club fell in line as well. Soon clubs fined members a shilling or in some cases two quarts of Scotch for not playing with red coats.[24] St. Andrews decided to really outdo the others, though, by adding a blue collar with the silver cross of St. Andrew, plus blue checked waistcoats, pearl gray hats with blue and white bands or blue checked cap for the links, gray knickers, scotch plaid hose and gray gaiters.[25]

St. Andrews Golf Club is the oldest existing club in the United States. The story had it that Robert Lockhart, in 1887, had brought back golf clubs from his trip to Scotland and tried them out along Riverside Drive in New York City. His friend, John Reid of Yonkers, called together a group of his friends, Tallmadge, Holbrook, Putnam and Upham. Together they formed the St. Andrews Golf Club on November 14, 1888, named after the famed 1754 Scottish club. The new St. Andrews was nicknamed "The Apple Tree Gang" because they played in an apple orchard. These men became instrumental in the development of golf in the United States.

There are written records of golf being played in Scotland as far back as the 12th century and in 1457 King James II of Scotland banning it and his grandson, James IV, did the same in 1491. But, James IV played the game in 1502, as did Mary, Queen of Scots, in 1567. The Dutch were also playing an early stick-and-ball game in 1297 in the Netherlands. Also, there are records of the game in the 13th century in Belgium and northern France. It is a point of conjecture as to which was the originator of the game, though Scotland claims it. Of late, China has also stepped forward as a possible originator of the game, playing a stick-and-ball game prior to the Western countries. The English, however, did not play it until the 17th century. King James VI of Scotland became King James I of England in 1603.

Golf had actually been played in the United States earlier than the 1890s, as well, perhaps as early as 1657 at Fort Orange and Beverwyck, New Netherlands, now the Albany area of New York. Koven (golf, or even hockey) was forbidden in streets because it broke too many windows and injured people, much like the early records of bat and ball games. Kolf was the more precise Dutch word for golf, meaning bat or club with klik as the actual word for the stick or the club.[26] The Scottish word for golf has run the gambit of spelling and pronunciation: "goff, goufe, goofe, goiff, gauff, gowff, goulf, golfe, golf."[27] Many of the Scottish and Dutch, playing during the Middle Ages, had embraced the same form of Calvinistic Protestant religion known as Reformed, which was also present in France and Belgium. The new world welcomed settlers from these countries bringing with them their games. Later, the 1786 Charleston Golf Club played the game as did the South Carolina and Savannah golf clubs, but the sport's coverage seemed to suffer after the War of 1812, and many early clubs folded,[28] perhaps as a response to things English.

The United States Golf Association (USGA) was formed in the winter of 1894. Henry O. Talmadge, on the Board of Governors for the St. Andrews Club, gave a dinner at the Calumet Club on 5th Avenue and 29th Street in New York City on December 22, 1894. He invited representatives from five clubs: St. Andrews, Brookline, Shinnecock Hills, Chicago, and Newport. They formed the USGA naming Theodore A. Havemeyer as president, Laurence Curtis as 1st vice president, Charles B. MacDonald as 2nd vice president, Samuel L. Parrish as treasurer, and Henry Talmadge as secretary.[29] MacDonald and Reid wrote the constitution and bylaws which were accepted on February 8, 1895. The idea was to set up championships. The Amateur Championship of the United States was held in 1894 at Newport with W. G. Lawrence winning. In 1895, also at Newport, Charles Blair MacDonald won the Amateur United States Open, the first Open. He is now called the "Father of American Golf" because even though he was born in Scotland and immigrated to the United States, he helped to foster the love of the game in the hearts of the

American public. He was the founding vice president of the USGA and greatly impacted golf architecture, designing a number of courses. Women also began competing. In 1895, Mrs. C. R. Brown won the Women's Championship of the United States. This was followed by three consecutive wins by Beatrix Hoyt in 1896, 1897 and 1898. She was only 16 in 1896.

Martin also mentioned in his book the fact that there were only a few writers during the 1890s who had actually played golf. Many times it was simply carried in the society pages, listing who was there, presumably because the details of the game were not fully understood. June, however, played the sport and played it well. He had a very good eye for fielding, pitching and batting in baseball. Drew Rankin actually called his father ambidextrous. He apparently could write with both hands at the same time and make his own copies.[30] Whatever his ability in that area might have been, it seemed to translate well into golf. Martin also mentioned that at first the press was served a luncheon at the clubs sponsoring a championship as a form of free advertising, but it was later dropped as admissions were charged and profits sought.[31]

H.L. Fitzpatrick, sportswriter for the New York *Sun*, also mentioned June Rankin writing on golf for the New York *World*, the *Brooklyn Daily Eagle*, and other papers during this period of 1895 in his 1916 article for *Golf Illustrated* titled "Early American Golf Reporters." One of the other papers was still the *Sunday Mercury*. Fitzpatrick also listed Crane of the *Herald* as writing on golf. The *Herald* would slowly add a number of golf reporters over time, as would other New York papers. In the article, Fitzpatrick recounted the early days of golf's emergence in the American press.[32] The public did not appear to be interested in the sport until the 1890s. With the increase of interest came positions for writers, and papers sought talent. Fitzpatrick and June Rankin became close friends.

Brooklyn had a number of places to play golf. Dyker Meadows Golf Club on 7th Avenue and 29th Street was built in 1895, near what is now Fort Hamilton Army Base. A nine-hole golf course was put in 1906. Daniel Chauncey was the first president of that club. He was on the original committee forming the Metropolitan Golf Association. Dyker Meadows eventually sold acreage to Brooklyn Polytechnical Institute. The golf course is now part of Dyker Beach Park. Marine and Field Golf Club was by Bath Beach in Brooklyn on 13th Avenue and 86th Street. It was organized in 1885, and golf was added in 1896. By 1900, it had 400 members. M.F. Spalding was the early president of the club. Marine and Field Golf Course merged, in 1909, with Dyker Meadows. Marine and Field was eventually plowed under in 1926 and formed into the present park, Marine Park. There is a newer Marine Park golf course at 2880 Flatbush Ave.

Seven. A Decade of Change (1890–1899)

The Brooklyn Golf Club, also known as Brooklyn Forest Park, was at Forest Park near Myrtle Avenue. Yes, there was a forest there. The individual lots were purchased by the city officials of Brooklyn on August 9, 1895, and developed into a recreational facility of 538 acres. At the turn of the century, the golf club had 280 members. When the City of Brooklyn merged with New York City, it became known simply as Forest Park. It is still the third largest park in Queens today.

The Crescent Athletic Club on 9th and 10th Streets and 9th Avenue and 8th Avenue went by a few names. In 1884 it was the Hills and the Athletic Grounds, and Long Island Athletic Club Grounds. In 1885 it was Adelphi Athletic Club Grounds. From 1886 to 1889 it was Crescent Athletic Club Grounds (I). It was long known for track and field, lacrosse, wicket, baseball, lawn tennis, football, rugby, shooting, archery, basketball, croquet and cycling. The Crescents Football Club began in 1884 after watching a Yale-Princeton game. They joined the American Foot Ball Union in 1887. This may have been the location where June Rankin saw football games. The club had over 300 members in 1900. In 1889 it also had merged with the Nereid Rowing Club and offered sailing and rowing. The nine-hole golf course was added in 1897 and expanded to 18 holes in 1898. The club later moved to Huntington, Long Island, in 1931. The grounds are now part of Fort Hamilton High School Athletic Field.

The A.G. Spalding & Brothers Company responded to the new interest in golf. They had branches of their store in the United States and Canada. The company published a Golf Guide in 1893. Then, they manufactured golf clubs in 1894, as a type of experiment, which proved successful. In 1898, they added golf balls, and by the early 1900s they would experiment with rubber cores for the balls, naming them the Wizard. They also introduced the dimples in golf balls in 1908.

The New York *Herald* covered a number of events in golf including colleges as they began to play the sport and women as they picked up the wooden clubs and began to leave their mark on tournaments called mixed with a man and woman paired.[33] June was writing at the point when American newspapers were just beginning to give space to the sport on home turf again with more prominence. He had helped foster baseball, was covering prizefighting as it made a transition into the modern gentleman's sport, and football as it emerged as a spectator sport out of college campuses, but golf became the second sport for which he developed a passion and the one he would help foster for the remainder of his life.

The first periodical on golf in the United States was *Golfing*, which was a monthly, published in New York City beginning in May 1895. The United

States Golf Association Bulletin, called *Golf,* began publication in 1897 at 213 East 24th Street in New York City. *Golf* cost $.25 an issue or $2.00 for the year. It was edited at that time by Van Tassel Sutphen, and carried news on a number of clubs in the country, with both men and women's golf prominently listed. They used Harper and Brothers Publishers which published out of Franklin Square in New York. *The Golfer* was also published during this time at 130 Fulton Street in New York. All of these emerging golf magazines were in the newspaper district where June and Will were writing. June, again, was in the right place at the right time.

June would continue writing on sports like golf for the *Brooklyn Daily Eagle*, and the New York *World*, which he wrote for until his death. The *World* had been founded as a Democratic paper, and it floundered until it came under the control of Joseph Pulitzer in 1883 until 1911. Pulitzer made it successful. The paper directly competed with the New York *Herald*. June wrote under the Pulitzer years. Control went to Joseph Pulitzer's three sons after his death, Ralph, Joseph and Herbert, and the paper ended in 1931. The New York *World* was known for yellow or sensational journalism and was the first paper to place reporters undercover for scoops. It was also the first paper to introduce a sports section with the large words "Best Sporting Page in New York" in a banner at the top. Golf was usually in the far-right column. The New York *World* building was the tallest building at the time of its construction. The paper also owned the Press Publication Company, which would be helpful to June in his need for self-expression. It appears as though the New York newspapers often served as publishing firms for authors. It is difficult to track the writing of June in the New York *World* because they often used the phrase special correspondent instead of the author of a story, or just left the byline blank. However, he was writing for them and usually covered items like boxing and golf while smoking his cigar.[34] William Abbott would later write on golf for the paper as well. The *World* had branch offices in Harlem, Brooklyn, and Washington, D.C.

The Metropolitan Golf Association was formed on March 31, 1897, at Delmonico's in New York City to discuss the governance of the sport in the local region and to set tournament dates. It worked closely with the USGA. It was first called The Metropolitan League of Golf Clubs and represented 23 clubs within a 55 mile radius from the city, including Greenwich, Connecticut, parts of New Jersey and all of Long Island. It would expand to 26 clubs. The formation committee was made up of Daniel Chauncey of Brooklyn's Dyker Meadow Golf Club, Oliver W. Bird of Meadow Brook Golf Club, Grenville Kane of Tuxedo Golf Course in New York State, Richard H. Williams of Morris County Golf Club in New Jersey, and T. Hope Simpson of State Island Cricket Club. These five drafted the constitution and bylaws which were adopted. At its formation, it represented about one fourth of the clubs in the USGA. The first president was H.B. Hollins of Westbrook; vice president was J.C. Ten Eyck of St. Andrews in Yonkers; treasurer was R. Bage Kerr of the Golf Club of Lakewood, New Jersey; and John du Fais of Baltusrol served as secretary. Of the five directors, four were on the original formation committee with R.H. Robertson of Shinnecock Hills, Long Island, replacing T. Hope Simpson. Their charter was dated April 14, 1897. The plan was to offer an amateur and open championship each year along with their other tournaments.

June would play golf in the metropolitan radius, and often cover this association. By 1898, the MGA set up the Metropolitan Amateur or Met Am for short. H.B. Hollins won the first one in Garden City, New York, and received a championship plate. By 1900 New York would lead the way in the number of golf courses with 165. Massachusetts was close behind with 157.[35] The Metropolitan Open began its first tournament in 1905 at Fox Hills Golf Club on Staten Island. It was considered one of the major golf tournaments.

Unfortunately, golf in the 1890s also ran into New York State's Blue Laws regarding games on Sunday. The American Association of Base Ball Clubs had managed to squeak by with Sunday baseball. The laws had been left unenforced, probably due to the betting and drinking going on. But, the City of Yonkers, in particular, made it very difficult for the early St. Andrews Golf Club. Locals were troubled seeing men playing golf in the fields instead of attending church on the Sabbath. Two members of the club insisted on being arrested to test the law, kind of like a sit-in. The case was ultimately dismissed.[36]

Will was still covering baseball. He remained constant in his devotion. The voice of the modern baseball reporter can be heard in the style of reporting in the New York *Clipper* during this period, which was under the editorial eye of Will. The paper seemed to set the tone of what reporting should sound like, which was later picked up by radio and television reporters.[37] The New York baseball world was largely focused at this time on gossipy stories about Giants owner Andrew Freedman and his bad behavior. He was a real estate lawyer who had purchased the Giants for $50,000 on January 17, 1895, from Edward Talcott. Freedman had half interest in the club. The New York *Clipper* had published an 1895 biography on Andrew Freedman, mentioning his "habit of thrift and industry." It also praised him for his intent to encourage the "patronage of ladies" by the "reserving of a section of the upper part of the grand stand" for ladies and their escorts. It was seen to be more conducive to woman with a no smoking section and vendors of "drinks" would not be allowed to "invade" it.[38] Most papers seemed to initially like him, but that changed rapidly, and his behavior was the major cause.

Andrew Freedman later attempted to secretly form a National League Base Ball Trust in 1901, placing a group of five men in control of the entire game.[39] It was called a syndicate by many. In the plan exposed by the press, the eight clubs were to merge into the National League Trust under a select, paid board of regents with a president, treasurer and secretary. New York would receive 30 percent of the stock; Cincinnati, St. Louis and Boston 12 percent; Philadelphia and Chicago 10 percent; Pittsburgh 8 percent; and Brooklyn 6 percent.[40] The plan, once exposed, failed. He was not well liked, but he had strong political connections with Tammany Hall. Freedman also had a bad temper which he often demonstrated publicly. For eight years he ranted at people, and brought forth one lawsuit after another. It made for good press but did the team little service. As a matter of fact, the primary focus of his rage seemed to be the press. He attempted to bar individual reporters from the Polo Grounds on a regular basis, and he tried to use political connections to intimidate writers. Samuel Crane, a baseball writer for the New York *Commercial Advertiser*, who had also played baseball for clubs like the Giants, wrote that Freeman was destroying the franchise. Freeman then blocked his access to the Polo Grounds. Freeman also went after blocks of writers from the *Cincinnati Enquirer*, New York *Sun*, punched a *New York Times* reporter, and even railed into Henry Chadwick. Chadwick led a boycott of Giants games. Ultimately, Albert Spalding was brought in to serve as a transitional president for the National League. By 1902 a peace was reached, and Freedman agreed to sell the Giants. Other New York area teams were, of course, followed by the public with great interest during this time, but the Giants appeared to be their local favorite. Saving the Giants was good news. The Giants would win the World's Series in 1905.

The Brooklyn club in the 1890s was known as the Bridegrooms, after the large number of newly married players. They joined the National League and won the National League Championship in 1890. Charles Ebbets, who had faithfully worked from the ground up, became the president, slowly acquiring stock in the club. The Bridegrooms would slowly strip the Baltimore Orioles of their best players as Harry B. Von der Horst, owner of the Orioles, bought controlling interest in the Brooklyn Club. Von der Horst had stock in two clubs in the same league at the same time. The nickname Bridegrooms for the Brooklyn club would be dropped during this shift and changed to Superbas, based upon a Vaudeville troupe by the name of Hanlon's Superbas. The press chose this nickname because the club's manager was Ned Hanlon from 1899 to 1905. The Brooklyn club would win the National League pennant in 1890, 1899, 1900, 1916, 1920, with many more following, including a number of World's Series.

Will's son Percy was married to Charlotte M. Tracey on June 17, 1897. The entire family was present at Charlotte's mother's house in Greenpoint. There had been a recent death in the Tracey family, so the Rev. William Hughes of the York Street Methodist Church performed the wedding in her home. Will's son Sydney served as best man. The bride carried daisies.[41] Will's son Harold would later marry Ethel Lydia Daisley, born January 12, 1882. Sydney would marry a woman named Mildred F. However, because June had married at age 35, his children were much younger than Will's.

By 1898, an aging Henry Chadwick wrote a series of wistful pieces about baseball for *Sporting Life* and the *Brooklyn Daily Eagle* in which he talked about being the only of the older contributors to that journal left. He mentioned June as a correspondent to *Sporting Life*, which is one of the few mentions of June writing for that paper, and then made a sarcastic comment about the young writers now writing for the paper.[42] The piece seems to show his respect for June as a writer, especially as the portion right before the excerpt mentions men Chadwick was glad were no longer writing. His respect for June appears to have begun when Chadwick chose June as his successor at the New York *Mercury* in the 1870s. Chadwick most likely opened the door for June to the New York *Herald* as well, since Chadwick had written for them prior to June. The article, written much later, still showed a professional bond between the two, even if he and Will had differences which seemed to be growing.

But by April 20, 1898, the Spanish-American War had begun, which greatly affected the entire country. Many New Yorkers enlisted to serve. The United States sought to intervene in helping Cuba in its War of Independence from Spain. The May 15, 1898, New York *World* covered the movement of troops from New York, New Jersey, and New England in 1,000 coaches using 90 locomotives as they prepared for the invasion.[43] The war was to prove difficult for baseball as many clubs were just not profitable.[44] Crowds stayed home, threatening many franchises financially. The war also stalled the expansion of golf.[45] War would continually affect sports in the future with the public uneasy and players enlisting in times of crisis.

Eight

Origins of Baseball (1885–1906)

The origin of baseball has been the subject of speculation since the early 1860s. In fact, it is still a topic of interest and research today among noted baseball historians. Some see its relationship to many bat-and-ball games and trace it back in time through many centuries in many cultures, defining it in a broader sense. Will Rankin weighed in on this topic in the 1870s and 1880s. He was the first one to publicly confront Henry Chadwick's 1860 statement on baseball coming from English rounders or town ball. Chadwick, an English immigrant born in Exeter in 1824, felt that the sport was similar to English sports played in his childhood there. He believed that rounders had been played for several centuries in England and stated repeatedly that it led to baseball.

Rounders consisted of two teams with anywhere from six to fifteen players. It had a pitcher, batter, a hitting square, a bowling square, and four posts for bases. The game lasted two innings with each player batting in each inning. The ball was tossed by the pitcher to the batter. The batter ran to the first post if he hit the ball, and points were given dependent upon the post reached. This, to Henry, was the root of American baseball. Town ball also involved trying to hit a thrown ball and trying to complete a square of bases made of wooden stakes without being struck by the ball or having one's hit ball caught. The first team to score one hundred talleys was declared the winner. It became known as the Massachusetts Game. Another popular game in America was called Old Cat, and it, too, used a batter and ball. The number of cats (two, three, four) increased with the number of players, making it Two Cat, Three Cat and so on.

Will wrote a piece called "Our National Game" or "Early History of Baseball" between 1885 and 1886, which was syndicated to nearly every major newspaper throughout the country.[1] The article listed some of his findings. He challenged the notion of baseball developing from rounders and town ball. Will wrote that just because these games had bats or paddles or sticks and balls did not mean that the particular game was the same as what had been formulated as the New York Game by the Knickerbockers Base Ball Club. This, he considered baseball. He did not see proof in an evolutionary process from games played in Europe leading to modern baseball. He could focus only on an American origin, more precisely Manhattan, and the New York Game with its diamond shaped infield and precise rules, which were drafted by William R. Wheaton and William H. Tucker in September 1845, and then adopted and published by the Knickerbockers Base Ball Club, between 1845 and 1846. Other clubs adopted these rules later, changing the ball games that they were playing to conform to this.

His article listed the reasons for not seeing a tie between rounders and baseball: rounders and town ball used a paddle or cricket style bat; the field had a square shaped infield instead of a diamond; the batsman was placed midway between first and fourth bases; any number of persons could play the older game, even up to twenty; there were only two infielders, the catcher and pitcher; a runner hit with the ball or a ball thrown between the runner and base constituted an out; and the rules governing the game were different. He did, however, concede that a rude form of baseball had been played in and around New York prior to the Knickerbockers, giving a "fifty years ago" phrase which placed it at about 1835. It was not played with any form of regularity, nor with a regular set of rules. It also set twenty-one aces or runs as the goal.

His findings showed the first scheduled game played at Elysian Fields in Hoboken, New Jersey, on June 19, 1846, between the Knickerbockers and New York Club with the New York Club winning. The Knickerbockers Base Ball Club, from New York City, had lost their playing fields in New York and rented the New Jersey field, taking the Barclay Street Ferry to cross the Hudson River. They first had played at 27th Street, where the Harlem Railroad Depot stood, and then at Murray Hill before using Elysian Fields. The first record of baseball in New York Will found in the New York *Sunday Mercury* on May 1, 1853. However, modern authors have actually found a New York *Herald* article mentioning the term base ball which pre-dates this, though details on the style of play were not given. The *Sunday Mercury* article only announced how healthy cricket and base ball were for players. Will wrote that the Knickerbockers and Gothams of New York City had informally played against each other a number of times, but these were more like practice games. The first formal match between them was the one set at Hoboken, New Jersey, on July

5, 1853, and covered in the *Sunday Mercury* by owner William Cauldwell on July 10, 1853. Cauldwell was the first baseball reporter to Will and he greatly admired him. The New York *Clipper* also covered it on July 16, 1853. He also admired Frank Queen, editor. The Knickerbockers won that game. Then, Will continued, the April 2, 1854, *Sunday Mercury* listed the existence of three baseball clubs: Gothams, New Yorks, and Knickerbockers. These clubs were all interrelated. The Knickerbockers were a younger group of men coming from the other two clubs. Their players were interchanged. Will also mentioned that in the November 5, 1854, *Sunday Mercury*, Cauldwell printed the first tabular score, which was between the Gotham and Eagle clubs. Henry Chadwick did not begin to write for the *Sunday Mercury* until 1858.

Will's article was based upon his investigations begun a decade prior to the 1885–1886 publication. He mentioned in a 1905 article for *Sporting News* that during the summer of 1877 he was standing on Fulton Street by City Hall with Robert Ferguson when Duncan F. Curry, the first president of the Knickerbockers Club, walked by. Ferguson was most likely the man born in Brooklyn who played on the early Atlantic Club and the New York Mutuals. Will was official scorer for the New York Mutuals in 1876 and baseball writer for the *Brooklyn Daily Eagle* at the time. Ferguson later went on to manage a few clubs, including Chicago and the Metropolitans; and served as an umpire.[2] Robert Ferguson, on that summer day, introduced Will to Curry. In the article, Will wrote that Curry began speaking about how he, Curry, found Chadwick's theories on baseball from rounders strange. Curry stated that he had never seen nor played rounders or town ball. It seemed, in the article, that Curry was the one wondering why people had not challenged Henry's rounders theory. Since Will was working with Henry Chadwick on the *Eagle*, it would seem logical to address this question to Will. Will went on to write that he, Curry, stated that he had played ball as a youth but it had "no name."[3]

On July 27, 1877, a historic game between the Excelsior's "old-timers" and the Knickerbockers was played. The *Brooklyn Daily Eagle*, where Will covered baseball, ran an article on this and mentioned that "all the 'vets' of the team of 1858 happened to be in Brooklyn the summer of 1877."[4] Will used the summer of 1877 as the date of his interview of the Knickerbockers team members, especially Duncan Curry. The members were all gathered in "Will's town," where he lived, that particular summer. He was most likely at that game and may have written the *Eagle* article.

The interview with Curry, he went on, changed his own personal position towards a Knickerbockers point of origin. At first he had accepted things that he had read in "dime baseball books," most of which would have been edited

Eight. Origins of Baseball (1885–1906)

by Henry Chadwick. In fact, the *Rockland County Journal*, during the time Will was writing for the paper (1870–1873) and playing baseball in the county (1866–1874), mentions Chadwick's books often as that county's point of reference on baseball. Will also mentioned in a 1904 article that he had "many extra-copies of Beadle's, DeWitt's, Spalding's and Reach's Guides" in his own personal library,[5] which shows that he did have books edited by Henry Chadwick at that time which were written by others. Though in 1907, he mentioned that the *Reach* guides were then his favorites and "the only real hand book that gives the actual doings in the baseball world for the preceding season."[6] Will and brother June were learning baseball in 1866, along with many local towns (Nyack being one) in Rockland County which did not know the game in that form prior to that date. It was new to them in that location close to New York City in New York State. He, and his Rockland County community, all believed what they read about the sport in the dime guides from those seeming to know it better.

It is also important to keep in mind that the 1870s were the period during which the United States celebrated its first centennial of independence from England. American origins for things were highly valued. In addition, many young men like Will and June had grandfathers who had fought the English during the War of 1812, and great-grandfathers who had fought them during the Revolutionary War. Baseball was considered an American sport. Releasing it from an English origin would have been very appealing to many in that particular decade.

Will, in 1877 when interviewing Curry, was working with Henry Chadwick on the *Brooklyn Daily Eagle* with Chadwick covering cricket and Will covering baseball. Curry mentioned having "played ball as a child" without a name for it, but then the "plan drawn upon paper" was presented at a lot where they, as adults, had "gathered for a game." It was a new idea which they agreed to try. There was a diamond shape on the field; 18 men played on two teams with a catcher, a pitcher, three basemen, a short fielder who merely assisted the pitcher, and three outfielders.[7]

Alexander Joy Cartwright (1820–1892) was a bank clerk and volunteer firefighter for the Knickerbocker Engine Company Number 12 of New York. He is credited as having organized the New York Knickerbockers Base Ball Club. The young men playing ball for that club were not familiar with the new style of play at that time. The original players for the club were men like James Fisher, Colonel James Lee, Dr. Ransom, Abraham Tucker, and W. Vail. In the spring of 1845, Cartwright organized the club and recruited new players including Duncan F. Curry, first president; William R. Wheaton, first vice president; William H. Tucker, first secretary-treasurer; Ebenezer R. Dupignac,

Jr.; and himself. More players were added in the next phases of the club including Daniel Lucius "Doc" Adams, Henry Tiebout Anthony, D. Anthony, Walter T. Avery, A.H. Drummond, Charles H. Birney, Paulding, Tryon, Turney, Eugene Plunkett, Edward W. Talman, William Bunker, Brodhead, B.C. Lee, Clare, James Whyte Davis, George A. Brown, Charles Schuyler DeBost, DeWitt, Gourlie, Fraley C. Neibuhr, Maltby, Moncrief, Paulding, Smith, Tryon, and so on.[8] John Ward pointed out, however, that Colonel Jason Lee stated in 1846, at age 60, that he had played the game as a boy.[9] That would place his playing back into the late 1700s.

Will mentioned in an April 8, 1905, article for *Sporting News*[10] that the theory of an origin with the Knickerbockers seemed strange to him at first, and it set him off investigating, asking questions of "many old-timers," all of whom refuted rounders and town ball as the beginning point for baseball. In fact, Will's *Sporting News* articles during the early 1900s are sprinkled with letters to the editor from early ball players in New York and Brooklyn who did not know the name rounders, and had never played town ball, even though Philadelphia and Massachusetts had a long history with town ball, not rounders.[11] The interview, followed by interviews of others involved in the formation of that particular club, led Will to believe that the game was formed by their club. He listed that some of those he had interviewed had passed on, but others included William Cauldwell, who had played for the Union Club and was owner and editor of the New York *Sunday Mercury* beginning in 1850; Thomas Tassie of the old Atlantic Club; Samuel Yates of the Eagles; John Prior; Richard J. "Dickey" Pearce, who played for the Atlantics, Brown Stockings and New York Mutuals; Sidney C. Smith; John Curtis "Jack" Chapman of the Atlantics Club, who served as a manager of the Louisville Grays at the time; and Andrew Peck, who had sold baseballs in New York from 1858 into the 1860s. In a 1908 article, Will also mentioned speaking with John W. Mott, vice president of the National Association of Base Ball Players and a member of the Eagles, who had also served early clubs as an umpire; W.V. Babcock, member of the Atlantics; A.J. Bixby from the Eagles; James W. Davis, chair of the Nominating Committee of the National Association of Base Ball Players and member of the Knickerbockers; Walter T. Avery from the Knickerbockers; John G. Price of the Atlantics; Henry Polhemus of the Excelsiors; and George Flanley of the Excelsiors, who also was a friend of Jim Creighton.[12] Each one sent him to another one, and the transition in his thinking happened while he was working with Henry Chadwick on the *Brooklyn Daily Eagle*. It appeared as though the name rounders was not familiar to those playing on early clubs in the area of New York City and Brooklyn, at least as per those who were interviewed and wrote letters to Will via the *Sporting News*. If Curry is an example, many ball players in the New York area just played a game hitting a ball without a name attached to it, though they did seem to know the name Old Cat. Stool ball was also played by the Dutch in New York, and that name was known. In that game, upside-down stools were used for bases.

The Knickerbockers' historic 1857 game at Elysian Fields in Hoboken, New Jersey, was then mentioned in detail in the *Brooklyn Daily Eagle* on August 18, 1879. This was two years after Will's interview with Curry and the others and may have been a time when Will was investigating and developing his own theories about the origin of the game. He became fascinated by that game. His theories were fully expressed much later, in 1885 and 1886, while again working with Henry Chadwick but on the New York *Clipper*. There was to be a parting of opinion between two co-writers on this issue of baseball's origin which became quite heated and unfortunately spilled into print.

Will did not appear to have had access to the research resources we have today, which actually do show forms of what was called base-ball being played in Europe prior to the New York Game, though not with its precise New York rules.[13] They did appear to have the hitting of a pitched ball by either a bat or the open hand, and the running to some form of a hole, post, or feature in nature as base. The game was usually played by children. Considering the fact that Will's research and article dated from 1877 to the mid–1880s, it would seem that he focused upon what he had access to, especially back issues of newspapers and journals, and live interviews with surviving players and reporters. He mentioned going through all the papers again, in a 1905 article, when writing the history of the Princeton College Base Ball Club in 1903.[14] He was looking for a precise starting point for the exact New York Game in print, rather than a gradual evolution into it through other similar forms. He noted that the Knickerbockers were the first to have their game score printed in New York *Sunday Mercury* and New York *Clipper* articles in 1853.[15] These reports became Will's texts for his theory. Editors of both papers became his secondary sources, the surviving players being the first.

Even John Montgomery Ward of the New York Giants in his book, *Base-Ball: How to Become a Player*, published in 1888, repeated the no rounders theme and wondered why writers in the first half of the century (early 1800s) had not mentioned anything about baseball being rooted in rounders before Chadwick's claim. He did not appear to have writings from Europe listing the words base-ball either, though some things were published in New England prior to this period.[16] Ward, a well educated man who cited ancient history, eventually sided with the Doubleday myth. Some modern writers, too, question the direct tie between rounders and baseball.[17] Will wrote in a June 25, 1904, article for *Sporting News* that John Ward and his wife had paid a call on him at his house "last Friday." Ward was preparing an article for a "book of sports." Ward needed information about early teams and "took a list of all the old clubs from 1845 to 1856," along with the "amended rules adopted in 1865."[18] So, Ward was another person using Will as a baseball reference person, though he differed in his conclusions. Ward also knew June Rankin well.

Interestingly, Henry Chadwick had written in the New York *Clipper* on October 26, 1861, that baseball was an American game exclusively,[19] and in the 1867 *Haney's Base Ball Book of Reference* that baseball, "as played according to the rules of the National Association of Base Ball Players," had "an originality as an American institution" just like the English people and their "national sport of the Fox Chase."[20] He continued, "What cricket is to an Englishman, Base Ball has become to an American."[21] His articles on rounders, however, became more frequent and emphatic during the time Will's writing on the Knickerbockers was circulating. Each used the other's articles as a forum for debate. Debate, for Will and June, had been part of their Latin-based education as children. You proved your point by using supportive data.

Will maintained that his original piece, "Our National Game," submitted for publication in 1885 and 1886, had been heavily edited before distribution by people most likely not wishing to offend Henry Chadwick. Will claimed that he did not see that version prior to printing. Had he viewed it, it would not have been run the way it was.[22] He tended to be methodical and precise and did not appear to like editing of his text when speaking about his passion, baseball. In fact, he often corrected colleagues when they had printed misinformation, even Henry Chadwick.[23] The Charles W. Mears Collection on Baseball at the Cleveland Public Library has a copy of this article in Volume One which may show some of the editorial changes. It is marked in places where the article may have been altered. In that copy, it appears rules of play on rounders might have been added, along with a few random words, and a section was taken out which may have referred to the Englishman in some form.

Alfred Spink printed Will's letter of March 13, 1909, to him in his book, *The National Game*. Will pointed to baseball's origin on Manhattan Island and the Knickerbockers Base Ball Club of 1853 in it and reaffirmed his no rounders position, but he also strongly debunked the "Doubleday Myth."[24] Will mentioned, in his letters, investigating the Knickerbockers baseball origin through interviews with the editors of the New York *Sunday Mercury* and New York *Clipper*, who were among the first to publish accounts of baseball. William Cauldwell, of the *Sunday Mercury*, started covering baseball as news in 1853, and he had accepted articles initially sent by the secretaries of the clubs. Material was published on both the Knickerbockers and Gothams. Will stated that he spoke with Cauldwell, who wrote the accounts of the early games himself. Frank Queen of the *Clipper* also began covering games in 1853. Will, as a writer for the *Clipper*, had access to the back issues of the paper, and his brother was baseball editor of the *Sunday Mercury*. The New York *Herald*, another paper for which June worked, actually printed the first account of baseball in New York, but Will did not mention it in his writings. Will, most likely, had known both editors of the *Mercury* and *Clipper* on a more personal level, making it easier to get their side of the story.

Will Rankin also claimed in a June 1, 1901, *Sporting News* article called "Base Ball's Birth," a possible link to American Indians. He cited the fact that tribes would gather, and friendly competition would follow in the form of sports between tribes which often used balls and sticks. The tribes mentioned were the Mohawks, Oneidas, Hurons, Abuakis (perhaps the Abenaki pronounced Ah-buh-na-ki), Seminoles and Cherokees and later Sioux, Creeks, and Comanche. It is interesting to see possible credit given to American Indians for baseball during a period when they were often marginalized. The prevalent thought was that anything of importance had to have had origin in the Western Hemisphere by white men. The article also quoted items from *Porter's Spirit* in September and November 1856. This reference was most likely to the weekly New York paper *Spirit of the Times: A Chronicle of the Turf, Agriculture, Field Sports, Literature and the Stage* founded by William T. Porter which was printed from 1831 to 1861. Interestingly, on December 6, 1858, the editor of that paper had people contacting him in great numbers from all over New York requesting rules to the game of baseball. The paper then offered the rules, and a diagram, since so many had requested more information on the new game.[25]

In a 1904 article for *Sporting News*, Will also quoted Judge William Van-Cott, an early ball player for the Washington club, an organizer of the old Gotham club, and president of the National Association of Base Ball Players, who felt the game may have had a Dutch origin since the Dutch played a form of the game in Bowling Green at the south end of Manhattan.[26] Thomas Tassie of the Atlantic club had given Will a letter of introduction to the judge while Will was making his searches. The inclusion of that material showed an opening in Will's position on a Knickerbockers point of origin to include pre-club influence. But, if the Dutch were a possibility, why not the English? Will added that the game "sprung up" and improved over time. Will was not able to concede, however, that the game might have origins outside of Manhattan Island.

By 1905, Albert Spalding had called together the Mills Commission, named after the chairman of the committee, Abraham G. Mills, former National League president and personal friend of Spalding. The three year commission was to come up with a definitive answer as to the origin of baseball, doing its own form of research. The commission was hand picked with great representation from the National League and no baseball historians. On the commission were Chairman Mills, National League president from 1882 to 1884; Morgan G. Bulkeley, the National League's first 1876 president; Arthur P. Gorman, former president of and player for the Washington Base Ball Club, and senator from Maryland; Nicholas E. Young, first secretary of the National League and its president from 1884 to 1902, also from Washington, D.C.; Alfred J. Reach, former player for the Philadelphia Athletics from 1871 to 1875 and owner of Reach Sporting Goods who would sell his business to Spalding in 1892; George Wright, former player for the 1869 Cincinnati Red Stockings, National Association and National League player from 1871 to 1882, and owner of Wright and Ditson Sporting Goods Company; and James E. Sullivan, president of the Amateur Athletic Union.

Initially, Mills had agreed with Will on the origin beginning with the 1845 Knickerbockers but later changed his position.[27] And ironically back in 1889, Albert Spalding and Abraham Mills had been present at a gathering at Delmonico's Restaurant in New York City to honor Spalding's baseball stars who had just returned from a triumphant 1888–1889 world tour. This was during the period called the Baseball Wars between the Players Union and the National League. During the tour, plans were developed by the National League's War Committee against the Players Union which also resulted in the subsequent removal of June from his position as baseball editor of the New York *Herald*. Delmonico's also was Bennett Jr.'s favorite hangout. Abraham G. Mills, the fourth president of the National League, spoke at the dinner on baseball as having an American origin with the crowd enthusiastically agreeing, and chanting "no rounders," which may have actually been a chant inspired by Will's 1886 article printed three years prior in many syndicated papers. It was widely read. Present at that dinner were the mayors of Brooklyn, New York and Jersey City as well as a number of representatives from major universities, United States senator and president of the New York Central Railroad System Chauncey Depew, Mark Twain (whose stories had been printed in both the New York *Sunday Mercury* and New York *Herald*) and Theodore Roosevelt. That dinner was the beginning of others trying to point to an American origin for the game. Will's article might have been one of the inspirations for the calling of a commission. "No rounders" would close Henry Chadwick out of the discussion.

In fact, Will wrote a number of letters to the commission on his own findings. In a letter written to Albert Spaulding during the investigations, Will repeated his belief that baseball did not originate in rounders or town ball, but he did not feel it necessarily began with the Knickerbockers either, since that team had other teams to play against. The Knickerbockers wrote down the rules for the game, but it was clear to him at that point that people were playing a form of the game before them.[28] This concession may have come after conversations with June, who also did historical research into the New York clubs in the early days of baseball. June was baseball editor of the *Sunday Mercury* as well as the *Herald*, and in 1889 appeared to have published commentary in the *Mercury* pointing to the conclusion that the Knickerbockers played against other teams who seemed to do quite well.[29] Will concluded that baseball "sprung up" on Manhattan very early as a childhood pastime in New York and improved each year to its present state.

In an article titled "Game's Pedigree," written in 1908,[30] Will also referred to an early drawing of a ball field, which had become a center of controversy with the commission. His interview in the summer of 1877 of Duncan Curry recorded Curry as stating that someone brought a diagram of a diamond-shaped field to their organizational meeting. Mr. Tassie stated that that someone was a Mr. Wadsworth who worked for the Custom House. Will printed what he had been told. Mills became very interested in interviewing Mr. Wadsworth about this matter, but no one seemed to be able to find a Mr. Wadsworth on the rolls of the Custom House. He wrote to Will in 1908 requesting more information. Will set out to investigate the matter, himself, and he found the same dead end and confessed that an error must have been made after speaking with Tassie again. Will recounted the matter to Abraham Mills, perhaps on January 16, 1908. Will then muddied the waters by finding a letter given to him by H.G. Crickmore during the summer of 1876. On the back Will had written "Mr. Alex J. Cartwright, father of baseball." This letter triggered his memory of that event.[31] He was looking up "records for a New York paper" when he saw the letter.

Will's interview with Duncan Curry, another man known as "The Father of Baseball," had been confirmed by Thomas Tassie of the old Atlantic Base Ball Club, who had initially stated that he witnessed the diamond-shaped field presented to the club by a Mr. Wadsworth, but later admitted that he must have been mistaken. In modern times, John Thorn, official baseball historian for Major League Baseball, in his book *Baseball in the Garden of Eden*, did his own investigation on Mr. Wadsworth and found that Mr. Louis Wadsworth was actually the attorney for the Custom House, and not an employee, which is why he could not be found on the employee rolls at the turn of the century. Wadsworth actually was on the committee which drafted the laws on the play of baseball for the Knickerbockers with Thomas Tassie.[32] Thorn credits Wadsworth with the nine innings and nine men used currently in baseball.[33] Wadsworth was present at those gatherings when the rules of play were being codified. He had also played ball for both the New York Gothams and the Knickerbockers. The possibility that he might have brought a diagram of the diamond to the gathering has been re-opened but not concluded.

This information was lost to the commission, however. Will mentioned a letter by Mr. Crickmore, sportswriter for the New York *World*, which brought things to light for him. He told the committee right away that it was "Tassie's blunder," and he was surprised that the issue kept coming up as proof of another beginning source for baseball. He had called on a number of persons to try to find the answer to the drawing and listed each one so others could question them as well, and he even offered to provide addresses for follow-up questioning. Henry G. Crickmore was not only a turf authority and author of turf guides, but also an authority on horse racing in general.[34] Will stated that when he found Crickmore's letter, he turned it over and found the words mentioning Cartwright as the "Father of Baseball." Cartwright became the center of baseball's creation for Will, since he formed the club, even though Will mentioned others on the Knickerbockers as having made decisions on a number of the actual rules. Cartwright was given the high honor of originator.

Henry Crickmore, in addition to writing on turf, had been baseball editor of the New York *World* after Mr. Ormsby. He knew horse racing and baseball. Crickmore became more than a person Will just knew professionally in the 1870 to 1880 sports world. In 1905, during all the letter writing to the commission, Henry's niece married one of Will's sons.[35] Ethel Lydia Daisley, daughter of Henry Crickmore's sister Sarah Crickmore Daisley, married Harold Rankin in April of that year. Will, however, was generally known to be a person of integrity. He usually presented the facts as clearly as possible. Just because the men knew each other did not mean there was any falseness to the letter.

Some see Will's words on the field design misquote with first one source and then another as backtracking, but given the size of William's baseball library, and the fact that he said that he found the original letter while searching for other things for a New York paper, it would not be improbable to believe that he had misplaced the original notes on the ball field from 1877 and had drawn on his memory in 1885. He had interviewed Curry, and did quote Curry's recollection of the Knickerbockers' formation of the club. Tassie was linked to the Mr. Wadsworth confusion, but in fairness, Tassie did work with Mr. Wadsworth on the committee establishing the baseball rules. A diamond shaped field was adopted by the club and Mr. Wadsworth was present at the formation meetings.

Given Will's twisted fingers, and the difficulty he may have had in sorting through material covering many decades, it might have been what actually happened. Will tried to track down the truth interviewing old players, publishers and anyone involved that might shed light on the issue. To his credit, he acknowledged to Mills and Spaulding, with whom he strongly disagreed about the origin of baseball, that the article must have printed a mistake about the playing field, which must have been humbling for someone intent on correct reporting. It must have been especially difficult writing to them, knowing what had happened to his brother June while scoring for the National League Giants and working on the New York *Herald* when Spaulding led the War Committee against the Player's Union. June was removed from scoring for the Giants and as baseball editor of the *Herald* because of the aggressive moves made by Albert Spalding in his three man committee.

The final report of the Mills Commission was dated December 30, 1907, and printed in *Spalding's Official Base Ball Guide*, which was edited by Henry Chadwick.[36] It claimed that General Abner Doubleday at Cooperstown, New York, invented the game in 1839, though they had little to back up the statement.[37] Their conclusion was based on the word of Abner Graves, a mining engineer, who stated that he saw Doubleday play baseball there when he was five. History later proved that Doubleday was, in fact, not in Cooperstown in 1839, but rather at West Point with no record of leave. But at the time, people like John Montgomery Ward endorsed the finding, with Henry Chadwick and Will Rankin emphatically disagreeing with it, and each other.[38] Will also commented that he wished the committee was "as anxious to find out General Doubleday's life" as they were in finding Mr. Wadsworth.[39] He had researched Doubleday and found that he could not have possibly invented the game at the time in question. Will actually published the letter he received from Captain J.S. Herron, at the United States Military Academy at West Point, which was dated April 4, 1908. The captain stated that a cadet in the first year of the academy could have leave only under exceptional circumstances like a death in the family or a business failure. Doubleday had entered the academy September 1, 1838, and graduated July 1, 1842. He could not possibly have had leave the first year to create baseball in Cooperstown, New York. Will also wrote that Abner Graves stated that he went to school with Doubleday in 1839. How could a man in the academy be in school with Graves at the same time? But Will's research into Doubleday was dismissed.[40] He still stands as one of the first to research the falsehood of Doubleday's role in baseball's origin. His research has since been affirmed.

We also know now that both Spalding and Mills had a relationship with Doubleday prior to the commission. Mills had served as a colonel during the Civil War and Doubleday as a general. Both were members of the same New York veterans organization. In fact, Mills arranged the military honor guard for his funeral. Spalding belonged to the same Theosophy Society as Doubleday. Doubleday had joined the group in 1878 and served as an interim president. The society was a self-awareness type of group with liberal ideas. Spalding's lover, Elizabeth, was a member of the group, and she had worked with Doubleday's associate. Spalding had a child with her which he had relatives adopt as an orphan while married to his first wife. When his first wife died, he married Elizabeth and adopted his orphan son. He officially joined the Theosophy Society in 1890 during the Baseball Wars.[41]

An interview found more recently in an 1887 San Francisco newspaper, presumably of William Rufus Wheaton, a member of the New York Gotham Base Ball Club, also sheds some light on the origins of the New York Game. In the article the Gotham club, playing in the mid–1830s, was listed as the first baseball club and they were said to have remodeled the game of Three-Corner Cat from a boys game to a game men could play with less ability for injury, given their strength in throwing and hitting the ball.[42] They replaced the hitting of the runner with the ball, to constitute an out, with a throw to the base and touch of the runner. They used bases instead of permanent objects in the landscape and used a diamond with home plate. The Knickerbockers, younger members later coming from that club, and the New York Club, then used this as their base for the New York Game. A number of members of the Knickerbockers did say that the game had been played before them, but the fact that it was not organized seemed to be the main issue, not the form in which it was being played. That earlier game may not have been exactly like the Knickerbockers' final set of rules, but it was considered baseball, and it was played in New York City. The California paper went on to say that the current 1887 game seemed to the person being interviewed to be very similar to the original game played by the Gothams. However, they did not have an umpire, shortstop, or nine men to a side. They used six or seven. So, even in trying to place a Knickerbockers origin to the New York Game we run into trouble. A team which formed that club apparently stated that they based the game currently being played on the children's game of Old Cat, adapting it to men's strength.

David Block, in *Baseball Before We Knew It*, has done an excellent job of tracing versions of bat-and-ball games back in time, showing versions played throughout Europe in many forms dating back to the Middle Ages.[43] Block is currently serving on the Major League Baseball committee seeking to study the origin of baseball. John Thorn is the chair of that committee along with distinguished people like filmmaker Ken Burns. In his book, Block wrote about how bat-and-ball games, in rude forms, appear to have been present in America as early as the arrival of the first Puritans on the 1621 Plymouth Plantation. Also mentioned was the Dutch prohibitions against playing near town in 1656; John Newbery's *A Little Pretty Pocket-Book*, published in England in 1744 and later in America in 1762 and 1787 which had a brief poem about children's base ball; notices against playing base ball near town windows were also published at colleges like the University of Pennsylvania in 1784 and Princeton in 1787,[44] and in towns like Pittsfield, Massachusetts, in 1791. Even in 1816 several other towns passed ordinances against it, but it was not played in the exact form we know today.[45] Following the Civil War, the game really took off across the country. So, games understood as base ball, bass ball, or baste ball were played prior to the Knickerbockers in America.

Block does show a relationship between these forms of ball and modern baseball, though they differed in fine points from the New York Game. He attempts to give a lineage for baseball in his book. The flow begins in Medieval Europe with a game called longball, which in England developed into trap-ball. Trap-ball then became the grandparent of baseball, with the cat–old cat family of games (one cat, two cat, three cat, four cat) parenting baseball, town ball and roundball. Town ball was played in both Massachusetts and Philadelphia and seen as a sibling to baseball. Roundball, also a sibling, was played in New England. Initially these games were played by children, but gradually adults found them to be a wonderful form of exercise.

English base ball and rounders, according to his study, developed in a parallel line with American baseball from the cat games. There was a great variety in the form in which the cat games had been played in England, depending upon the local interpretation of number of players, lengths of bats and distance between bases.[46] He states that the term base ball pre-dated the term rounders in England by nearly 100 years, and cites his evidence.[47] Block also does not see evidence of the word rounders in England prior to 1828 and it appears, at that time, to be another regional name for base ball.[48] Rounders and baseball by the early 1870s, however, became two separate sports. He felt that the multi-ethnic mix in New York City may have influenced the development of the baseball in that location.

Old-cat, in America, seemed to surface along with baseball, with printed records dated to 1837.[49] This is the date Will referred to in his "fifty years ago" statement which came from the early player's comments and letters to him in *Sporting News*. The fact that it is not from rounders also backs up Will's position. Block wrote that there appears to be no evidence in the New

York City vicinity of playing town ball or roundball, which also corroborates the letters published in the *Sporting News*.[50] They merely reported playing ball. Modern writers also are seeking to find an origin, or origins, for baseball. They tend now, however, to look at the family of games which led to the current game and define it more loosely than Will did. They look at games involving two teams "pitching, hitting, and rounding a certain number of bases in order to score runs."[51]

Block also sites another interesting tie in baseball between the English and the Germans, which also predates the Knickerbockers, in a book written by Johann Christoph Friedrich Gutsmuths called *Spiele zur Ubung und Erholung des Korpers und Geistes fur die Jugend, ihre Erzieher und alle Freunde Unschuldiger Jugendfreuden*; or in English: *Games for Exercise and Recreation of Body and Spirit for the Youth and His Educator and All Friends of Innocent Joys of Youth*. The German book on sports was published in Schrepfenthal, Duchy of Gotha, central Germany, in 1796.[52] It was a book on sports for young people which lists rules for an English game of baseball. The rules are similar to our modern baseball. The game was being introduced into Germany at that time, with credit to England as the point of origin.

One thing that is interesting about the location of the publication is its own tie to England. Six British monarchs, including Queen Victoria, King George III and the current house of Windsor, were members of the German House of Hanover. King George III was reigning during the American Revolution.[53] Where in Germany, you might ask, was the House of Hanover located? The answer is in the Duchy of Gotha, which ties the English monarchy, beginning in 1714 under George I, who spoke mainly German, to the publishing location of the German book listing English baseball in 1796. At that early date, the name base ball was tied to the English.

Many of the early ballplayers in New York were also second generation German. The Dutch and British colonies in America were refuge places for a number of groups in Europe fleeing persecution. The Germans were among the early immigrants to the colonies held by the British. The mixed religious groups of German immigrants (Lutheran, Reformed, Mennonite, Moravian) coming to the British colonies in America mainly settled in Pennsylvania, two-thirds of them, along with hundreds of thousands of Scotch Presbyterians, all due to that state's tolerance of religious groups. Pennsylvania also had numerous bat-and-ball games recorded early in its history. Philadelphia, in particular, produced a multitude of clubs.

It would seem that a number of games with bats, paddles, sticks and balls were played in Europe during the Middle Ages and during the early colonial period in America. Some appear to be closely related to the New

York Game, and others more distant. A crude form of the game was called base-ball and was played in England in the early 1700s. Many groups moving within Europe during the Middle Ages, with its religious persecutions, who later played versions of bat-and-ball games in America seemed to have had direct or indirect contact with England in one way or another. Even the Dutch gained independence from Spain with the help of the English in the 1500s. In New York, a number of these cultures converged during the early colonial times, and each may have brought particular rules of games to local ball fields.

Early ballplayers, not only the Knickerbockers but clubs like the Gothams, and the New York Club from which their members came, the Brooklyn Ball Club, the Magnolia Ball Club, and the Philadelphia Olympic Club looked over all the possibilities for the game. Members of the Knickerbockers, however, should be credited with organizing the game with a regular playing schedule and publishing the standardized rules of the distinctive New York Game of 1845 with nine players and nine innings. After that publication, it became easier for others to follow that version of baseball.[54]

Another point which seems to be controversial regarding Will was listed in the obituary written about him in *The Sporting Life* April 5, 1913. It stated that Will "felt" that he should have had the title of "Father of Base Ball" instead of Henry Chadwick.[55] How they found that to be the case was not mentioned. Will did, however, often comment on Chadwick's writing on cricket while he wrote on baseball. Again, this might refer to the work each did for the *Brooklyn Daily Eagle* in the 1870s and early 1880s. Teddy Roosevelt was actually the one who formally named Chadwick the "Father of Baseball" in 1904, though the nickname had caught on prior to that. Will was not the only one to challenge Chadwick's receipt of the title; *The Sporting News*, published by Alfred Spink, also tried to debunk his claim as father of the game, but dropped the attack after Chadwick was given a column in their paper.[56]

Chadwick had begun his journalism career in 1848 and specialized in sports, though cricket was his main focus at that time. However, by the late 1850s he *was* writing on baseball and editing manuals and guides on the game.[57] He *did* promote the game of baseball early, and *did* encourage its play. He did not, however, give birth to the game. Also, Will gives credit for many of the scoring changes to a number of different newspaper editors prior to Chadwick's final formula.[58] As early as February 17, 1879, the *Brooklyn Daily Eagle* commented on the *Clipper*'s new method of scoring.[59] That most likely was Will's writing. And in Will's 1886 *Early History of Baseball*, Will detailed M.J. Kelly's scoring system, which had been published in the 1868 and 1869 *DeWitt's Guides*.

Will began playing baseball in 1866 and wrote on baseball during his entire journalistic career, beginning in 1870. He meticulously kept records on the one sport, which others used as reference, including Henry Chadwick. He was a co-writer with Chadwick on the *Brooklyn Daily Eagle*, hired to report only on baseball, and a co-writer with him on the New York *Clipper*, specializing again only in baseball. He often corrected Chadwick on misstatements about historic games and also found inconsistencies in Chadwick's claims about involvement in a number of formative meetings, obsessing over records which seemed to have omitted Chadwick's name while listing everyone else. Inaccuracy may have been his main point of frustration with Chadwick, outside of a rounders origin.

June, on the other hand, also had worked closely with Chadwick. He had been placed by Chadwick at the New York *Sunday Mercury*, in 1875, to succeed him and write only on baseball, and did the same on the New York *Herald*. June dearly loved Henry and saw him as a type of father figure. They socialized together. Neither said a negative word against the other. June and Henry remained close, as mentor and student, and in many ways seemed to have had more similar personalities. Both were extroverts, social and expressive.

Chadwick maintained that "base ball never had a father but like Topsey, the game just *growed*."[60] In the end, Chadwick's promotion of the game was found to be a great value, and his presence won out. It is difficult to know if Will really thought he should have had the title of "Father of Baseball" or just thought Chadwick should not have had it. He probably would have voted for members of the Knickerbockers Base Ball Club, or Alexander Cartwright in particular. Unfortunately, Will has been interpreted by sports historians as being petty, though there were a number of people who did not like Chadwick at the time because they felt that he always seemed to be moralizing and had a style of writing they did not care for.[61] W.A. Hulbert of the National League did not like him. Abraham Mills disliked him, and Albert Spalding was later dismissive of him as an American origin for the game was selected.[62]

Frank Phelps in an article on Will, from *Baseball's First Stars* in 1996, mentions a humorous story told by Will. It seems Henry Chadwick told his friends that he only had one enemy, namely Will, but later that same night Chadwick went to Will's house to get information "for the last guide he ever edited."[63] Even though they disagreed with each other, sometimes very strongly, they still worked professionally together on baseball projects and saw each other regularly. Will did give Chadwick credit for all of his work he had done in baseball, but having worked so closely with him over all of those years, he may not have had the same starry-eyed view of him that others had. In the long run, neither of them was the true father of baseball, but all three, Henry, Will and June, deserve credit for helping to promote and record the game.

NINE

A Century Turns (1900–1910)

In March 1900, New York celebrated the ground breaking for a subway line from city hall to 145th Street. It would be open for business on October 27, 1904. The subway was to travel at 45 miles per hour. Prior to that, the elevated train rumbled along at only 25 miles an hour. This helped New Yorkers travel quickly to work and shopping in that area, and it also helped baseball with many able to now make it to the two hour games and home within a reasonable amount of time. Newspaper writers clustered around city hall found it very helpful in traveling to games as well.

William had three sons: Percy B., Sydney Irvine, and Harold Emerson. He lost his youngest son, William, in infancy. Will was devoted to his family. Percy had married Charlotte in 1897. Sydney had married a woman named Mildred and they would have a daughter named Mildred in about 1904. Sydney also became a reporter for the New York *Clipper* and then an advertising manager.[1] Little Mildred's photo is actually in a newspaper article within the Mears Collection, in Vol. 8 on the last page. She looks to be about five or six in the 1909 photo. A portrait of Will's son, Sydney, is on the same page in the collection in an 1890 news article from the New York *World*. At that time, he was in seventh grade and had just won a math contest. The two pictures of father and daughter as children in Will's scrapbook is touching. Harold was still single, but not for long.

Will's family had lived in a number of dwellings, but near the end of his life, Will was living at 2503 Claredon Road in Flatbush, Brooklyn, New York. Everything in the home had revolved around baseball and Will's passion for the sport. His baseball library was continually growing, containing pamphlets, histories, letters, scoresheets, articles, notes on individual clubs, and notes on the sport in general. He had all the baseball dime booklets and guides for each year and booklets from the original National Association of Professional Base Ball Players' meetings. He had newspapers and many books, including Charles A. Peverelly's 1886 book, *The Book of American Pastimes*, which gave the complete minutes of the early clubs.[2] The Charles W. Mears Baseball Collection of the Cleveland Public Library holds some of his scrapbooks, showing extensive clippings of game reports and scores secured on heavier paper, from across the nation and Canada. Will mentioned in 1907 that he sat with his scrapbooks and used them as historical reference in his columns.[3] He acknowledged that most people liked to hear stories about players, but he also had interest in legislation and actions done by the "Magnates."[4] He might have had an interest in baseball law, had the practice existed. The Mears Collection is an interesting testament to Will's hobby of collecting game scores.

- Volume 1 contains newspaper articles and box scores from 1857 to 1870. Many are from the New York *Clipper*, which may have been collected while he was working for that paper later, though he claims to have first read it in the summer of 1865. This particular period, 1857–1870, was during the time when Will was playing baseball and writing for the *Rockland County Journal* in Nyack, New York. There is, however, a copy of his "Early History of Baseball" stuck into the volume. He wrote it between 1885 and 1886 while writing for the New York *Clipper*. This was, presumably, because it dealt with the early period in baseball history, like so many of the clippings. That particular copy is very interesting because it has edit marks on it showing where someone may have changed Will's original text, something he always asserted. It would appear that the lines describing the play of rounders were added, as were a few random words. Text also was removed which may have alluded to Henry Chadwick.
- Volume 2 covers articles and box scores from 1870 to 1877, when Will moved from writing for the *Rockland County Journal* to the *Brooklyn Daily Eagle*. These "*Clipper*" articles would not have been his.
- Volume 3 contains *Clipper* articles and box scores from 1878 to 1883, which was when Will was writing for the *Brooklyn Daily Eagle*.
- Volume 4 contains articles, mostly from the New York *Clipper* from 1855 to 1878 and 1907, but Will was not writing for the *Clipper* during those periods either. The New York *Clipper* discontinued direct coverage of baseball in 1901 with Will remaining on staff as manager of the routing department until his death while writing for other papers on baseball. They did print baseball biographies until 1903.
- Volume 5 contains box scores for Western clubs from 1875 to 1879.
- Volume 6 contains articles and box scores from 1879, 1881, and 1882.

Will was writing for the *Brooklyn Daily Eagle* at this time but wrote for other New York papers as well.
- Volume 7 contains stories and box scores from 1871 to 1881 which, again, was when Will was writing for the *Brooklyn Daily Eagle*.
- Volume 8 is particularly interesting. It contains articles written by Will, but not really from the *Clipper* as the collection states from 1904 to 1912. These, mainly, are from the *Sporting News* for which he wrote on baseball during that exact period of time, beginning in 1903. He also wrote for *Baseball Magazine* in 1909 and 1910. When the *Clipper* stopped publishing baseball coverage in 1901, it continued to publish biographies on managers and players until 1903, but these are not biographies in this collection. Will is listed on the articles in the collection as special correspondent from New York. *Sporting News* was published in St. Louis. The journal actually advertised him as one of their correspondents. The collection contains many baseball histories, articles on the origin of baseball, and reports on the New York and Brooklyn clubs. Will also began complaining that the Polo Grounds were too small for the large crowds trying to attend games, and that a number of fans were being turned away.[5] Will's period of writing on baseball for the *Clipper* appears to be missing from the volume 1885–1903, with him on staff until 1913.
- Volume 9 contains articles from New York and Philadelphia papers from 1901 to 1905. Will was writing for a number of papers during this time.
- Volume 10 contains articles and box scores for the New York *Clipper* from 1879 to 1881 which, again, was before Will was writing for them.
- Volumes 11–42 appear to be those of Charles W. Mears.

What is interesting about his turn of the century writing is that fact that he revealed the full extent of his research in more of a teaching manner. He was 51 in 1900, and his attention was drawn to recording and preserving the conversations he had had with ballplayers, managers and reporters from 1870 on. He published letters sent to him by those people. He also mentioned the editors of both the New York *Clipper* and New York *Mercury* frequently, people to whom he and his brother had had access. They had been some of the earliest baseball writers. Will captured moments when interviews were held with them and with members of the original clubs, like the Knickerbockers, recording their words.

The National League was now made up of the Boston Nationals-Doves-

Braves, Brooklyn Superbas-Dodgers, Chicago Colts-Orphans-Cubs, Cincinnati Reds, New York Giants, Philadelphia Phillies, Pittsburgh Pirates, and St. Louis Cardinals. However, a new league surfaced. In 1899, Byron Bancroft "Ban" Johnson oversaw the Western League. He helped to turn it around. The Western League then decided to challenge the National League in the new century by moving from a first rate minor league into a major league. They chose the name American League, since the American Association was no longer functioning. The National League had cut a number of clubs in 1900 to regain its eight-club structure and to focus on making clubs more profitable in wealthier cities. Baltimore, Cleveland, Louisville and Washington had been dropped from the National. The American League picked up those clubs and players. The American League then installed clubs in Detroit, Cleveland, Chicago, Milwaukee, Minneapolis, Kansas City, and Indianapolis. Their league would be made of the Baltimore Orioles (who would become the New York Highlanders in 1903), Boston Americans-Pilgrims-Puritans-Plymouth Rocks-Somersets-Red Sox, Chicago White Stockings–White Sox, Cleveland Blues-Bronchos-Napoleans or Naps, Detroit Tigers, Milwaukee Brewers (who became the St. Louis Browns-Ravens in 1902), Philadelphia Athletics, and Washington Senators-Nationals. Both leagues raided players from each other in an attempt to put together a winning combination. The New York *Clipper* published a baseball biography on "B.B. Johnson" on March 10, 1894, mentioning his "genial" character, and "fairness and excellent judgment." "Candor and honesty" were his attributes. Johnson had also served as an official scorer for the Cincinnati club and had written for the Cincinnati *Commercial Gazette*.[6]

Ultimately, the National Commission was formed to end the disputes between the American League and National League. The National Commission was a three-person committee made up of a chairman, August Herrman being the first; the president of the National League; and the president of the American League. The National Agreement was signed in January 1903 between the National League, American League, and the National Association of Minor Leagues. The first World Series happened that year. The commission functioned from 1903 to 1920. The Commission carried out the mandates of the National Agreement, enforcing fines and the suspension of players.

June Rankin had waited to marry until he was 35. He had four children: Andrew, Herbert, Elizabeth, and Marguerite, who was born about 1900. Marguerite, called Peggy, was deaf like her aunt, though some felt that Annie also contributed to the loss by hitting the child by the ears and rupturing her eardrums. Peggy was a "bird-like" creature who was under five feet in height when fully grown, with tiny feet and a huge collection of store sample shoes, size 4B. She would sit perched on a chair, trying to follow what was going on. She was called "good-hearted and sweet" by the family.[7] June was living at 172 Elton Street, Brooklyn in 1900. It was just south of the intersection with Fulton Street. He would ultimately move to 115 Elton Street by the time of his death.

June's son, Andrew Brown Rankin VI, called "Drew," was sent as a boy to live with his aunts, June's sisters, on Long Island. June was very protective of his sisters; his son would later be the same. The sisters lavished attention on young Drew, much to the jealous eye of his siblings. Since the sisters of June had not been allowed to marry "beneath their station," they had no children of their own. For all intents and purposes, Drew became their son. Drew learned to sing from one aunt, and dance from another. He was known for his "sailor's hornpipe and tap dance," which he would break out into as an adult when he was having fun.[8] He also played the mandolin and sang. The sisters supported themselves but may also have had some financial support from June. Drew would continue to help them when they aged.

Annie, June's wife, had fallen down a flight of stairs sometime between 1893 and 1895, which resulted in severe brain damage. Not much was known about brain damage at the time. She was deemed "never quite right" after that, with some family members feeling that she was mentally ill, but her daughter Elizabeth, called Betty, maintained that it was the fall that caused the change in her behavior. June was always on the road, covering tournaments and matches. Betty helped care for her younger deaf sister, Marguerite, and older brother Herbert.[9] Annie was very difficult with violent outbursts which were unpredictable. Though Betty was very patient, the three children living at home had a completely different childhood from their oldest brother, Drew. Frustration began to grow in June's children.

June's travels associated with his writing were not limited to the New York geographic area either. He was covering golf with long travel to tournaments, and prizefights with travels to matches where it was legal. He had been reported as still writing for the New York *Sunday Mercury* in 1896, and he continued writing for the New York *Herald* until about 1898 while also beginning to write for papers like the *Brooklyn Daily Eagle* and the New York *World*. He would end his writing for the *Eagle* prior to 1916 and continue writing for the *World* until his death. The New York *World* was published from 1830 to 1931, and its publisher from 1883 to 1911 was Joseph Pulitzer. In 1894 it began using a four-color printing press and launched a color supplement. Pulitzer's sons Ralph, Joseph and Herbert administered the paper after Joseph's senior's death in 1911.

In golf 1900 was all about Harry Vardon's win of the U.S. Open. He was considered the standard for English players at the time due to his grace and style. He was a long hitter. He toured America that year, and Spalding's staff member Charles S. Cox acted as his manager. The A. G. Spalding & Brothers Company quickly developed the Vardon Flyer Ball.[10] Vardon would win the British Open in 1896, 1898, 1899, 1903, 1911 and 1913. Walter Travis' win of the U.S. Amateur also happened in 1900. Travis, born in Australia and a United States citizen, would win the United States Amateur title in 1900, 1901, and 1903; the Metropolitan Amateur in 1900, 1902, 1909, and 1915; and in 1904 would become the first foreigner to win the British Amateur. He was called the "greatest putter of all time," and was considered very consistent in his play.

However, the July 3, 1900, issue of the *Brooklyn Daily Eagle* listed June at the Paris *Eagle* Bureau at 53 Rue Cambon. The reason for the Paris trip was not mentioned, but 1900 was the second Summer Olympics played in Paris (May 14–October 28), as well as the Paris Exposition or World's Fair. He most likely was covering sports for the *Eagle* and perhaps also for the New York *World*. The Eiffel Tower, built by Gustave Eiffel, had been completed in 1889. It was an iron lattice structure, which was a marvel at 1,063 feet in height, making it the tallest building in the world. It maintained that title until the 1930 Chrysler Building in New York took the title.

The *Eagle* covered much of the pre–Olympic qualifying in field events with particular mention of the colleges involved.[11] This may have been June's writing, though his name is not on the pages. A June 17, 1900, article in the paper focused on "American Athletes Abroad" listed the colleges sending full teams: Pennsylvania and Princeton with representatives from the University of Chicago, Cornell, Syracuse, Columbia, Georgetown and Yale also competing.[12] Track and field events were a major part of the story such as assorted races, high and broad jump, discus throwing, and also steeplechase, etc. The athletes were to sail on an oil steamer donated by the Standard Oil Company.[13] An issue was raised and addressed with reference to Sunday sports. Albert Spaulding was the American director of athletics at the Paris Exposition. He apparently encouraged the Paris officials to "respect the Americans and change, whenever it is possible, the Sunday dates."[14]

One of the games included in the 1900 Olympics for the first time was golf, with two events being played on October 2. Twenty-two golfers from four countries competed in two events: men's individual golf and women's individual golf. The four countries represented were the United States, France, Great Britain and Greece. Charles Sands of the St. Andrews Golf Club in Yonkers, New York, won the gold. Walter Rutherford and David Robertson of Great Britain won the silver and bronze, respectively. On the women's side, Margaret Ives Abbott of the Chicago Golf Club won the gold. Pauline "Polly"

Nine. A Century Turns (1900–1910) 145

Whittier of Boston won the silver, and Daria Pratt of the United States won the bronze. Polly Whittier had been born in Calcutta, India, to wealthy parents and was studying art in Paris. Daria Pratt later became Princess Karageorgevitch of Serbia. No medals were given in these Olympics, only works of art and cash. Golf would also be played in the 1904 Olympics.

June was always on the move and sometimes gone for long periods of time, staying in hotels and rooming houses while completing an assignment.[15] The New York *Daily Tribune* mentioned June a number of times in their society pages as having come in a "driving party," with others like the New York *Sun* writer H.L. Fitzpatrick, and staying in a local hotel by a resort; presumably all were covering a golf match, called "field games" in the 1900–1901 period.[16] In 1895 there had been only about 300 automobiles in New York, but by 1905 there would be 78,000. Driving parties were probably done for safety reasons, just in case of breakdowns. Driving became highly popular for recreation for the more affluent.

An example of June's golf writing during this early turn of the century period for the *Brooklyn Daily Eagle* might be the November 13, 1900, article on golf, "Golf Caddies at Play." His name is not printed; however, after listing the role of caddies in filling in for missing partners and competing in their own tournament, it does go on to relate details on the national sport as played at various clubs during his period of writing for the paper.[17]

Sister Adela, age 57, continued to perform recitations. One was listed in December 1901 as "An Evening with Sir Walter Scott," and the other was simply listed in January 1902 as recitations within a larger program. Both, reviewed in the *Brooklyn Daily Eagle*, may have used some of the same material, since they were only a month apart.[18] It is likely that her sister, Arie, age 45, played the piano at these same events. Arie did not, however, receive press notices. She seemed to prefer supportive roles.

The New York *Clipper* discontinued coverage of baseball in 1901, the same year Guglielmo Marconi sent the first wireless transatlantic radio signal from England to Newfoundland making the world feel smaller. Will became a route department manager for the *Clipper* instead,[19] while continuing to write on baseball for a number of other papers and journals. The January 19, 1901, edition of the *Sporting Life* made the comment: "Long may both the "Clipper" and Will Rankin remain in baseball."[20] At least one of the two things came true. The *Clipper* did, however, continue printing biographical sketches on baseball players, managers and teams until February 28, 1903, when it dropped sports to focus on the theater and circus trades. It adopted the subtitle "The Oldest American Theatrical Journal" in place of "The Oldest American Sporting and Theatrical Journal" at that time.

There was a new baseball club in town now, belonging to the American League. The 1901 Baltimore Orioles were sold to gambler and illegal bookmaker Frank Farrell and former New York City police chief William Devery in 1903 for $18,000; it was an interesting pairing. The club moved to New York and was initially named The Greater New York Base Ball Club; it played at American League Park at 168th Street and Broadway. The club park was dubbed Hilltop Park because of its elevation. The New York press named the Greater New York Club the New York Highlanders, or the Americans, both for the location in Washington Heights, and the American League. Joseph W. Gordon was the club's president. He had been New York City's inspector of buildings, and was the brother-in-law of John B. Day. And, the Gordon Highlanders were a well known British infantry regiment which existed from 1794 to 1994. They were recruited mainly from Aberdeen and Northeast Scotland and chose Clan Gordon for their tartan. The press felt that Gordon's Highlanders seemed to fit for the new baseball club. Their ballpark was considered one of the largest parks at the time. Columbia Presbyterian Medical Center sits on top of the site now. Later, the newspapers would nickname the club again. The term Yankees would relate to the club's Americans name. The team struggled initially as it tried to find its place in the metropolitan area.

Between 1902 and 1903 Andrew Freedman sold the Giants to John Tomlinson Brush (1845–1912). Brush had been the one who sold his American Association Indianapolis Hoosiers Base Ball Club players to John B. Day. He was partial owner of the Giants beginning in 1890 and continued as owner until 1912. Brush would be the leader in the formation of a set of rules to govern the World Series. In 1902 John McGraw (1873–1934), who was nicknamed "Muggsy" and "Little Napoleon," was hired as a player-manager for the club. He would bring the club to greatness by completely rebuilding it from scratch. McGraw had played for the Baltimore Orioles and St. Louis Cardinals, and he knew what he wanted in a baseball club. The New York *Clipper* biography on him in 1893 called him a "very young and promising professional."[21] Christy Mathewson also surfaced as a star pitcher and perfect gentleman in 1902. He would become idealized as a ballplayer, held up for his virtue and fine playing record. The *Clipper* biography on him in 1901 called him "a fair haired youth, handsome in features and physique, and pleasant in manner." However, there was a fear at that time that he would not be strong enough for the club. He proved them wrong. He was filling the void left by pitchers Carrick, Mercer and Hawley who had joined the American League.[22] The combination of McGraw and Mathewson would seem unstoppable. Also hired at the turn of the century was a player named Luther Haden Taylor, dubbed "Dummy Taylor." This unfortunate nickname was due to the fact that he was a deaf-mute, but he was an excellent player and no dummy. When John McGraw came to work for the club, he made the entire team learn sign language, and they began using it to communicate on the field. This was the beginning use of communication signs in baseball. Taylor would play for the major leagues from 1900 to 1908.

In 1903 the compromise or National Agreement was finally established to resolve conflicts between the American and National leagues. New York had representation in both. The agreement laid the foundation for what is now known as the World Series. It was the same year Orville and Wilbur Wright recorded first flight in North Carolina. During this period, from 1903 to 1912, Will was the New York correspondent for *The Sporting News*, a paper owned by Alfred Spink of the St. Louis Browns.[23] He wrote a weekly column. In it were a number of pieces on the history of baseball and his research on the early clubs. This also was the period of the Mills Commission, and Will's columns were reflective of his letters to that commission, with explanations for his position on the subject. He also wrote extensively on the two New York clubs, the Giants and Highlanders, slipping in stories on the Brooklyn Trolley Dodgers-Superbas, their close neighbor. Since he was a New York correspondent for the *Sporting News*, his focus was on a smaller target in baseball, though he did comment on the clubs in the national game.

Will mentioned how nice it was to have easy access to the American League Park several times. It must have seemed very modern to him to travel by elevated trains, and then the subway line, especially since he began work using a horse and buggy. During those early years of the new century, he recorded the slow progress of the Highlanders as they developed into a really great club. The public seemed to root for them.[24] He also began using the Yankee term for them in 1904 and 1905, which was still relatively new.[25] The press, in general, began using it in 1904, but the team did not officially accept it until 1913. Will often pushed for a game between the Giants and Highlanders,[26] commenting that the Giants would undoubtedly win because of the management of McGraw, whom he greatly admired.[27] Will called McGraw the "man of the hour." He felt the Giants excelled in general teamwork.[28] But, he also commented that "the American League has shown that it is not a dependent upon the National League for its existence."[29] With so many teams in the metropolitan area, his columns always had material.

One of the things that made Will popular in his writing was the fact that he did analysis which was pointed at the playing of a better overall game. Peter Morris, in *A Game of Inches: The Stories Behind the Innovations That Shaped Baseball*, mentions a number of Will's articles in *Sporting News* during this period. Will would often mention people who had introduced innovations in the play of baseball, and he could recount the details of those innovations within the context of a particular game or event. Will had the names and dates associated with the first of many things like the curveball, the spitball, catchers playing close to the batter, use of chest protectors and such.[30]

Will mentioned in an article for the *New York Times*, back in September 1900, that he would be handed requests to give early histories on a subject. He would research these and respond. In that particular article the issue of the origin of the curveball was discussed, putting an argument between writers Joseph McElroy Mann and A.C. Anson to rest.[31] Anson held that Arthur Cummings of the Star Nines used it in the early 1870s and Will agreed, giving quotes to back it up. Will became the reference person for many newspapers on issues relating to early baseball. He also mentioned in 1905 that he kept his collection of scorebooks and used them for reference on players.[32] During this period the general public also would keep score on games they attended, so Will's scorebooks might have been on any or all of the games he witnessed, and not just on those he served as a professional scorer. He also mentioned bringing players from the Brooklyn club to games played in New York with him on their off days.

A "Baseball Summary" written in May 1911 gives a little insight into Will's love of the game. In it he begins by trying to explain the real enjoyment "lovers of the game" derive from watching the sport. He mentions the "nervous energy," "stir in the people," and the "highest pitch of enthusiasm" which happen particularly in the ninth inning finishes. He basically watched the sport as a great fan and recorded games with the same enjoyment readers sensed when reliving the feats of their heroes.[33] His comments for *Sporting News* also pointed to his feelings behind the writing: "I am in baseball for the game itself and always have been,"[34] and "baseball is the most uncertain game known to the public,"[35] which probably spoke the closest to the fascination it held for him. One could never tell what might happen on the field during a particular game.

Will also wrote a history of baseball for Princeton College in 1903. He had witnessed a game played by members of the college in 1866, when he was just learning to play amateur baseball. His account for the college went all the way back to 1858, when freshmen from Brooklyn formed the first Princeton nine. The game, in his words, was not "highly developed." The first game was played April 19, 1862, between the college and seminary, now Princeton Theological Seminary, with the college winning 45 to 13; using the live ball.[36] We do also have records, however, that individuals played what they understood to be baseball as early as the 1770s at Princeton. The college banned the play of bat-and-ball games by windows in 1787, and a student named

John Rhea Smith recorded playing "baste ball" in 1786.[37] It would not have been the formal New York game, but it may have been one of the earlier forms involving pitching, batting and rounding of some type of bases.

The *Brooklyn Daily Eagle* carried the wedding announcement for Will's son Harold on Friday, April 7, 1905. Harold Emerson Rankin married Ethel Lydia Daisley. She was dressed in a crepe de chine gown. The wedding took place at her parents' house on 125th Street and Felix Street. The article gives us a window into traditions of the time. The parlor was decked with palms and an altar was set up in the corner of the room. The Rev. Dudley Austerheld of the Warren Street Methodist Episcopal Church performed the service with the couple leaving afterward on a Florida honeymoon. Present were members of the Daisley family, Will and his wife, Will's sons Percy B. and Sydney J. with their wives, and June and his wife. Harold, though blind, became a paymaster for the Southern Pacific Rail Road. Harold and Ethel would have a son named David on February 21, 1907.

Meanwhile, Henry Chadwick was growing even weaker and seemed to write many pieces bemoaning the passage of time and remembering writers from the past. In January 1904, June sent him a letter to congratulate him on reaching his eightieth birthday. It was published in *Spalding's Official Base Ball Guide* for that year, which was edited by Chadwick, and must have held meaning for Chadwick since it was included with other letters of best wishes. The letter showed June's affection for Henry Chadwick. It is ironic to see it in a guide published by someone who helped to push June from baseball, but Henry obviously wanted it in there. June greeted Chadwick as his "Dear Old Friend: My teacher, mentor and guide." He congratulated him on reaching age 80 and set him up as his faithful instructor, Gamaliel, with himself as Paul.[38] The Gamaliel and Paul quote would have been familiar to readers in the 1800s, knowing their Bible (Acts 5:34–40; 22:3). Gamaliel was a renowned Jewish scholar teaching in Jerusalem in the first century who was revered for his legal knowledge. He trained the Apostle Paul in Jewish law during the period when Paul was still persecuting Christians as a member of the Sanhedrin. June set Chadwick up as the respected scholar and teacher, Gamaliel. He had trained June in the field of baseball writing and both had watched the old style of baseball pass, with a quicker style of play in vogue. Baseball entered the modern era just as Albert Einstein published his theory of relativity in 1905, which changed science forever.

Will, on the other hand, seemed somewhat obsessed with Henry's misquotes and perceived misrepresentations. Will mentioned in a 1907 article that he had "about everything the veteran gentleman has written from 1858 to date," feeling that it would be enough for a book. But, he used it to find inconsistencies in Henry's claims and inaccuracies in his reporting. Will called William Cauldwell of the *Sunday Mercury* the first baseball reporter. Cauldwell also helped organize the Union Club of Morrisania (Bronx) in New York and served as their secretary and represented the club at the annual convention, also serving on the rules committee. Cauldwell had a Mr. Whitney doing the outside baseball work until he became sick and Henry Chadwick, who was writing on cricket for a number of papers, was employed to write on baseball, though William Cauldwell had never seen him on a ball field prior to that. Cauldwell, to Will, was a hero and a truthful man. He covered games in Hoboken. Cauldwell was the expert for Will on the goings-on in early New York baseball.

Will focused on the fact that there were only two clubs playing baseball in Hoboken when Chadwick claimed to have played the position of shortstop there, and his name was not listed on either team roster, nor in any paper. So, where was Chadwick playing ball in 1847 and with what club? Will did not seem to be able to accept that Chadwick may have just played in pick up practice games. Instead, Will looked at the fact that clubs like the Knickerbockers, and the area cricket clubs, kept detailed minutes which included lists of their membership and who played in a given game. They did not play a great number of games either, so the games were highlighted in the minutes. Henry Chadwick's name does surface, however, on October 12, 1863, when he served as scorer for one game between the Excelsiors and Knickerbockers. The former won 42–13, but that was the only place in the early years of the clubs that Will saw his name, outside of reporting.

Will mentioned in his *Sporting News* articles having a copy of Charles A. Peverelly's 1866 work, *The Book of American Pastimes: Containing a History of the Principal Base-Ball, Cricket, Rowing, and Yachting Clubs of the United States.* It was dedicated to the members of the Atalanta Boat Club by the author and contained very interesting information on a number of organizations. Under Yachting for example, the New York Yacht Club is listed with all of their membership and races up to that point. June's publisher, James Gorden Bennett, Jr., is in that book with his yacht's history. Also mentioned is the fact that they had a summer rendezvous at Elysian Fields every July, and the Hoboken Yacht Club had its clubhouse at "old Atlantic Garden" near Hoboken and the Barclay Street Ferry."[39] They would have been able to see the ballplayers making their way to the field. Peverelly must have had Henry Chadwick's theory on rounders at that time because he begins his section on the national game with the assumption that baseball came from English rounders. What would have really been interesting to a baseball historian like Will was the fact that Peverelly had minutes to original baseball clubs under his section on the National Game. It shows when a given club was formed;

who was inducted into membership; who the leaders were; who the club played against, and when, with the scores. It went year by year, giving a detailed view of baseball through the eyes of the recording secretaries. Will Rankin could see Henry Chadwick in the minutes of the Knickerbockers only on October 12, 1863, as scorer.[40]

Chadwick also claimed to have been at the meeting of the original association's rules committee in 1859, but Will could not find his name listed with those attending. P. Remsen Chadwick was treasurer for the Excelsior Club of Brooklyn from 1855 to 1856 and president of the club in 1857 (pp. 400–401). The club had organized on December 8, 1854, and was one of the original members of the NABBP. P. Remsen Chadwick was listed as a delegate to the NABBP at its formation,[41] but not Henry.

The only references to his participation at that earlier date were in books edited by Henry Chadwick himself, or from persons repeating what Henry Chadwick had stated in his books. Will had the original booklets of the National Association of Base Ball Players in his library. The formal list also had been furnished to the New York *Clipper* and published there. Will continued by writing that Chadwick's name did not show up until 186, merely as a delegate, and in November 1879 even he, Henry Chadwick, also had stated in print that that 1863 meeting was his first meeting. He then was on the rules committee from 1867 to 1874.

Chadwick also had claimed in his guides to have been the one who organized the Professional Association, dividing the clubs into two classes, which many writers contradicted. Will printed the names of those dispelling that claim. He tried to go line for line in his *Sporting News* articles showing that Chadwick was not where he claimed to be in a number of instances and, unfortunately, instead of proving his point, he came across a little too small and punitive.[42] Henry was a fixture at that point and a beloved old man. He had served on the committees in the early years. Nobody seemed to care about the date, but Will cared very much. It is almost as though his initial idol had fallen and he wanted everyone to know how. Having worked in his father's law office, he had learned that minutes and printed news articles all had more value than a person's assertions. Unfortunately, modern writers sometimes miss some of Will's real contribution to baseball because of his obsession in proving that Henry Chadwick might have misrepresented himself at times. The more Will attacked rounders as the foundation of baseball, the more Chadwick flaunted it, calling himself the "gardener" helping the "little acorn of rounders" develop into a "great oak tree" of baseball.[43] It became awkward.

June remained close to many sportswriters throughout his life. Just as he had played on the New York Reporters' Base Ball Club, he now joined the

New York Newspaper Men's Golf Club. They played in the Newspaper Men's Golf Tournament, which may have been a tournament June helped organize. The tournaments are mentioned in the magazine *Golf*, the United States Golf Association Bulletin, for November 1904 and November 1905 as having been played the end of October or thereabout. It seems that the tournament began in 1903, with the New York group showing great strength in a game played at Garden City, winning 7 to 3. It alternated between the New York and the Boston area, competing against other newspaper writers. The second year the game was played at Wollaston, Massachusetts, with the New England club winning 4 to 2. In 1905, New York again won 7 to 3. The winning team took the trophy until the next match. After each tournament, teams gathered together for dinner and some form of entertainment. This was the fraternity June was seeking, the one he cherished from his teen years.[44] Playing for the 1904 New York Newspaper Men's Golf Club were W.W. Harris, R.W. Boorum, Jason Rogers, J.J. Worrell, H.I. Fitzpatrick, and A.B. Rankin, though they game him an L. middle initial in the article.[45] The tournaments continued through the 1920s.[46]

This club of writers was active within the Metropolitan Golf Association, which was an organization of clubs within a 55 mile radius of New York City, plus Long Island as well as parts of New Jersey. The mile limit was extended to also cover a club in Greenwich, Connecticut. Their focus was on local arrangement of tournaments under the United States Golf Association. In 1905 the MGA instituted the Met Open which was held at fox Hills Golf Club on Staten Island. In the association's 1997 book, *Golf Clubs of the MGA: A Centennial History of Golf in the New York Metropolitan Area*, they actually mention the fact that the New York Newspaper Golf Club played at Van Cortlandt Park, which does seem like a good fit. However, according to that book, the New York Newspaper Golf Club was formed by Grantland Rice, the famous syndicated sportswriter, and Harry Brownlaw "H.B." Martin, golf writer for the New York *Globe*, New York *World*, and *The American*. The club was considered "stalwarts" at Van Cortlandt.[47] Yet, Tennessean Grantland Rice (1880–1965) was initially writing in the South. He did not begin writing in New York until 1911 when he was on staff at the New York *Evening Mail*. He then, in 1914, wrote for the New York *Tribune*. The club was clearly playing prior to his arrival in New York with records about them in major golf magazines from 1903 through 1905. Rice may have been in a second wave of reporters gathered to play golf. H.B. Martin (1873–1965) clearly states in his book that Fitzpatrick and Rankin were in the first group of golf reporters. Both of them were listed in golf magazines as members of the initial club. Rice and Martin were not listed at that time.

Van Cortlandt Park was the first municipal golf course in the United States, built in 1895. It is between Broadway and Jerome Avenue in the Bronx. Jacobus Van Cortlandt bought the original tract of land in 1699, and the city obtained the property in 1888 and later created the golf course.[48] In 1896 the St. Andrews Golf Club fostered a tournament on that links for players who were not members of clubs in the USGA. Van Cortlandt Park seemed to attract newspapermen, writers, actors and artists who enjoyed the game,[49] making it an exciting place for the public who were curious to see how golf was played. Demonstrations were often set up to encourage others. The park was set up with a "9th hole with a fairway from tee to green of 700 yards. It was the longest hole ever to be installed in America" at the time.[50] The park hosted a number of tournaments for pros as well, like Jim Barnes in 1916, but it declined in the 1960s and was taken over by The American Golf Corporation in 1992 which renovated the clubhouse, tees and greens.[51] There were less than 50 courses in the United States in 1894, but by 1900 there were 1,040 courses with at least one in each state.[52]

In July 1905, June traveled in a special train from Jersey City to Cleveland with members of the American Golf Association of Advertising Interests, and a host of reporters. Eighty to ninety people filled a baggage car, dining car, and three or four sleeping cars to witness a tourney at Cleveland from July 18 to 20. The train cars were attached to the Erie line's Train Number Three, which was called the *Chicago Limited*. The writers represented on this particular train to Cleveland not only included major newspapers and sports papers, but also college newspapers and religious papers.[53] Golf was becoming a big business, or as June would say large business.

In the article, June was listed as covering the event for *The Rider and Driver* magazine. Its full name was *The Rider and Driver: An Illustrated Weekly of Outdoor Sport*, and it was edited by Samuel Walter Taylor. It was, as the title suggests, a weekly published on Saturdays. Its offices were at 1123 Broadway at the corner of 25th Street in New York City. The 20 page magazine began in 1890. It was about 9½ inches by 13¾ inches in size. *The Rider and Driver* specialized in things pertaining to horses, especially fox hunts, horse riding, horse racing, horse shows, breeding, harness horses, polo ponies, jumping and related activities. Most people in America still used horses for transportation, and June and Will had grown up with horses. In fact, their father often had horses for sale in the area newspapers. The magazine also showed riding fashions, automobiles, and dog shows.

In the late 1890s, *The Rider and Driver* cost $.10 an issue and $4 for a yearly subscription. Golf fell under the subheading of coaching. Coaching was very popular. Grand coaches drawn by horses would bring larger numbers of patrons to events. Coaching parties were a regular form of entertainment. Apparently, coaches were used to deliver persons to golf events as well. Under the subheading was a short list of tournaments throughout the country. It is unknown how long June wrote for this magazine. H.I. Fitzpatrick, apparently, also wrote for this magazine as per a March 13, 1903, *Golf Illustrated* article.[54]

In 1905, an MGA golfer named Leighton Calkins from Plainfield Country Club developed the first national handicap system. It would be modified later and adopted by the USGA in 1911. Each course was "assigned a par score based on the expected score of the U.S. Amateur Champion."[55] And, in 1906, Jerry Travers began his lucky streak in golf. He won the Met Am in 1906, 1907, 1911, 1912, 1913; the United States Amateurs in 1907, 1908, 1912 and 1913; and the 1915 United States Open.

In baseball, the New York Giants were being called the greatest of all baseball clubs in 1905 as far away as California, as papers in that state followed reports furnished through the *Associated Press*. The New York Giants won the World's Championship series over Philadelphia and it seemed to matter to readers on the West Coast.[56] The nation was beginning to relate to itself on a broader level instead of as isolated regional pockets, and sports like baseball, as covered through local newspapers, helped to begin the process of Americans thinking of themselves as a collective unit.

Will, in his writing, predicted a win by the Giants in the World Series due the management of McGraw.[57] It does appear that Will wrote often on the Giants during this turn of the century. He, of course, did columns on other teams, but the Giants were headline news and McGraw was the reason. By 1905 New York reporters would travel with the club, and by 1906 the club would replace their shirts with ones bearing the phrase "World's Champions." During the summer of 1905 when Will was 56, he wrote another complete history of the New York club. He also wrote short baseball histories which were widely circulated as letters in a variety of newspapers, including *Baseball Magazine*.[58] These were very popular with the public. Baseball and stories about the old clubs were accepted as part of American culture by then.

As for June Rankin, the February 2, 1907, issue of *Sporting Life*, mentioned that June had "acquired national celebrity" status from the 1880s on as the sporting editor of the New York *Herald*. Francis C. Richter was the founder and editor of *Sporting Life*. *Sporting Life* had supported the Players Union during the Baseball Wars. Richter had also started as an amateur baseball player like both Will and June and had helped form the American Association in 1882, an association for which both June and Will had scored. *Sporting Life* was published between 1883 and 1917 and then 1922 to 1924 and had a number of references to both brothers. Their publication address

Nine. A Century Turns (1900–1910)

The *Official Golf Record* was published weekly by June Rankin beginning in June 1906 at the *World* building in New York City. It contained news on tournaments from across the country and photographs of players (courtesy USGA. All rights reserved).

was 34 South Third Street in Philadelphia. The article on New York sports mentioned yet another magazine at which June was busily writing and serving as editor in 1906 and 1907 called *The Official Golf Record*. It was published in New York City. The magazine was dedicated, as you might think, to the game of golf.[59] This was the fifth journal edited by June. He had edited and published the *Official Record* and *Sporting Critic*. He also had served as editor for the New York *Sunday Mercury* and New York *Herald*. This magazine must have had some level of recognition in the New York sports world to have been mentioned as "news from New York" in a Philadelphia paper.

The *Official Golf Record* was focused upon June's area of expertise in golf. The baseball writing, editing, scoring and committee work he had done for baseball for many years certainly did qualify him as a baseball expert, and the reporting on boxing qualified him as an expert on that sport as well, though he never boxed. But, golf was to be his passion for the remainder of his life. There are two very rare copies of *The Official Golf Record* in the United States Golf Association Museum Library in Bernards Township, New Jersey. The copies are dated June 22, 1906 (Vol. 1, no. 4) and November 16, 1906 (Vol. 1, no. 25). The paper was published every Friday, which points to a beginning date of Friday, June 1, 1906. The reference in *Sporting Life* was printed in February 1907, so there is at least backing for its existence within those two years from the spring of 1906 through, at least, the winter of 1907. It is unclear how long it lasted.

The journal was published in New York at the World building, which would have been on Park Row. June was covering golf for the New York *World*,[60] as well as other papers, at this time and most likely leased press time. The *World* did have a publishing company, like many New York papers. June is listed as editor in this particular journal. The paper was published by the *Official Golf Record Publishing Company*, which sounds similar to the *Official Record Publishing Company* of 1885 and 1886, which published *Official Record–Official Baseball Record*. Single copies of the golf paper sold for $.10, and an annual subscription cost $3.00. The paper was offered in both the United States and Canada and featured schedules of events, announcements and notes on players as well as advertisements.

The Official Golf Record was printed on eight glossy white pages folded in half and stapled to make a sixteen page journal with quite a bit of text on golf, plenty of black and white photos, and period advertisements. It measured about 12 3/8 inches in height, and 9 1/8 inches in width, which most likely fit the presses of the time. The cover had the name of the journal in hollow letters at top with *The Official Golf* in the first row and a decorative *Record* in the second row. A picture frame beneath the title was made of golf clubs on the sides, a finial with a golf ball at the top, and, at the bottom, was a lying, filled, golf case and also a loose club in the lower left with five golf balls placed about. Inside the frame each week was a golfer with his name beneath and the championship won. It is assumed that other issues reflect the same format of the copies available.

What is particularly interesting about the advertisements is the fact that the A.G. Spalding & Brothers Company had a number of ads. Whatever June's feelings may have been towards the War Committee of the National League, he seemed to have set them aside at this point and solicited Spalding for representation in his journal. Spalding placed prominent ads. Spalding's goods were everywhere and covered every sport. His Spalding Athletic Library covered more than the following sports: archery; baseball, indoor and outdoor; basketball; bicycling; bowling; boxing; canoeing; cricket; croquet; curling; fencing; football; golf; gymnastics; handball; hockey, both field and ice; lacrosse; lawn games; lawn tennis; marathon running; marching drills; polo — equestrian and water; racquets; roller skating; rowing; soccer; swimming and speed swimming; and tumbling. The list went on and on. There was no way to avoid interaction with him if you were a sportswriter.

Each copy of *The Official Golf Record* carried extensive lists of clubs, tournaments and winners with statistics. June printed a request for secretaries of clubs to send their "fixtures"— meaning tournaments or championships — "yearbooks" and "announcements." The lists of tournaments include many states and Europe. The quantity of photos of golfers must have made it popular, particularly with amateur and semi-pro players who had a chance to see themselves in the news. It seemed that groups were forming everywhere. There was even a group from the New York Stock Exchange.[61] There is a good deal of information on the St. Andrew's Golf Club as well, which had been formed in 1888 in Yonkers and is still the oldest surviving club in America.[62]

In the November 16, 1906, issue June mentioned a closing dinner between the members of the Brooklyn and Forest Park Golf Clubs, which was to be held in Brooklyn on December 1. He highlights "the best of good-fellowship exists between the members" which points again to his view of sports as a fraternal and bonding experience.[63] The picture he painted in that small notice is of a festive dinner with the extension of warm wishes in the midst of competition. Women's golf also played a prominent part in his golf journal. Golf was a sport which welcomed female players, and their tournaments and photos were listed along with those of men in a matter-of-fact way, with the same respect.

The *Sporting Life* article listing this journal, mentioned earlier, went on to call June "still the smiling, genial, whole-souled man he was in his youth," but went on to try to tie this to his nickname June. The writer from *Sporting Life* did not seem to know, nor did a number of others writing at the time, that the nickname June was simply for Junior. Many tried to figure out the meaning behind the name, and some gave up exasperated, stating that nobody could figure it out. In 1889 a book with a long title had been published called *Athletic Sports in America, England and Australia: Comprising History, Characteristics, Sketches of Famous Leaders, Organization and Great Contests of Baseball, Cricket, Football, La Crosse, Tennis, Rowing and Cycling* by Harry Clay Palmer, James Austin Fynes, Francis C. Richter, and William Ingraham Harris and an introduction by Henry Chadwick, in which the name seemed to cause confusion. They pointed to it being his childhood nickname which nobody could figure out but must be related to his "sunny disposition and balmy temper." They said he was so popular that he was given every sporting summary in the city.[64] It is particularly humorous to see their puzzlement over the name considering the fact that Harry Palmer represented the New York *Herald* and Henry Chadwick knew June on a personal level. James Fynes worked on the *Clipper* with Will, and Francis Richter was editor of *Sporting Life*, which had reported extensively on both brothers. June had a large following on the East Coast, and was generally well liked,[65] but the name was not chosen based upon his personality, just his rank in the family.

Meanwhile, Will corresponded frequently with Abraham G. Mills and Albert Spalding during this period,[66] especially during their Special Base Ball Commission on the origin of baseball, often called the Mills Commission. They were also seeking an American origin to baseball, though they differed from Will Rankin on the results. They developed a stream of correspondence between them on matters relating to baseball's origin. Will sent his thoughts, which were read and then largely ignored, as were Henry Chadwick's. The commission appeared to have already come to their own conclusion: Doubleday as inventor of baseball.

Will's duties at the *Clipper* were no longer on baseball, but he was still publishing in other papers, and according to the August 24, 1907, issue of *Sporting Life*, William was selected to supervise the Bowler's Day field event in Cincinnati. There were five baseball events set into this exhibition. It was limited to players belonging to the National Agreement. The events were in the areas of long distance hitting, accuracy in throwing, running out a fair bunt, long distance throwing, and circulating bases, all for a cash prize of $100. The choice of Will was seen in the article as a sign that it would be conducted correctly.[67] Those officiating at the event were:

The judges: President Harry C. Pulliam of the National League, President

Ban B. Johnson of the American League, and Secretary John E. Bruce of the National Commission and of the American League.

REFEREE: William Rankin
JUDGES: B.B. Johnson, Harry C. Pulliam and John E. Bruce
STARTER: Starbuck Smith
TIMERS: M.C. Longnecker, E.W. Murphy and Charles Walters
MEASURERS: Prof. Al. Brodbeck, Prof. N.C. Seuss, and Ed. Brendamour
CLERK OF COURSE: Morris H. Iswes
SCORER: Ren. Mulford, Jr.[68]

Many recognize 1908 as the year Ford's Model T, or Tin Lizzie, went into production, costing $850 and opening up travel within cities and towns. June's son would eventually own a Model A, which was produced between 1928 and 1931. Automobiles had been around prior to this, but the Model T popularized travel. Driving was a major form of recreation. As news writers traveled in driving parties to the sporting destination, and stayed at local hotels with the local press listing their arrival,[69] papers also would be sure to advertise new roads now available near the country clubs. The popularity of sports and development of the automobile impacted the infrastructure of many small towns and cities with the demand for better access by the public to the sports facility. Golf and baseball were among the sports demanding space for courses, fields, and roads to accommodate fans.

In early April 1908, almost as a premonition, Samuel Karpf wrote a letter to the *Brooklyn Daily Eagle* mourning the death of John H. Mandigo, sporting editor of the New York *Sun*. In that letter, he spoke of the old guard of baseball scorers from the 1880s who were now gone. Listed were Stackhouse, Donohue, Caylor and Mandigo. The only New York scorers remaining alive from that period in his article were "Papa" Chadwick, Will Rankin, June Rankin and himself.[70] Of course, Chadwick and the Rankin brothers were well known to each other. Stackhouse and Mandigo also had played on the same baseball club with June. A few short weeks after the article was published, on April 23, 1908, baseball suffered a loss when the legendary Henry Chadwick died after catching a bad cold watching a game. It was the end of an era, and the circle was closing in. Chadwick was buried in Green-Wood Cemetery in Brooklyn. It was the same cemetery in which William M. Rankin, Jr., and Andrew Nerva Rankin had been buried. Chadwick had watched baseball in its early beginnings on into the more modern sport, which was as popular as ever. By 1909, there would be 14 new ballparks. William, at Chadwick's passing, was given by some the title of "the next father of baseball."[71] Will did write about Chadwick's passing in *The Sporting News* on April 30, 1908. In the article, he spoke of how Chadwick was "highly esteemed," and "gained renown" after fifty years of writing about baseball. He then gave a detailed biography on him.[72]

Sporting Life began including Will's statements in their list of *Wise Sayings of Great Men*. His sayings were printed from 1905 to 1910. Others also contributing sayings during this period included people like Connie Mack (Cornelius McGillicuddy, Sr.), Charles Sebastian "Red" Dooin, William Klem, Charles Comiskey, John Kling, Charles W. Murphy, William J. Murray, Thomas J. Lynch, Harry Saliee, and August Herrmann. Most of Will's statements have to do with being positive and the down side of being a pessimist. One statement, "The world generally hates a man who can prove his assertions by statistics," seems to be especially true for Will.[73] A series of statements were most likely written at one time, sent to the journal together, and then divided up by the editor for individual issues. The five year block of short statements gave him a steady presence in *Sporting Life*. Both Will and June had personal bonds with the publisher. Will's letter to the editor in 1908 mentions the fact that he began reading that paper in 1883, when a copy came to the Old Washington Park in Brooklyn where he was serving as official scorer for the Brooklyn Club.[74] Will began reading it regularly after that and eventually developed a friendship with the editor. He wished the paper well in their publishing ventures.

A number of things happened in baseball between 1908 and 1910. First, the Baseball Writers Association of America was formed at the World Series on October 14, 1908. The organization looked at working conditions related to writers: the press boxes and access to players for stories. Joe S. Jackson served as the first president. Second, baseballs used the cork-center ball. Third, Ty Cobb, of the Detroit club, won the Triple Crown in October of that year: .377 average, 9 home runs, and 107 RBI. And sadly fourth, the sport mourned the suicide of National League president Harry Pulliam in July 1909 at age forty.

Will Rankin began writing a monthly letter for *Baseball Magazine*, from 1909 to 1910, which repeated his love of baseball history with little facts about the game and the players. He also participated in fundraisers like the Jones Relief Benefit given for aging Charles W. Jones to raise money for his care in a sanatorium. Jones had played for the Cincinnati, Boston, Metropolitans, Brooklyn and Kansas City Clubs as a left fielder. Will was on the executive committee for the event along with John J. McGraw, manager of the New York Giants; two other newspapermen; and Jack Campbell, an actor.[75] A game was played by a number of old-time ball players, many of whom were on the committee, and was held at South Beach on Staten Island, New York. Little did Will know at that time that the clock was beginning to tick for him.

Ten

Working to Death (1910–1913)

In 1910, 59-year-old June Rankin was still writing on golf and playing golf. He sported his straw hat and scribbled notes in his notebook along with the mass of writers and spectators on the course. He appeared to derive great pleasure from his work and enjoyed the fellowship of other golf writers, telling jokes and still being the life of the party. Newspapers added golf writers as they recorded J.J. McDermott's win of the 1911 Open Championship of the United States. He would win it again in 1912. More coverage was given to women in the sport as well. Lillian Hyde Feitner won the WMGA title in 1910, 1911, and would win it again in 1914, 1915, 1916, and 1920. She won a total of six titles. It was the beginning of a shifting in roles for women as they actively participated in sports and successfully won championships. They were still somewhat hampered by their floor-length skirts, which would shorten over the decade as they made a lasting mark in what had been a man's world.

As Will aged, he helped other writers edit their work. When Alfred H. Spink, owner of *Sporting News* in St. Louis, set out in 1910 to write his own history of the game, *The National Game*, he sent one of the first copies to Will for his edits. Will was the New York baseball correspondent for that paper at the time. Spink mentioned that Will carefully went over the book and sent his corrections and comments; adding biographies on the baseball writers which appear in the finished book.[1] The book tried to faithfully record baseball history up to that time and has been used as an excellent resource to this day.

Will also continued to write baseball letters for various papers. What was interesting about Will's writing on baseball and baseball personalities was that he often recorded events much like a secretary of an organization. His concerns over recording correct dates in baseball history, with the persons

June Rankin covered golf for the *Brooklyn Daily Eagle*, the New York *World*, and a number of other papers in the early 1900s. He also played on the New York Reporters Golf Club with other celebrity writers. They competed in a number of tournaments alternating between New York and New England (used by permission, Rankin Family Archives).

involved, along with collecting baseball writings and scorecards, seemed to place him in an archivist position. For example, in his 1911 coverage of the gathering of the three leagues in New York, he not only mentioned the Eastern League at the Hotel Victoria changing its name to the International League to include Canadian teams, the National League at the Waldorf-Astoria, and the American League at the Hotel Aster, but he also carefully listed their resolutions. Persons present were recorded so that the average reader would have a clear idea of the events occurring which governed the very management of baseball at the time, and future readers would be able to have an accurate account.[2] His interest in the sport had spanned decades, and his collection of facts and trivia was legendary.

William McDowell Rankin wrote on baseball for numerous newspapers from 1870 until his death in 1913. He was considered an expert and was often sent difficult questions to unravel. His large library provided reference sources for a number of baseball writers. This photograph is of Will Rankin with his grandson, David Rankin (used by permission of Arthur Rankin, great-grandson of W.M. Rankin).

Between 1910 and 1914 the baseball news in the east was about the American League Philadelphia Athletics, under the management of Connie Mack, and the National League New York Giants, under the management of John McGraw. The Athletics won the World Series in 1910, 1911, 1913, and would go on to win the American League Pennant in 1914 but lose the World Series to the Boston Braves. The New York Giants, under John McGraw, won the

National League Pennant in 1911, 1912, 1913, 1917, 1921, 1922, 1923, and 1924 and would win the World Series in 1921 and 1922. Connie Mack's club had been established in the American League to compete with the Philadelphia Phillies. McGraw of the Giants had originally been a member of the Baltimore Orioles, which was a member of the American League, prior to joining a National League club. His change of allegiance from one league to another seemed to be quite strong. He called the "A's" white elephants, which they embraced as a team logo. Mack and McGraw fought. Their spats were legendary and often printed in the newspaper. However Mack insisted that he loved McGraw, calling him the "life of the party."[3] One thing that united the leagues, however, during this time of competition was the adoption of the cork-centered baseball in 1911. Will commented during this time about how wonderful it was to have three good teams in New York,[4] though he always pushed for the Giants to add some young pitchers to help Mathewson and to help more young pitchers develop their skills.[5]

In New York City, the big news was the fact that Polo Grounds III burned down on April 14, 1911. Apparently it began in the right center field bleachers, attributed to a smoldering cigarette. The only thing remaining after the fire was the outfield bleachers. The Giants were given permission to play for a time at the Highlanders' field at Hilltop Park while a fourth Polo Grounds stadium was constructed. Even though polo was never played at Polo Grounds number two or three, nor would it be at number four, the name took on its own identity with baseball based upon the first field where June Rankin had scored, which was the only one initially used for polo. Will had witnessed baseball at all three of the older Polo Grounds and would witness it at the new field as well. Polo Grounds IV opened on June 28, 1911. The management learned from the fire. This stadium was constructed of concrete and steel as a preventative.

Will wrote weekly "Professional Baseball Summaries" for newspapers.[6] His summaries tied together the National Game in many cities, giving a larger picture of the world of baseball. He commented on how the sport had moved from an American pastime to a "gigantic American enterprise."[7] Those, like himself, who had played amateur and semi-professional baseball in local cow pastures, had been replaced by professionals playing on elaborate fields with glorious stadiums. Amid the overarching accounts about the sport, by 1913 the Highlanders formally took on the name Yankees, a name originating in the press and now commonly used. Will had called them that in 1904. They sported their signature pinstripe uniforms and would eventually move from Hilltop Park to play at the Polo Grounds IV.

Other news in the New York area focused first on the sinking of the steamship *Titanic* on April 15, 1912, with the loss of approximately 1500 lives due to a lack of lifeboats, and then on Jacobus Franciscus "Jim" Thorpe, called Wa-Tho-Huk or "Bright Path" in Pottawatomie, who won gold medals in the pentathlon and decathlon in the 1912 Olympics in Stockholm. He was of mixed heritage: Caucasian and American Indian. For six years he played professional baseball as an outfielder. The New York Giants hired him to play in 1912, and then he was traded a number of times to other teams but returned time and again to the Giants. Thorpe was considered the most versatile athlete of all time, playing baseball, basketball, football, and a number of track events for which he held the gold medal.

In 1913, Will Rankin was age 64. He had been suffering from asthma and had complained of acute indigestion prior to March 29. In the morning of that day, he readied himself for work at the New York *Clipper*, as he had done the day before. He boarded a railcar on Flatbush Avenue near his home. But while traveling, he suddenly slumped forward and then fell to the floor.[8] He was dead. His body was taken to a local police station where his son Harold later identified him. The official diagnosis was apoplexy, like Andrew Nerva Rankin. The term was used commonly in that day for sudden death and was most likely a sign of some type of stroke. Will left behind his wife, three sons with their wives, and two grandchildren.[9]

Will had been present at the July 6, 1912, dedication of Ebbets Field in the Crown Heights section of Brooklyn, but he missed the opening of the major league baseball park in Flatbush by only a few days.[10] He died March 29 and the park officially opened April 9 with a game between the Brooklyn Dodgers and the Philadelphia Phillies. He stated in an August 17, 1912, article that the dedication in July had been a "glorious day." He felt that the building of the Ebbets Field had been a "great undertaking," and that Mr. Ebbets deserved "all the nice things that have been said about him and his wonderful scheme."[11] He recounted the origins of Brooklyn baseball from the old Union Grounds, Washington Park, Eastern Park and again Washington Park to Ebbets Field. The game in Brooklyn was now a necessity. The people were "brought to it with the march of improvement." The park was named after Charles Ebbets, the owner of the Brooklyn Dodgers who had worked himself up from the bottom of the organization. Will had scored for the Brooklyn club in 1883 and 1884, and had written many columns on them over the years.

Will also missed an exhibition game before the opening of the field, which had been played April 5 between the Brooklyn Dodgers and New York Yankees. The park seated 25,000 in 1913 and became the home of the Dodgers as well as a number of New York football teams. Oddly, the press box had been left out of the design, befitting his absence. It would not be added until 1929. Ebbets Field was eventually closed and demolished on February 23, 1960.

When Will died, he had amassed the largest baseball library in existence at that time, with details on players and clubs dating back to his very first entrance into the sport, and back into the mid–1850s.[12] Some of the library was eventually sold to Charles Willard Mears (1874–1942) and some of the scrapbooks are now part of the Charles W. Mears Baseball Collection of the Cleveland Public Library. The forty cases in the collection, and numerous microfilms, contain some of William's clippings, box scores, articles, stories, and personal letters, along with those of Charles Mears, though much of Will's library is still missing. The Abner Library at the National Baseball Hall of Fame and Museum, in Cooperstown, New York, has a scrapbook made by him which was supplied by his great-grandson, Arthur. Other libraries around the country carry back issues of the papers for which he wrote, but the location of the complete library is unknown.

William was buried in Green-Wood Cemetery in Brooklyn, on the same 8th Avenue axis as Henry Chadwick. Chadwick's plot is lot 32004, section 131. William is on the direct opposite side of the cemetery in lot 21072, section 4. It is though they were equals with polar views even in death. However, Will's plot was the same lot and section as his young son, William, who had been buried on July 3, 1887, and Will's father had been buried in the cemetery as well. It was not chosen to relate to Henry Chadwick in any way.

The cemetery was long famous for burials of baseball players, writers, and managers. Along with Chadwick and Will, are men like Charles Ebbets, members of the original New York Knickerbockers, Gothams, Eagles and Putnam baseball clubs, as well as members of Brooklyn's Excelsior and Atlantic baseball clubs, to name a few.[13] Ren Mulford, Jr., in a July 1913 article in *Sporting Life* listed Will with those who had parted, the "old guard reporting across the mystic river." He mentioned them as being those "whose word pictures were among the finest ever counted as baseball literature."[14]

Eleven

June Writes Alone (1913–1930)

By 1904, three million phones were in use in the United States. They used manual switchboard exchanges. The first long-distance telephone call would be made by A.G. Bell in New York City in 1915 to his former assistant Thomas Augustus Watson in San Francisco, California. The telephone would become indispensable for sports. Also, even as silent movies made stars of people like Charlie Chaplin, so too they opened up the possibility of recording more sports on film with moving figures.

Sports had been largely relayed through teletype to newspapers in the past. However, beginning in 1899, the *Associated Press* had used Guglielmo Marconi's wireless telegraph to cover the America's Cup yacht race off Sandy Hook, New Jersey. Marconi developed ship to shore radio following his successful transatlantic transmission in 1901. And, in 1914 the *Associated Press* introduced the teleprinter, which used telegraph wires to transmit directly to printers. It could record 60 words per minute. Melville E. Stone (1848–1929) was the general manager of the *Associated Press* from 1893 to 1921. He had been the founder of the Chicago *Daily News* in 1875. The teleprinter changed the process of timely delivery of information to the major newspapers, making it easier to receive information for publication from reporters in the field. Golf newspaper writers set up media tents at tournaments. They were often equipped with telegraph centers with journalists buzzing in and out.

In 1914, the feats of Walter Hagen (1892–1969) were heralded. He won the U.S. Open Championship and would win it again in 1919. Hagen, from Rochester, New York, almost tried out for the Philadelphia Phillies Baseball Club that year as a pitcher and shortstop. The decision to enter the golf championship changed his life forever. H.B. "Dickey" Martin, a friend of June's, would become his manager. Oswald Kirkby won the Met Am that year, and then again in 1916 and 1919. Reporters busily relayed the news around the country as their stories were printed long distance.

Nineteen fourteen was also the year the United States completed the Panama Canal connecting the Atlantic and Pacific oceans, and the two coasts. The real construction had begun in 1904. When completed, a 48-mile-long waterway saved the shipping industry not only the 8,000 mile trip around South America, but also the danger of the Cape Horn passage with rough waters colliding into each other from the two oceans.

In June's family, changes were happening as the children grew up. His daughter, Betty, was now age 20. She had started working after school doing gift wrapping at a local department store at 14. She did such a good job that she was eventually noticed and hired by the Norcross Company, a gift wrap manufacturer. They encouraged her to go to night school to get a bookkeeping-accounting degree, which she did. This would come in very useful in her future. In fact, three of June's children would get the same degree, which would help all of them in the business world.

In baseball, the Federal League of Base Ball Clubs, or Federal League, was formed (1913–1914). It lasted only two years and was embroiled in litigation. The Federal League was set up to be a rival to both the American and National leagues. They called it, however, the "outlaw league" due to its payment scales for players. The six initial teams on the Federal League expanded to include eight clubs: Baltimore Terrapins; Brooklyn Tip-Tops or Brookfeds; Buffalo Buffeds; Chicago Whales or Chifeds, who played at Weeghman Park which was later called Wrigley Field; Indianapolis Hoosiers or Federals (who became the Newark Peps in 1915); Kansas City Packers; Pittsburg Rebels; and St. Louis Terriers. The presence of the Tip-Tops added stress to the existing Brooklyn club, now called the Robins, and cost both owners money. The Tip-Tops and Robins had to compete not only with each other, but also with two really great New York clubs nearby.

In 1916, golf changed. The Professional Golfers Association of America (PGA) was founded. Rodman Wanamaker, of the department store fame, wanted to increase sales of golf equipment. He felt that forming an association of professionals would do that. He held a luncheon at the Taplow Club in the Martinique Hotel on Broadway and West 32nd Street in New York City on January 17, 1916. James Hepburn, John Hobens, Jack Mackie, James Maiden, Gilbert Nicholls, Herbert Strong and Robert White organized the PGA of America. April 10 is the date of its actual founding in New York City with its initial 35 members. The PGA Championship was inaugurated October 10 to 14 at Siwanoy Country Club in Bronxville, New York, with James M. "Jim" Barnes as the first champion, defeating Jock Hutchison. Wanamaker awarded a trophy and $2,580 in cash. Barnes, also nicknamed "Long Jim," would win the PGA in 1919, the U.S. Open in 1921, and the British Open in 1925. Alexa Stirling Fraser won the Women's Amateurs in 1916, and again in 1919, and 1920, and two WMGA championships. June was covering these developments as his son Herbert married Kathryn Dexter on June 11, 1916. Drew Rankin, Hub's brother, served as best man. Herbert was 24 and he would have a son named Robert, but his poor choices ultimately resulted in a divorce.

Drew won many medals in long distance running. He had been on the Commercial High School track team. He had chosen running so as to not compete with his father or uncle in either baseball or golf. This was a sport they knew less about, and he was very good at it. He also had gone to business school after high school and learned bookkeeping, typing and shorthand. But in 1916, Drew enlisted in the New York National Guard and was sent to the Mexican Expedition at McAllen, Texas, fighting Pancho Villa. Mexican leader Pancho Villa had raided the American border, which resulted in a dispatch of American forces to the south. It could have resulted in a war between Mexico and the United States, but didn't.

Under President Wilson, the National Defense Act was passed in June 1916. Local militias became National Guard units, and under the new act the federal government recruits took a double oath to the federal and state governments. The troops sent to Texas largely patrolled the area, with some fighting with Villa's forces, but they were unprepared for the climate. The uniforms were made of wool, and the temperature was over 100 degrees in Texas, sometimes reaching as high as 120. The forces also came with little training, receiving instruction in the process of serving, while dealing with shortages of supplies. Drew complained about the fact that since he had some skill in building, he seemed to be building things all the time in camp. The style of warfare used in the United States was based on systems put in place during the Civil War. This group of National Guard became, in a sense, a transitional force from the older style of warfare to the more modern age. They still traveled on horseback and in railroad cars, but the guard troops became the best trained for what was yet to come.[1] Drew served in the artillery with cannons pulled by horses.

Drew's New York National Guard unit became Battery F, 104th Field Artillery, 27th Division, 52nd Brigade of 186 men from the 12th Infantry, 1st New York Field Artillery in 1817 and was the first unit sent in to fight World War I in France. He stayed the entire length of the war in mud-filled trenches, sleeping in simple tents. The war was largely fought using artillery. He achieved the rank of sergeant and lost some of his hearing due to the shelling.

However, Drew did make lifelong friends during the war, and later, after retiring from doing bookkeeping and working for the National City Bank as an appraiser, served the army as a civil engineer inspecting and evaluating properties until the day he died. He literally died on the job. At his funeral, his entire company, those living, attended with deep respect.[2] Will Rankin's sons also were drafted during World War I. Harold did not serve due to his blindness, but Sydney, who also became a reporter for the New York *Clipper*, registered for the draft on September 13, 1918, and later, at age 65, registered to fight in World War II.[3]

In 1918, when the secretary of war put out a call for men to either work for the war efforts or join the army, it had a large impact on sports, particularly baseball where 227 major leaguers joined the military. Since many of the men on the teams enlisted, ball clubs faltered. Also, the U.S. Open and the U.S. Amateur were not held during the war, so golf had no winners to highlight. Instead, the headlines in papers contained reports from the War Department with lists of officers and enlisted men who were killed, wounded, or taken prisoner. June's son was on the front lines in the field artillery, and his nephew was fighting as well. The war became the news of the nation and the news of the family. Interestingly, soldiers from the American Expeditionary Force in France did play baseball at the YMCA hut during the war. Drew was very active in the YMCA in both Texas and in France, but it is unknown if he or Will's son, Sydney, participated in, or witnessed these games. Drew did, however, sing with the YMCA chorus.

While the country searched the papers for loved ones, in 1918 the influenza virus killed between 20 million and 40 million people. It is difficult for us to imagine the impact of what was called the Spanish flu on the population, but about one fourth of the people in the United States caught it, and about one fifth of everyone in the world. It has been called a pandemic, and it killed more people than World War I with people dying quickly after exposure, particularly those in the 20-to-40-year-old bracket.[4] Current studies are still inconclusive as to its origin, perhaps China, though the dampness and location near possibly infected livestock may have contributed. Cities like New York were particularly vulnerable with their dense populations. Antibiotics were in their infant stages with penicillin not discovered until 1928 and not put into general use until 1946. Crowded sporting events were places to avoid when diseases were present.

In October 1919, the Volstead Act was passed prohibiting the sale of alcoholic beverages effective in January 1920. June's younger sister had worked hard to push for prohibition through the temperance movement. She, and others, believed that it would solve some of the problems associated with alcoholism in the country. Little did she, or they, know that it would also spark a massive trade in illegal goods and sleazy speakeasies. Organized crime would be the winner of that battle.

The Red Scare was also front page news. Fear of insurrection led by groups of communists and socialists was the center of columns. Alexander Mitchell Palmer (1872–1936), attorney general under Woodrow Wilson, began rounding up groups deemed dangerous to the United States. There were bitter strikes, and an explosion on Wall Street killed 38 people and wounded 200. The New York area public was uneasy because it seemed that major institutions in America were no longer safe.[5] The country was trying hard to stabilize after World War I and reports of groups deemed unpatriotic were shocking.

The beginning of the 1920s was a blur of activity in sports. Sporting reports were beginning to be relayed to a small number of fledgling radio stations in the early 1920s, but radio did not have the technology for live broadcasts at those events. For the most part, a reporter in a small box was given an announcement to read into the microphone. Very few homes had radios. This would change by the 1930s. In the news in 1920 was the formation of the American Professional Football Association made up of 32 teams. The name was changed to the National Football League in 1922. June had reported on the sport when it was still at the college activity level. Now it claimed its own place in the hearts of the people. Also, in 1919 the Black Sox Scandal had begun to surface. By September 1920, it was made public. Seven players were on trial for "complicity in a conspiracy with gamblers to fix the outcome of the series."[6] Ed Cicotte, pitcher; Hap Felsch, outfielder; Chick Gandil, first baseman; Joe Jackson, outfielder; Fred McMullin, utility player; Sweede Risberg, shortstop; Buck Weaver third baseman; and Lefty Williams, pitcher, were tried before the grand jury in Cook County, Illinois. They were ultimately found not guilty in August 1921; however, Commissioner Kenesaw Mountain Landis banned them from the league for life.

However in New York, the 1920s were a gift in baseball. It was the banner year that Babe Ruth made history playing for the New York Yankees. He was purchased by the club from the Boston Red Sox for a whopping $125,000. Ruth drew over one million fans to the stadium. He hit 54 home runs in that one year, a record that no person had ever come close to achieving at the time. He dominated the sport for a number of years and changed it forever. It was the beginning of what was to be called the golden age of baseball. Ruth would become a legend. On April 18, 1923, Yankee Stadium opened. The club had used the Polo Grounds up until then. The new stadium was called "The House That Ruth Built" because Babe Ruth was so popular that large crowds came to see him play, paying their admission price gladly.

The New York Yankees would win the American League Pennant in 1921, 1922, 1923, 1926, 1927, 1928, and win the World Series against the New York Giants in 1923, against the Pittsburgh Pirates in 1927, and the St. Louis Cardinals in 1928. Coupled with this was the New York Giants' winning of the National League Pennant in 1921, 1922, 1923, 1924 and winning of the World's Series against the Yankees in 1921 and 1922, and against the Washington Senators in 1924. New York baseball fans were in heaven. Not to forget the fact, of course, that in 1920 the Brooklyn Robins (Dodgers) also won the National League Pennant. Baseball was the topic of conversation in New York, but June was now on the outside looking in.

Another beginning happened in 1920: the Negro National League was formed during February. Rube Foster was the chief organizer. It included eight franchises: Chicago American Giants, Chicago Giants, Cuban Stars, Dayton Marcos, Detroit Stars, Indianapolis ABCs, Kansas City Monarchs and the St. Louis Giants. It became the league in which persons of color finally had their talent and contributions recognized. Their opening day was in May.

At the end of World War I, newspapers began to pick up more coverage of sports like golf. In fact, the "press-tent became a major part of the game" with "an army of correspondents." The Metropolitan district had "the largest number of writers on the game."[7] An attempt was made in 1920 to form a Golf Writers Association with Harry West as president and Francis Powers as secretary, but it did not function well.[8] There are currently many active associations for golf writers, including one using that name. In 1920, the USGA also began research on turfgrass and published their first magazine in May titled *The Professional Golfer of America*. It is known today as *PGA Magazine*. Percy C. Pulver, a golf writer for the New York *Evening Sun*, was editor.

June was 69 in 1920, and still writing on sports for papers like the New York *World* while living in Brooklyn and playing golf.[9] The New York *World* continued to add golf writers as did all the New York papers. But to June, the summer of 1920 was focused on the wedding of his son Drew to Anne Schwartz, with the marriage announcement listed in the *Brooklyn Daily Eagle*. Drew Rankin was now 35 years old, the same age his father had been when he married. Drew met his wife at work. Anne's maternal family, the Schaefflers, had come to America in 1881 as German Moravian missionaries to the German population in New York City. Her grandfather, a lay preacher, founded a number of New York City churches which are now part of the United Methodist Church. On her father's side, the Schwartz family came from Rheinland Pfalz in Germany as Methodists and had been told numerous times to remove the "t" from their name, since it indicated a Jewish background instead of a Christian one. They emphatically refused, and the "t" was proudly kept, though her father was harassed for it with teachers pronouncing his name like they were spitting. Anti-Semitism was very much a problem in New York City. The Schwartz family was one of the founding members of St. Marks Methodist Church in Brooklyn, which Drew and Anne joined. However, Anne, with a rheumatic heart, was never really well and unfortunately died young. Drew remarried later in life, a lovely woman named Francis.

In 1921, the New York *World* covered the gathering of "Champions of Three Continents in Play for 'Met' Open Title." The three champions competing in the Metropolitan Golf Association's annual open were Jim Barnes of the United States, Joseph Kirkwood of Australia, and Jock Hutchison of Great Britain.[10] The July event paired Jim Barnes with Tommy Kerrigan and Walter Hagen with Cyril Walker. They were golf stars in their day. Jim Barnes won the U.S. Open in 1921. That also was the year that the official golf ball was adopted. It was 1.62 inches in diameter and weighed 1.62 ounces. It would eventually be replaced in January 1931 with the 1.68 inch ball which weighed 1.55 ounces, but not without years of testing and protests over the new ball by the public to the local newspapers.[11] The acceptance of a standardized ball led towards more uniformity in the game.

In 1921, Walter Hagen (1892–1969) was the first United States–born winner of the PGA Championship. He defeated James M. Barnes. Walter Hagen went on to win eleven professional majors and break down the social barrier between the professional and amateur ranks. He won the United States Open twice (1914 and 1919). He also became the first United States–born winner of the British Open in 1922. It was the inaugural international competition between the United States and Britain. Jock Hutchison had been the first American citizen to win the British Open before him. Hagen then won the British Open in 1924, 1928 and 1929. He won the PGA championship five times (1921, 1924–1927) and the Western Open five times. Finally, he was the Ryder Cup Captain six times and would win the cup which was named after Samuel A. Ryder, in 1927, 1929, 1931, 1933 and 1935. He was the non-playing captain in 1937. Hagen, the almost baseball player, would be linked with Wilson Sports in the development of golf gear. He is still considered instrumental in the development of professional golf, cutting through the barriers in a sport largely supported by amateurs. H.B. "Dickey" Martin served as his manager.

There were other golf wonders in the 1920s. Gene Sarazen would also rack up trophies. He won the U.S. Open in 1922 and 1932; PGA in 1922, 1923 and 1933; Masters in 1935; and British Open in 1925. He also would win the Ryder Cup in 1927, 1929, 1931, 1933, 1935 and 1937. Women also did well in golf. Marion Hollins won the U.S. Women's Amateur in 1921. Glenna Collett Vare was a six time winner of the United States Women's Amateur Championship from 1922 to 1935.[12] And, in 1922 the Walker Cup was founded by George Herbert Walker. His grandson is George H.W. Bush, and his great-grandson is George W. Bush.

Bobby Jones would come to dominate the sport as well. Jones won the British Open in 1926, 1927 and 1930; the Amateur Championship in 1930; U.S. Open in 1923, 1926, 1929 and 1930; U.S. Amateur in 1924, 1925, 1927, 1928 and 1930; and the Walker Cup in 1922, 1924, 1926, 1928 and 1930. Because Bobby Jones was a very well educated man, he had a fan base in both the United States and in Britain.

Boxing in New York largely centered on Jack Dempsey in the '20s. He held the heavyweight title in 1920 and 1921. The sport was now legal and a match against Luis Firpo in September 1923 was called the most dramatic sports moment by the *Associated Press*. The New York *World* called it an "Epic Battle of Knockdowns." Dempsey hit the floor, followed by Firpo hitting the floor seven times, in the first round. Dempsey also went "through the ropes" into the "press stands." The crowd was said to be "in a frenzy." In the second round, Firpo hit the floor two times. Dempsey was declared winner and retained his heavyweight title.[13]

Nineteen twenty-five, however, was a devastating year for June, who was now 74 and still writing. Sister Adda died April 9, and Margaret died June 18. Both sisters were buried with their mother, as would later be Lizzie and Etta. Adda, the great public speaker and performer, and Margaret, the quiet deaf sister, were both gone. Three out of the original six children remained. June's son, Drew, also lost his first child, but June was able to see Andrew Charles "Andy" Rankin born, the seventh Andrew Rankin, on September 16, 1927.

Also, on April 18, 1925, Charles Ebbets, president of the Brooklyn club, died, and Ed McKeever became president of the club. The Dodgers were playing the Giants that day. Ebbets had worked for the club beginning in 1883 when it was formed as a member of the Inter-state Association. Will had been the official scorer then. June had had the idea for a Brooklyn club and had been present at their formation. However, in a stranger-than-life occurrence, the day of Ebbets' burial at Green-Wood Cemetery, where Will had been buried in April 1913, the weather was very cold and windy. Ed McKeever caught a cold at the gravesite and died the following week from pneumonia. It was startling. Two presidents of the club were gone within a week of each other.

June Rankin was always active and athletic, and continued playing golf and reporting on it for the New York *World* until the day he died at age 79 (used by permission, Rankin Family Archives).

October 24, 1929, was the stock market crash, which was called Black Thursday. It ushered in the Great Depression with its devastating effects felt in almost every country around the globe for a decade. This impacted a number of golf magazines which folded under their patrons' economic stress. The Depression era was generally very difficult on sports, however, the *Associated Press* in 1931 reported that the sport of golf "showed steady gains in its followers and equipment, despite widespread factors of depression in many sports." In fact, 1930 was seen as a "boom year in golf,"[14] which may show the economic barrier associated with those playing the sport. Golf had an appeal for the upper class and was considered the "rich man's game." The high membership fees not only supported the greens, but also "palatial club houses, with grand ballrooms, card rooms, squash courts, bowling alleys and lounging rooms."[15] The club became a place for socialization, and a place where business was conducted. The country club was purely an American addition to golf; neither Scotland nor the Netherlands had it.[16] It became an exclusive place for only those deemed acceptable by the individual club association. The press' choice to play on municipal courts, thereby avoiding the high fees, also provided a certain level of privacy for the wealthy.

In 1929 and 1930, Robert Trent "Bobby" Jones (1902–1971) was the focus of attention. The Atlanta native, who was a lawyer by profession and amateur golfer, won what was called the Grand Slam, winning the United States and British Opens, and the United States and British Amateur titles. He had won his first children's championship at age six. He won the U.S. Open in 1923, 1926, 1929 and 1930; and the U.S. Amateur in 1924, 1925, 1927 and 1928, ultimately winning 13 major championships before retiring from competition at the ripe old age of 28. He would also write a book, *Down the Fairway*, in 1927 which became a classic, combining his personal memoirs and instruction on golf. It was also the year that the PGA moved from New York to Chicago, and Bobby would go on to help the A.G. Spalding & Brothers Company sell golf gear; however, A.G. Spalding had died in 1915.

June's second son, Herbert, called Hub, had a son named Robert by his first marriage. He remained single for a long time after his divorce and then eventually married again, late in life, a woman named Marguerite. He found his mission as an accountant at a home for mentally challenged elderly persons in New York. His second wife worked for a girls' home. They were quite happy together, helping others. June's youngest daughter, also named Marguerite, who was deaf, did not live independently.

June's third grandchild, and Drew's second child, Ruth Ann, was born on February 28, 1930, but he would miss Lois Carol's birth on December 9, 1932. On April 25, 1930, at 10:15 P.M., after covering a sporting event, June died a tragic death from carbon monoxide poisoning in a rooming house. Many houses still used gas lamps and this one, apparently, leaked. June had been the oldest living baseball reporter in America up to that point covering sports from 1875 to 1930, the last of the old guard.[17] He had worked to the end of his life in the field of sportswriting what he dearly loved, just like his brother. Some papers listed his death in the hospital from a lingering illness, but it was carbon monoxide poisoning and an accident. The funeral service was held at Fairchild Chapel in Brooklyn. June was 79 years old.

June also missed seeing his daughter, Elizabeth, as she came into her own. From 1939 to 1959, she became the first female business manager of *Woman's Day* magazine, earning more than most men in the United States at that time. She also became treasurer of Advertising Women of New York (AWNY) for many years, an organization which was founded in 1912 to promote women in the communications industry. She lived in a luxurious apartment-hotel on 10 Park Avenue with a beautiful view of the avenue.[18] She was the one who carried on the family love of publishing rather than her brothers. She would also support her mother and younger sister after her father's death. Her years of serving her family resulted in great managerial skills. She carried herself well in her New York designer clothes with French seams.

June was not buried at Green-Wood Cemetery in Brooklyn with his brother and father and many other baseball heroes, however. Instead, he was buried with his sisters and mother in the Springfield Cemetery in Queens. The plot is very humble, with only a marker number over the grave of their bodies, Plot 418. His wife, Annie, died a few years later in her early 70s. She and June's two younger sisters, Lizzie and Etta, would also be buried there, as would be Drew's first wife.

Will and June Rankin had served the world of sports from 1870 to 1930 combined. Their location in New York and Brooklyn set them in the middle of many developments in a number of sports, and they wrote not only for local newspapers but for papers all over the country, especially through work done with the *Associated Press* and early *United Press*. They had covered transitions in baseball from its days as a gentleman's activity directly following the Civil War to its becoming a professional modern sport, writing volumes of columns and multiple histories on clubs and players. They recorded scores and unraveled difficult plays. June also was present as boxing transitioned into a legal professional sport with guidelines made to minimize injury; football moved from college activity to professional sport; and American golf transitioned from the apple orchard to plush country clubs. Will and June covered the developments not only as professional writers, but also as fans who enjoyed the celebration of life found in the meeting of athletes in the course of competition. Their legacy as early scribes has helped the world of sports remember the contributions made by individual players and managers. Their histories have saved moments for posterity. They joined the fellowship of other writers watching and recording the sports readers have grown to love.

Appendix

It is fitting to close the book with comments from authors and newspaper obituaries since both brothers spent their lives writing. Will's obituary went out through the *Associated Press*, so many papers across the country carried the same basic material, though some chose to add their extra thoughts. The comments about William and Andrew by their peers are very telling. Listed here are also the papers for which they wrote and their contribution to the sports of baseball and golf.

William M. Rankin

"The accuracy of his reports soon attracted attention, and in a short time he became recognized as one of the leading writers on baseball. He reported the game for several of the leading New York dailies, and also for a number of years furnished the Associated Press with the game scores, which were sent all over the country.... Mr. Rankin had long been regarded as the leading authority on baseball, and many knotty questions were referred to him to be straightened out.... During all the years of his active service as a baseball writer, and even up to the time of his death, Mr. Rankin kept a record of professional baseball, and his records of the game are acknowledged to be the most complete in existence.... In Wm. Rankin's death THE CLIPPER loses a conscientious member of its staff. His loss is also doubly regretted by the officials of both the New York as well as the Brooklyn ball clubs, and the entire leagues, as well as by all newspaper men that knew him."[1]

— The New York *Clipper*, April 5, 1913

"[A] semi-professional in the early days of base ball ... [he] acquired a considerable reputation as an authority on the sport. [He was] closely associated with the late Henry Chadwick.... Rankin leaves one of the most complete base ball libraries in existence. He kept a record of everything of interest from the time he first became identified with the game, and after Chadwick's death he assumed the latter's title."[2]

—*Sporting Life*, April 5, 1913

"Several members spoke of W.M. Rankin's ability as a base ball writer.... [He] contributed numerous interesting articles on the origin and progress of base ball, as well as reporting the games and scores of the Old New York and Brooklyn teams. He was also connected at one time with the sporting department of the World and the Sun always as a baseball writer, and was highly respected among players.... The news of his death will be learned with deep regret by base ball writers and players everywhere."[3]
— Elmira *Telegram*, April 6, 1913

"One of the oldest and best informed authorities on baseball ... early ... was a semi-professional player ... frequently practiced with the Metropolitans ... first official baseball scorer ... 30 years on staff at the New York Clipper ... highly respected among players, who valued his praise and feared his criticism ... a indefatigable worker.... The news of his death will be learned with deep regret by baseball writers and players everywhere."[4]
— *Brooklyn Daily Eagle*, March 29, 1913

"For thirty years Mr. Rankin had been a member of the staff of 'the New York Clipper' and recently he had held an editorial position. He was an authority on baseball. In his early days he was a semi-professional player."[5]
— New York *Tribune*, March 30, 1913

"He had a host of friends among ball players, club owners, and sporting writers."[6]
— Washington *Post*, March 30, 1913

"[He was a] semiprofessional in the early days of baseball, followed the game closely as a writer, and acquired a reputation as an authority on the sport. He was connected with the New York Clipper for the past 30 years, closely associated, with Henry Chadwick."[7]
— *Boston Daily Globe*, March 30, 1913

"He has been connected with the New York Times, Daily Witness, Tribune, World, Mail and Express, Sporting World, Evening Sun, and the Clipper, besides doing the baseball work for the United Press, as well as for many daily and weekly papers. He also writes special sporting letters every week, which are syndicated. Mr. Rankin has written a history, 'Our National Game,' which was printed in nearly all the leading newspapers of the country. His collection of baseball literature is a rare one, and embraces everything of importance up to date from the year 1853, when the game was yet in its infancy, and when Senator Cauldwell, of the New York *Sunday Mercury*, first gave it prominence in his paper."[8]
— *Sporting Life*, April 5, 1913

"Rankin leaves one of the most complete base ball libraries in exis-

tence. He kept a record of everything of interest from the time he first became identified with the game, and after Chadwick's death he assumed the latter's title [father of baseball]."⁹
— Alfred H. Spink, *The National Game*, 1910

"Will Rankin perhaps exemplifies the ideal SABR [Society for American Baseball Research] researcher better than any of his peers, even the famous Chadwick, frequently his antagonist."¹⁰
— Frank Phelps in *Baseball's First Stars*, 1996

"He had a reputation for being thorough and conscientious in his work.... His contribution to [the New York Clipper] was enormous."¹¹
— Andrew J. Schiff, *"The Father of Baseball": A Biography of Henry Chadwick*, 2008

Newspapers with Which William Was Associated

Baltimore *American*
Boston *Herald* and *Boston Globe* (New York baseball correspondent)
Brooklyn *Citizen*
Brooklyn *Daily Eagle* (baseball writer and editor 1874 to 1883, writing with Henry Chadwick)
Daily Witness (baseball writer 1876–?, paper ended in 1878)
Detroit Daily Free Press
Evening Journal of Detroit
New York *Evening Sun*
New York *Clipper* (baseball writer-editor-staff 1885–1913, initially working with Chadwick)
New York Times (occasional pieces 1876–1913)
New York Tribune (occasional pieces 1876–1913)
New York World (occasional pieces 1876–1913)
Mail and Express (baseball writer 1887–?)
Rockland County Journal (baseball writer 1870–1873)
Sporting Life (wise sayings 1905–1910)
The Sporting News (New York baseball correspondent 1904–1913)
The Sporting World (baseball writer-editor 1886–?)
United Press (correspondent with the first United Press)
Special work for many weekly and monthly papers
New England, Northwestern and Associated presses
The New York Press Association

William Was Scorer for the Following Baseball Clubs

- First official scorer; working for the Mutual Base Ball Club in the National League (1876).
- Official scorer for the Brooklyn Club-Grays-Atlantics in the Inter-State and American Associations (at their inception 1883–1884). They became the Dodgers.

- Scorer for the Inter-State Association (1883–1884).
- Scorer for the American Association (1884).

Baseball Histories

- William compiled numerous histories on the national game and individual baseball clubs like the Metropolitan, Brooklyn, Chelsea, and New York clubs. "Our National Game" was a syndicated history of baseball. He also wrote smaller histories in the form of letters for various newspapers.[12]
- New York Clippers biographies on a number of players, managers, and umpires.
- Many of the New York papers for which he wrote are in the New York Public Library.
- Multiple scrapbooks with club scores and statistics. Many in the Charles W. Mears Baseball Collection of the Cleveland Public Library.

Firsts

- First official scorer for major league baseball in 1876.
- First to publicly confront Henry Chadwick on the origin of baseball beginning in rounders or town ball. First to debunk and investigate Doubleday as founder of baseball. First to delve into an American origin for the New York game.
- First to set up reporting networks for baseball in major cities to provide accurate and timely information for the public, perhaps as early as 1874.

Andrew B. "June" Rankin

"Best known all-round newspaperman in New York City."[13]
— Palmer et al., *Athletic Sports in America, England and Australia*, 1889

"He was a bright and ready writer, and for years, while he had entire control of the Herald's baseball, made it interesting and reliable. June Rankin was a delegate to the National Association when it was formed in 1877.... [He] entered the golf field where he soon became as well-known an authority on it, as he had been while connected with baseball."[14]
— Spink, *The National Game*, 1910

"[He was an] early ... semi-professional player"[15]
— *Brooklyn Daily Eagle*, March 20, 1913

"'June' Rankin became an expert on golf and wrote various articles for the Brooklyn Eagle and other papers and magazines on the subject, as well as reporting golf tournaments."[16]
— Elmira *Telegram*, April 6, 1913

"The best known all-round newspaper man in New York City ... an expert on golf ... wrote various articles for the Eagle and other

papers and magazines on the subject, as well as reporting golf tournaments." [17]
—*Brooklyn Daily Eagle*, Saturday March 29, 1913

"The oldest living baseball reporter in America."[18]
—*Brooklyn Daily Eagle*, October 29, 1922

"[He was] the Associated Press representative at the Corbett and Sulivan Championship bout ... wrote for the Eagle on golf and baseball topics."[19]
—*Brooklyn Daily Eagle*, April 26, 1930

Newspapers and Journals with Which Andrew Was Associated

Associated Press (beginning with baseball and then on many sports, especially boxing)
Brooklyn Daily Eagle (writing on golf and baseball 1895–1916)[20]
New York *Herald* (baseball writer-editor 1876–1889; sporting editor on various sports including football, boxing and golf 1889–1898). The *Herald* had editions in other major cities and in Europe.
New York *World* (writing on golf and sometimes boxing 1895–1930)
New York *Sunday Mercury* (baseball writer-editor 1875–1896/7)
The National Police Gazette ("expert on sports" merely answering questions from the public, 1884)
The News (writing on baseball 1887 range)
The Official Record–Official Baseball Record, the baseball daily (editor-publisher, 1885–1886 seasons)
The Official Golf Record, golf weekly (editor-publisher, June 1,1906 through 1907–?)
The Rider and Driver (writer on golf, 1905 range)
The Sporting Critic (editor-publisher, present in 1890, began after 1889–1890)
The Sporting Life (writing on baseball)

Andrew Was Scorer for the Following Baseball Clubs

- Official scorer for the New York Metropolitans Base Ball Club (at their inception 1880–1883)
- Official scorer for the New York Base Ball Club/Giants (at their inception 1883–1889)

Baseball and Golf Histories

- Editor and publisher of *Official Record–Official Baseball Record* (summer of 1885 to fall of 1886).[21]
- *The New York Baseball Club.*
- *The New York and Brooklyn Baseball Clubs.*[22]
- Editor and publisher of *Sporting Critic* (1890)
- Editor and publisher of *The Official Golf Record* (1906–1907–?)

- New York newspapers in the New York Public Library, but wrote for the Associate Press as well.

FIRSTS

- Official scorer for the Metropolitan Base Ball Club at their inception.
- Official scorer for the New York Base Ball Club-Giants at their inception.
- Published the first daily dedicated entirely to baseball: *Official Record–Official Baseball Record*.
- Among the first group of New York newspapermen to cover the sport of golf in America for the New York *Herald*, New York *World* and the *Brooklyn Daily Eagle* beginning in the 1895 range as the current associations were being formed. Editor and publisher of one of the early 1906 weeklies on golf: *The Official Golf Record*.

Combined Comments on the Brothers

> "Will Rankin and his brother, June Rankin, in New York for the past thirty years have been known as the best boosters of the game in that section. They were never known to knock a player but were always trying to help some poor fellow along. They will be known forever as the two best friends the game has ever had in the Eastern Metropolis."[23]
>
> — Spink, *The National Game*, 1910

William McDowell Rankin and Andrew Brown Rankin V were inducted into the Helms Hall of Fame in 1952, at its beginning. Also inducted at that time were Oliver Perry Caylor of Cincinnati, manager of the Cincinnati Red Stockings and then the New York Metropolitans; Henry Chadwick of New York; Michael Kelly of New York; Hugh Keough of Chicago; Louis Meacham of Chicago; David Reid of St. Louis; Alfred Spink of St. Louis; William MacDonald Spink of St. Louis; and Alfred Wright of New York.

William was considered an expert on baseball, and heir, by some, to the "Father of Baseball" title when Chadwick died. Andrew was considered the best all-round newspaperman of his time by many, and he had been called the oldest living sports and baseball writer at his death, connecting the old game of baseball to the modern era. Both Will and June have been widely quoted by baseball historians ever since.

Will Rankin's scrapbooks, which were in his extensive library, were purchased by Charles W. Mears (1874–1942). Some of it is now in the Charles W. Mears Baseball Collection of the Cleveland Public Library. A copy of a scrapbook by William, belonging to his great-grandson Arthur, is also at the Abner Library at the National Baseball Hall of Fame and Museum. June Rankin's two baseball books are there as well. The United States Golf Association (USGA) museum library has two copies of June's *The Official Golf Record*. Microfilm of June's *Official Record–The Official Baseball Record* is in numerous libraries around the country as are hard copies of the papers for which they both wrote. Will and June are still quoted today by modern baseball historians, and their material is referenced when looking at the early life of baseball clubs and American golf. The two men left a lasting impression in New York on sports.

Notes

Chapter One

1. James G. Leyburn, *The Scotch-Irish: A Social History* (Chapel Hill: University of North Carolina Press, 1962), 169, 185.
2. Cyrus Cort, ed., *Fort McDowell Monument Dedicatory Services, October 5, 1916* (Union Bridge, MD: Pilot Print, 1917).
3. Franklin *Repository*, February 9, 1830. William and Andrew Rankin's father, Andrew Nerva Rankin, Esq., owned the same paper under the name *Repository and Transcript*. Virginia Shannon Fendrick, *American Revolutionary Soldiers of Franklin County, Pennsylvania* (Chambersburg, PA: Historical Works Committee of the Franklin County Chapter, 1944), 15, 134, 175, 188, 253, 291.
4. *Chambersburg Gazette*, June 19, 1798, as per Samuel Bates, *History of Franklin County, Pennsylvania* (Chicago: Warner, Beers, 1887), 223.
5. This information was printed by Ann Rankin Robinson, the daughter of Colonel John Rankin who was the grandson of Andrew Brown Rankin III, on the back of a photograph of Andrew Brown Rankin III with his wife. It is now in the possession of Doug Torrence of Ohio (Ann Robinson's descendant). Also see Pamela A. Bakker, "Franklin County, Pennsylvania, Abolitionist, Andrew Nerva Rankin, Esq.," in *Franklin County Historical Society: The Civil War Issue*, Vol. 23 (Chambersburg, PA: Franklin County Historical Society, 2011): 40–48.
6. Cyrus Cort, *Memorial of Enoch Brown and Eleven Scholars Who Were Massacred in Antrim Township, Franklin County, PA., by the Indians During the Pontiac War* (Lancaster, PA: Hensel, 1886).
7. Samuel Bates, *History of Franklin County, Pennsylvania* (Chicago: Warner, Beers, 1887), Chapter 8. I.H. M'Cauley, *Historical Sketch of Franklin County, Pennsylvania* (Harrisburg, PA: Patriot, 1878), 84–85. Israel Daniel Rupp, *The History and Topography of Dauphin, Cumberland, Franklin, Bedford, Adams, Perry, Somerset, Cambria and Indiana Counties* (Lancaster, PA: Hills, 1846), 149–51.
8. Pennsylvania Constitutional Convention with John Agg reporting, *Proceedings and Debates of the Convention of the Commonwealth of Pennsylvania to propose Amendments to the Constitution Commenced and Held at Harrisburg*, Vol. 3 (Harrisburg, PA: Packer, Bariett, and Park, 1837), 557. Andrew Brown Rankin III is listed as being appointed to the elected office of justice of the peace in Franklin County on June 2, 1821. He served in this office for 50 years, having been continually re-elected.
9. Alfred H. Spink, *The National Game*, (Reprint: Carbondale: Southern Illinois University Press, 2000), 342.
10. *Repository and Transcript*, 1856–63. Obituary notice of Andrew N. Rankin. *The Public Opinion*, September 24, 1890.

Chapter Two

1. "Underground Railroad" on *http://www.explorefranklincountypa.com/history/indexcfm?id=3* mentions the fact that the Franklin County African American free population was the fifth largest in the country at this time. The town of Mercersburg had the largest free population within the county.
2. Franklin *Repository and Transcript*, May 9, 1864. This was the name of the paper prior to Andrew N. Rankin's purchase of the paper.
3. As per "Underground Railroad," *http://www.explorefranklincountypa.com/history/index.cfm?id=3*.

4. I.H. M'Cauley, *Historical Sketch of Franklin County, Pennsylvania* (Chambersburg, PA: Pursel, 1878), 43–44.
5. Samuel Bates, *History of Franklin County, Pennsylvania* (Chicago: Warner, Beers, 1887), 323.
6. *Repository and Transcript*, May 5, 1860; July 18, 1860; August 1, 1860; September 5, 1860.
7. *Chicago Tribune*, October 3, 1860.
8. Edward L. Ayers and William G. Thomas III, "Two American Communities on the Eve of Civil War: An Experiment in Form and Analysis," reprint from *The American Historical Review*, January 11, 2002, p. 5.
9. Ibid.
10. George B. Kirsch, *Baseball in Blue and Gray* (Princeton: Princeton University Press, 2003), 54–55.
11. *Kittochtinny Historical Society Newsletter* 21, no. 5 (May 2005), 3.
12. Ayers and Thomas, p. 59. *Repository and Transcript*, September 12, 1860.
13. *Repository and Transcript*, April 18, 1861.
14. As per Ruth Rankin Leaper and Lois Rankin Prior, granddaughters of Andrew Brown Rankin V, in interviews with the author in 2010–2011.
15. I.H. M'Cauley and J.L. Suesserott, *Historical Sketch of Franklin County, Pennsylvania* (Chambersburg, PA: Pursel, 878). J. Hoke, *Reminiscence of the War* (Chambersburg, PA: Folte, 1884), 22–30.
16. *Harper's Weekly*, November 1, 1862, at http://www.sonofthesouth.net/leefoundation/civil-war/1862/november/chambersburg.htm.
17. Alfred Spink, *The National Game* (Carbondale: Southern Illinois University Press, 2000), 342.
18. Benjamin Shroder Schneck, *The Burning of Chambersburg, Pennsylvania* (Memphis: General Books, 2010), 8–9.
19. Pamela A. Bakker, "Franklin County, Pennsylvania, Abolitionist: Andrew Nerva Rankin, Esq.," in *Franklin County History: The Civil War Issue*, Beate A. Schiwek, ed., Vol. 23, (Chambersburg, PA: Franklin County Historical Society-Kittochtinny, 2011), 40–48.
20. W. Powell Ware and A.N. Rankin, *Professor Ware's $10,000 Prize Rule for the Equation of Payments* (New York: Francis and Loutrel, 1890). Andrew Nerva Rankin's *Perpetual Almanac* is appended to the book, which was a $10,000 prize winning presentation of the "best rule for equation of payments." Both men had their work entered by Act of Congress.
21. Edward L. Ayers and Anne S. Rubin, *Valley of the Shadow* (New York: Norton, 2000).
22. *Valley Spirit*, January 29, 1864.
23. Ibid., February 10, 1864.
24. Schneck, 7.
25. Franklin *Repository and Transcript*, July 3, 1864.
26. As per Ruth Rankin Leaper, granddaughter of Andrew Brown "June" Rankin V.
27. *Central Press*, August 5, 1864, and Lancaster *Intelligencer*, August 4, 1864. Also, Hoke, 114–115.
28. Hoke, 114–115.
29. Schneck, 10.
30. Ibid., 5–6.
31. Ibid., 6.
32. Franklin *Repository and Transcript*, August 25, 1864.
33. Ibid., August 31, 1864.

Chapter Three

1. Alfred H. Spink, *The National Game* (Carbondale: Southern Illinois University Press, 2000), 342.
2. Pamela A. Bakker, "Franklin County, Pennsylvania, Abolitionist, Andrew Nerva Rankin, Esq.," in *Franklin County Historical Society: The Civil War Issue*, Vol. 23 (Chambersburg, PA: Franklin County Historical Society, 2011): 40–48.
3. American Union Commission, *The American Union Commission: Its Origin, Operations and Purposes* (New York: Sanford Harroun and Co., Printers, October 1865), 3–6. Also, http://faculty.assumption.edu/aas/Reports/amunioncomorigin.html.
4. Some of the patents of Andrew Nerva Rankin, Esq., include:
5/22/1860 (Philadelphia) *Improved Lock*, Patent #28,406.
12/10/1861 (Philadelphia) *Improvement in Manacles*, Patent #33,917.

2/17/1863 (Philadelphia) *Improved Annunciator,* Patent #37,706.

1863 (Philadelphia) *The Excelsior Perpetual Calendar* which listed the days of the week for every year from 1/1/1401 to 12/31/2100. By looking at the one-page chart, you are able to see what day of the week an event happened on or will happen.

11/28/1865 (New York) *Improved Deodorizing Composition,* Patent #51,216 Series .

6/5/1866 (New York) *Improved Chamber-Vessell* (first urinal), Patent #55,361.

6/4/1867 (New York) *Water-Closet,* Patent #65,505.

8/10/1886 (New York) *Cold-Packed Pipe-Joint and Method of Producing the Same,* Patent #347,060 series 131, 649.

10/4/1870 (Philadelphia) *Improvement in Shutter-Fasteners,* Patent #108,052.

1/17/1888 (New York, filed 1887) *Tool for Forming Cold-Packed Pipe-Joint* Patent #376,609 series 230,246.

1/21/1890 (New York, filed 1888) *Apparatus Constructing for Constructiong Cold-Packed Pipe-Joint,* Patent #419,995 Series #294,242.

12/23/1902 (Brooklyn, NY — deceased, with Andrew Brown Rankin V as administrator) other *Apparatus for Constructing Cold-Packed Pipe-Joint,* Patent #716,579 Series 104,232.

Andrew Nerva Rankin also patented railroad switches after working as secretary for the railroad committee in Rockland County, New York, which sought to bring the Erie Railroad to Monsey, New York, for an express run between Monsey and New York City. They were successful in that endeavor.

    5. *Rockland County Journal,* January 5, 1867.
    6. Frank Phelps, "Baseball's First Stars: William M. Rankin," *The Baseball Research Journal,* Vol. 25 (Cleveland: Society for American Baseball Research, 1996), 134. An example of this might be the *Brooklyn Daily Eagle* baseball article of June 14, 1876, which mentions the Duke of Gloucester.
    7. Spink, 342.
    8. *Rockland County Journal,* July 14, 1866; August 4, 1866; August 11, 1866; August 25, 1866; September 2, 1866; September 29, 1866; April 20, 1867; May 25, 1867; July 27, 1867; August 10, 1867; August 17, 1867, August 31, 1867; September 21, 1867; October 12, 1867, and October 19, 1867.
    9. Ibid., March 19, 1870.
    10. Ibid., August 21, 1869.
    11. The *Rockland County Journal* ran John H. Blauvelt's ad for "Bat-Proof Balls" during the 1869 season.
    12. "Cannot Take Base on Balk, Says Rankin," Nyack *Star,* August 17, 1905. This is in a scrapbook compiled by William Rankin which is in the possession of Arthur Rankin, his great-grandson. A copy of this scrapbook also is in the National Baseball Hall of Fame Museum and Library.
    13. *Rockland County Journal,* September 11, 1869.
    14. Ibid., September 17, 1870, 5.
    15. Henry Chadwick, *Haney's Base Ball Book of Reference* (Boston: Applewood Books, 1867), 73–111.
    16. Henry Chadwick, *Beadle's Dime Base Ball Book of Reference* (New York: Beadle, 1860).
    17. *Rockland County Journal,* October 1, 1870.
    18. Ibid., August 14, 1869.
    19. http://www.irs.gov. The history of the agency is listed.
    20. *Rockland County Journal,* March 19, 1870.
    21. Warren Goldstein, *Playing for Keeps: A History of Early Baseball* (Ithaca: Cornell University Press, 1989), 17–18. *Rockland County Journal,* September 17, 1870, mentions Alex Milne of the Sylvan Star Club of New York City as umpire. That particular game took only two hours to play, perhaps using the dead ball.
    22. W.M. Rankin, "Letter to the Editor," *Rockland County Journal,* July 9, 1870.
    23. Goldstein, 23–26. The *Rockland County Journal,* April 9, 1870, mentions Will and June as being on the first nine.
    24. *Rockland County Journal,* July 31, 1869; August 21, 1869; September 11, 1869; November 27, 1869; April 9, 1870; July 9, 1870; August, 27, 1870; October 1, 1870; September 17, 1870; April 15, 1871; May 6, 1871; June 10, 1871.
    25. Nyack *Evening Journal,* July 28, 1877.
    26. *Rockland County Journal,* August 19, 1871.
    27. Ibid., June 10, 1871.
    28. Ibid., January 21, 1871.
    29. Nyack *Villager,* October 2011.
    30. *Rockland County Journal,* July 6, 1872; August 31, 1872; September 7, 1872; August 16, 1873.

31. Nyack *Villager*, September 2010.
32. *Rockland County Journal*, July 6, 1872; August 31, 1872; September 7, 1872. They played the Active Base Ball Club of Tarrytown in one game.
33. Kevin Walsh, *Forgotten New York: Views of a Lost Metropolis* (New York: Collins, 2006), 155. Sing Sing Street is now called Charles Lane and is between West and Washington streets.
34. *http://www.villageofossining.org//*
35. Spink, 342.
36. Ibid.
37. *Rockland County Journal*, February 4, 1871.
38. Ibid., September 18, 1869.
39. Ibid., April 29, 1871.
40. Ibid., June, 4, 1870, and May 28, 1870. The Rev. Walter Chamberlain was the one quoted as not being in favor of women's rights, "per se," but he would listen to women present from the community for the area Sunday School Association meeting. Andrew N. Rankin jumped to his feet declaring himself in favor of it and inviting the women present into the discussion.
41. *Rockland County Journal*, January 1, 1870.

Chapter Four

1. Alfred H. Spink, *The National Game* (Carbondale: Southern Illinois University Press, 2000), 342.
2. Noel Hynd, *The Giants of the Polo Grounds: The Glorious Times of Baseball's New York Giants* (Dallas: Taylor, 1995), 4–5.
3. David Q. Voigt, *American Baseball: From the Gentleman's Sport to the Commissioner System*, Vol. 1 (University Park: Pennsylvania State University Press, 1992), 90–91.
4. New York *Tribune*, March 30, 1913.
5. *Sporting Life*, April 5, 1913.
6. George P. Rowell, *American Newspaper Directory* (New York: Rowell, 1887).
7. *Brooklyn Daily Eagle*, March 29, 1913.
8. Frank Phelps, "William M. Rankin," in *Baseball's First Stars*, Frederick Ivor-Campbell, Robert L. Tiemann and Mark Rucker, eds. (Birmingham: Society for American Baseball Research, 1996), 134.
9. *Brooklyn Daily Eagle*, February 6, 1873. Also, Chadwick printed English newspaper's response to the American players during the tour of England. He stressed the playing of an "improvement of rounders or touch ball," which was printed August 17, 1874.
10. Voigt, 89.
11. *Brooklyn Daily Eagle*, July 16, 1874.
12. Ibid., March 15, 1875.
13. Voigt, 94.
14. Ibid., 95–96.
15. Connie Mack, *My 66 Years in the Big Leagues* (New York: Dover, 2009, reprint), 147–150.
16. Andrew J. Schiff, *The Father of Baseball: A Biography of Henry Chadwick* (Jefferson, NC: McFarland, 2008), 169.
17. *The Commissioners of Patent's Journal* by the Great Britain Patent Office, August 21, 1874, lists Andrew N. Rankin's inventions of both. The *Rockland County Journal* lists his patent for fastenings for window sashes in the August 8, 1874, edition.
18. *Rockland County Journal*, October 25, 1873; August 5, 1875; July 29, 1876; November 25, 1876.
19. Samuel Bates, *History of Franklin County, Pennsylvania* (Chicago: Warner, Beers, 1887), 712.
20. *Brooklyn Daily Eagle*, October 25, 1885.
21. Henry Chadwick, "Almost Alone: Mr. Chadwick's Experience in the Sixties," *The Sporting News*, March 27, 1897.
22. Daniel J. Kenny, *The American Newspaper Directory and Record of the Press: Containing an Accurate List of All the Newspapers, Magazines, Reviews, Periodicals, etc. in the United States & British Provinces of North America* (New York: Watson, 1861).
23. As per W. M. Rankin in Spink, 356.
24. Ibid.
25. *Brooklyn Daily Eagle*, June 15, 1896. This article mentions how June was placed on the *Sunday Mercury* newspaper by Henry Chadwick, and that he was still there in 1896. He was called "the oldest of the young class" of writers.

26. Voigt, 64.
27. W. M. Rankin, "Played Politics," *Sporting News*, December 29, 1906.
28. W. Stewart Wallace, ed., *The Encyclopedia of Canada*, Vol. 2 (Toronto: University Associates of Canada, 1948), 228. This mentions the history of the New York *Sunday Mercury*.
29. *The Register*, March 4, 1876.
30. Spink, 342.
31. Henry Chadwick, ed., *Haney's Base Ball Book of Reference* (Boston: Applewood Books, 1867), 66–71.
32. Paul Dickson, *The Joy of Keeping Score* (New York: Walker, 1996), 7.
33. Ibid., 15–35. The Knickerbockers had a simple box score system with names, outs, and innings.
34. Ibid., 14–15.
35. *Brooklyn Daily Eagle*, May 24, 1875; June 3, 1876.
36. Harold Seymour, *Baseball: The Early Years* (New York: Oxford University Press, 1960), 86.
37. W.M. Rankin, "Still in Running," *Sporting News*, June 16, 1908.
38. The list was compiled by Baseball Almanac at *http://www.baseball-almanac.com/teamstats/ roster.php?y=1876&t=NY3*.
39. New York *Clipper*, January 1, 1887; October 13, 1883.
40. Ibid., June 28, 1879.
41. Jean-Pierre Caillault, *The Complete New York Clipper Baseball Biographies* (Jefferson, NC: McFarland, 2009), 721.
42. *Brooklyn Daily Eagle*, October 5, 1876.
43. Voigt, 39.
44. *Brooklyn Daily Eagle*, November 16, 1876.
45. Peter Morris, *But Didn't We Have Fun? An Informal History of Baseball's Pioneer Era, 1843–1870* (Chicago: Dee, 2008), 36.
46. *Brooklyn Daily Eagle*, Saturday, March 29, 1913, 18.
47. As per W.M. Rankin in Spink, 357.
48. Henry Chadwick, "Almost Alone."
49. James L. Crouthamel, *Bennett's New York Herald and the Rise of the Popular Press* (Syracuse: Syracuse University Press, 1989), 158.
50. Ibid., 120.
51. Ibid., 162.
52. Don Seitz, *The James Gordon Bennetts, Father and Son: Proprietors of the New York Herald* (Indianapolis: Bobbs-Merrill, 1928), 217–218.
53. Ibid., 222–226, 240.
54. Crouthamel, 46.
55. Ibid., 50.
56. *http://www.facstaff.elon.edu/dcopeland/mhm/mhmjour4-2.htm*. Abstract: William Anderson, "Creating the National Pastime: The Antecedents of Major League Baseball Public Relations," *Media History Monographs*, Vol. 4, no. 2, (Baton Rouge: Louisiana State University Press, 2000–2001).
57. Kenny, op. cit.
58. George P. Rowell, *American Newspaper Directory: Containing a Description of all the Newspapers and Periodicals Published in the United States and Territories, Dominion of Canada and Newfoundland, and of the Towns and Cities in Which They Are Published*, March 1900, Vol. 32, Issue 1 (New York: Rowell, 1900).
59. The New York *Herald*, Saturday, September 16, 1876. This same issue mentions the first carrier rope being set for the cable to be used to begin the process of building the Brooklyn Bridge.
60. Mark Rucker, *150 Years of Baseball* (Lincolnwood, IL: Publications International), 1989, 56.
61. Dean Sullivan, *Early Innings: A Documentary History of Baseball, 1825–1908* (Lincoln: University of Nebraska Press, 1997), 100–105.
62. *Brooklyn Daily Eagle*, November 19, 1877, 3.
63. John Thorn, *Baseball in the Garden of Eden* (New York: Simon and Schuster, 2011), 196.
64. *Rockland County Journal*, July 22, 1876; December 2, 1876.
65. *Brooklyn Daily Eagle*, December 14, 1878.
66. There is an article on Sydney Rankin, son of Will, in the New York *World* dated Tuesday, October 14, 1890, when Sydney was "nearly 13" and in 7th grade. He figured out a math puzzle presented by the paper and was visited by a correspondent at his school.
67. *Brooklyn Daily Eagle*, August 5, 1879, 3.
68. Ibid., August 24, 1879.
69. New York *Sunday Mercury*, December 6, 1879.

Chapter Five

1. As per W. M. Rankin in Alfred H. Spink, *The National Game* (Carbondale: Southern Illinois University Press, 2000), 357.
2. Harold Seymour, *Baseball: The Early Years* (New York: Oxford University Press, 1960), 24.
3. W.M. Rankin, "Grip of Gamblers On Base Ball Broken by the National League," *Sporting News*, November 19, 1904, in Charles W. Mears Collection of the Cleveland Public Library, Vol. 8. The day, 19, is not on this article, however, the article pasted before it in the collection, and the one after it are dated which leads to the conclusion that this one was from that date, since they were seven-day intervals. Also, "Marvelous Growth of Baseball in New York City from its Humble Origins," New York *Press*, July 30, 1905.
4. Noel Hynd, *The Giants of the Polo Grounds: The Glorious Times of Baseball's New York Giants* (Dallas: Taylor, 1995), 22–25.
5. Ibid., 23.
6. June Rankin, *The New York and Brooklyn Baseball Clubs: Brief and Authentic Sketches of the Clubs with Portraits of the Managers and Individual Players* (New York: Fox, 1888). The book is not paginated, however James Mutrie has his own woodcut portrait and the information is listed on the next page. If the first section on "Our National Game" is taken as a preface, it would be page 3.
7. Ibid., 136.
8. Ibid.
9. New York *Clipper*, August 26, 1882.
10. Ibid., May 24, 1884.
11. Ibid., October 8, 1881.
12. Ibid., June 14, 1884.
13. Ibid., July 8, 1882.
14. Hynd, 24.
15. David Q. Voight, *American Baseball: From The Gentleman's Sport to the Commissioner System*, Vol. 1 (University Park: Pennsylvania State University Press, 1992), 124–5.
16. David Nemec, *The Beer and Whiskey League: The Illustrated History of the American Association-Baseball's Renegade Major League* (Guilford, CT: Lyons Press, 2004), 1.
17. Ibid., 214.
18. *Brooklyn Daily Eagle,* March 29, 1913; April 23, 1886.
19. *Sporting Life,* May 17, 1913.
20. Ibid., March 29, 1913.
21. Peter Morris, *Catcher: How the Man Behind the Plate Became an American Folk Hero* (Chicago: Dee, 2010), 53–56, 28.
22. John P. Rossi, *The National Game: Baseball and American Culture* (Chicago: Dee, 2000), 18.
23. Spalding, p. 81.
24. Voigt, p. 87.
25. Morris, p. 75.
26. Seymour, p. 64.
27. *Brooklyn Daily Eagle,* Saturday April 26, 1930.
28. Voigt, p. 86.
29. *Brooklyn Daily Eagle*, August 24, 1879, p. 3.
30. Albert Goodwill Spalding, *America's National Game; Historic Facts Concerning the Beginning, Evolution, Development and Popularity of Base Ball, with Personal Reminiscences of its Vicissitudes, Its Victories and Its Votaries* (Memphis: General Books, 2010), 188–189.
31. Ibid.
32. The Great American Egg Company was listed in the *Rockland County Journal*, June 5, 1880, the *Newtown Register*, June 10, 1880, and the Utica *Morning Herald*, June 10, 1880. *American Machinist*, September 3, 1881, listed the other companies.
33. *Rockland County Journal*, July 10 and 17, 1880.
34. Seymour, 102–103. Benjamin G. Rader, *Baseball: A History of America's Game* (Urbana: University of Illinois Press, 2008), 52.
35. New York *Clipper Annual*, (New York: Clipper, 1880): 30.
36. Frank Graham, *The Brooklyn Dodgers: An Informal History* (Carbondale, Southern Illinois University Press, 1945; 2002), 3.
37. W.M. Rankin, "Snow in New York Five Days After Start of 1905 Pennant Race," *Sporting News*, January 20, 1906.

38. W. M. Rankin, "Technical Point: Hanlon Questions Right of Ebbets to Office," *Sporting News*, November 24, 1906.
39. http://www.baseball-reference.com/minors/team.
40. Biography of George Taylor in the New York *Clipper*, December 1, 1883.
41. Graham, 5.
42. Biography of Charles H. Ebbets in the New York *Clipper*, April 16, 1892.
43. *Brooklyn Daily Eagle*, Wednesday, December 12, 1883.
44. Frank Deford, *The Old Ball Game: How John McGraw, Christy Mathewson, and the New York Giants Created Modern Baseball* (New York: Grove Press, 2005).
45. Hynd, 35.
46. Frank Graham, *The New York Giants: An Informal History of a Great Baseball Club* (Carbondale: Southern Illinois University Press, 1952, reprint 2002), 4–5.
47. Voigt, 115.
48. New York *Clipper*, September 10, 1881.
49. Graham, 9.
50. Will Rankin felt that P.J. Donahue of the New York *World* was the first to record Mutrie's Giants term for his team in an April 14, 1885, article.
51. Voigt, 115–116.
52. Hynd, 39.
53. Ibid., 60.
54. Edward Van Every, *Sins of New York as "Exposed" by the Police Gazette* (New York: Stokes, 1930),15.
55. Examples of letters held for June Rankin by the editor include *The National Police Gazette*, January 12, 1884; January 19, 1884; April 12, 1884; August 2, 1884.

Chapter Six

1. *The Sporting News*, September 30, 1905.
2. John Thorn gives a wonderful history on the New York *Clipper* in the forward of Jean-Pierre Caillault, *The Complete New York Clipper Baseball Biographies*, Vol. 1 (Jefferson, NC: McFarland, 2009), 2–5.
3. Ibid.
4. New York *Clipper*, August 1, 1885.
5. Caillault, 8.
6. New York *Clipper*, September 15, 1888 this is an example of the type of box scores pasted into William Rankin's scrapbooks in the Charles W. Mears Baseball Collection of the Cleveland Public Library.
7. New York *Clipper Annual*, 1887, 7–10.
8. Henry Chadwick, The *Sporting Life*, January 19, 1887.
9. *Brooklyn Daily Eagle*, October 25, 1885.
10. Ibid.
11. As per W. M. Rankin, in Alfred H. Spink, *The National Game* (Carbondale: Southern Illinois University Press, 2000), 356.
12. *Brooklyn Daily Eagle*, October 25, 1885.
13. *Sporting Life*, February 17, 1886. *Brooklyn Daily Eagle*, February 28, 1886.
14. *Sporting Life*, op. cit.
15. *Official Record/Official Baseball Record* (New York), Monday July 26, 1886.
16. Ibid., September 28, 1886, October 4, 1886.
17. *Official Record*, October 9, 1886. It was to be available as of October 12 as per page 3.
18. Timothy Hughes Rare and Early Newspapers (http://www.rarenewspapers.com/) listed *Official Record/Official Baseball Record* as the very first daily sports newspaper dedicated entirely to professional baseball.
19. *Official Record*, August 6, 1886.
20. Ibid., September 28, 1886.
21. Ibid., August 9, 1886.
22. Ibid., June 15, 1886.
23. Ibid., October 7, 1886.
24. Ibid.
25. Ibid., May 3, 1886.
26. Ibid., May 24, 1886.

27. Ibid., April 24, 1886.
28. Ibid., May 17, 1886.
29. Ibid.
30. Ibid., September 3, 1885.
31. *Official Record*, August 16, 1886.
32. Noel Hynd, *The Giants of the Polo Grounds: The Glorious Times of Baseball's New York Giants* (Dallas: Taylor, 1995), 38–39.
33. *Official Record*, August 4, 1885.
34. *Sporting Life*, February 2, 1907.
35. Nerva Pipe Protecting Company in Camden, New Jersey, was formed as a corporation by Andrew N. Rankin, Martin V. Bergen and Samuel D. Bergen using Andrew Nerva Rankin's cold pipe inventions. The company is listed in *American Machinist*, October 8, 1881: 9, as making jacketing for water pipes to prevent them from freezing.
36. *The Official Gazette of the United States Patent Office*, July 6 — September 28, 1886, Vol. 36 (Washington, DC: Government Printing Office, 1887), 621; *The American Engineer: An Illustrated Weekly Journal*, Vol. 12, (Chicago: Cowles and Weston, 1886), 76.
37. *Brooklyn Daily Eagle*, April 23, 1886, lists a sample of what might be Will's corrections of players.
38. *Brooklyn Daily Eagle*, Feb. 28, 1886.
39. Henry Chadwick, "Tobogganing," *Brooklyn Daily Eagle*, December 12, 1886. David A. Curtis, Auburn, New York, *Weekly News and Democrat*, January 13, 1892.
40. *Sporting Life*, July 13, 1887, mentions the death of Will's son occurring "last week," which points to early in July.
41. As per the records of Arthur Rankin, great-grandson of Will Rankin. Harold was Arthur's grandfather.
42. *Brooklyn Daily Eagle*, February 29, 1896.
43. *Sporting Life*, April 27, 1887; and January 11, 1888.
44. *Brooklyn Daily Eagle*, February 28, 1886.
45. David Q. Voigt, *American Baseball: From The Gentleman's Sport to the Commissioner System*, Vol. 1 (University Park, PA: Pennsylvania State University Press, 1992), 195. New York *Clipper*, March 19, 1892. *The Sporting News*, September 15, 1888, reported: "Henry Chadwick, the father of base ball stands pre-eminent among the writers of the Metropolis as a base ball authority. He has been base ball editor of both the New York Clipper and the Brooklyn Eagle for over a score of years. The base ball work is pretty well divided up among six or seven men. George E. Stackhouse represents both the Tribune and Morning Journal, and finds time to send a gossipy letter to The Sporting Life every week. John H. Mandigo does the Sun base ball and does it well. Both he and 'Stack' — 'the twins' — were at the Cincinnati meeting. June Rankin is on both The Herald and News. Mike Lane has the Star and Sporting World; Will M. Rankin, the Mail and Express; J.C. Kennedy, The Times, and Pete Donahue The World. O.P. Caylor, now a New Yorker, is a free lance whom everybody knows, and whose worth is universally acknowledged."
46. Voigt, 195 ; *The Sporting News*, September 15, 1888; and The New York *Clipper*, March 19, 1892.
47. *Sporting Life*, April 27, 1887.
48. Thomas Richter, *Richter's History and Records of Base Ball: The American Nation's Chief Sport* (Jefferson, NC: McFarland, 2005), p. 422–423.
49. *Brooklyn Daily Eagle*, May 17, 1887.
50. June Rankin, *The New York and Brooklyn Baseball Clubs: Brief and Authentic Sketches of the Clubs with Portraits of the Managers and Individual Players* (New York: Fox, 1888), i–x.
51. *Brooklyn Daily Eagle*, July 29, 1888.
52. Alfred H. Spink, *The National Game*, (Carbondale: Southern Illinois University Press, 2000), 356.
53. Jean-Pierre Caillault, "Appendix: Chronology of the Biographies," in *The Complete New York Clipper Baseball Biographies* (Jefferson, NC: McFarland, 2009), 721–729.
54. An example of this is the March 11, 1898, issue of the *Brooklyn Daily Eagle* which stated that it was using Will Rankin's sketch of Jack Ryan, catcher for the Brooklyn Club.
55. *National Police Gazette*, February 26, 1888, 10.
56. "A Comedy of Errors: Yesterday's Benefit Ball Game Between Actors and Journalists," *The New York Times*, September 8, 1888.
57. Andrew Ross posted a page called 1890 and the Orphan Teams of Brooklyn at http://www.covehurst.net/ddyte/brooklyn/1890.html.
58. *Brooklyn Daily Eagle*, August 16, 1889.

59. *Hudson Evening Daily Register*, July 10, 1889.
60. Voigt, 196–197.
61. Harold Seymour, *Baseball: The Early Years* (New York: Oxford University Press, 1960), 198.
62. *Sporting Life*, February 16, 1887.
63. Ibid., April 27, 1887. This piece mentions that Henry Chadwick, Andrew Rankin V, and William M. Rankin sat in the same press box together to watch games.
64. As per Ruth Rankin Leaper, June's granddaughter, and as per the author of this book from her conversations with Andrew Brown Rankin VI "Drew," her grandfather.
65. *The Boston Daily Globe*, August 1, 1889.
66. Harry Clay Palmer; James Austin Fynes; Francis C. Richter; William Ingraham Harris; Henry Chadwick, *Athletic Sports in America, England and Australia: Comprising History, Characteristics, Sketches of Famous Leaders, Organization and Great Contests of Baseball, Cricket, Football, LaCrosse, Tennis, Rowing and Cycling* (New York: Union, 1889), 607.
67. Spink, 357.
68. Daniel M. Pearson, *Baseball in 1889: Players Vs. Owners* (Bowling Green, OH: Bowling Green State University Popular Press, 1993), 3.
69. Frank Graham, *The New York Giants: An Informal History of a Great Baseball Club* (Carbondale: Southern Illinois University Press, 1952; 2002), 13–14.
70. Hynd, 48.
71. Albert Spalding, *America's National Game; Historic Facts Concerning the Beginning, Evolution, Development and Popularity of Base Ball, with Personal Reminiscences of its Vicissitudes, Its Victories and Its Votaries* (Memphis: General Books, 2010), 99–104.
72. Rucker, *150 Years of Baseball* (Lincolnwood, IL: Publications International, 1989), 68.
73. Pearson, 28–32.
74. Ibid., 28, 45–46.
75. New York *Clipper*, March 2, 1889, as per Pearson, 30.
76. Hynd, 66.
77. Pearson, 147.
78. New York *Clipper*, July 20, 1889, as per Pearson, 95.
79. Pearson, 187.
80. Spalding, 108–111.
81. Ibid., 109.
82. Benjamin Rader, *Baseball: A History of America's Game* (Chicago: Illinois Press, 2008), 49.
83. Seymour, 221.
84. *Sporting Life*, September 14, 1887.
85. Voigt, 157.
86. John P. Rossi, *The National Game: Baseball and American Culture* (Chicago: Dee, 2000), 58–59.
87. David Nemec, *The Beer & Whiskey League* (Guilford, CT: Lyons Press, 2004), 39.
88. J.H. McDonough, "The Centre of the War: Some Facts About the Scoring in New York—How Newspaper Reporters are Coerced Through League Influence and How Papers are Manipulated," *The Sporting Life*, June 7, 1890.
89. Hynd, 65–67.
90. W.M. Rankin, "Rivals Relations. National Magnates Selfish and Shrewd, *Sporting News*, January 7, 1905, in Charles W. Mears Collection of the Cleveland Public Library, Vol. 8.
91. W. M. Rankin, "The Baseball Slaves," New York *Clipper*, April 29, 1893.
92. Rem Mulford Jr., "Redland Lights: The Prophecy of a Coming Big Trade," *The Sporting News*, August 20, 1904. Boston *Daily Globe*, December 10, 1889, also mentions those remaining in baseball work at that time.
93. Sam Crane, "Rudolph's Ability," *The Sporting Life*, December 5, 1914.

Chapter Seven

1. New York *Clipper*, July 29, 1893.
2. Frank Graham, *The Brooklyn Dodgers* (Carbondale: Southern Illinois University Press, 1945), 5.
3. W. M. Rankin, "Marvelous Growth of Baseball in New York City from its Humble Origin," *Sporting Life*, July 30, 1905.
4. *Sporting Life*, September 20, 1890.
5. *The National Police Gazette*, May 17, 1890. Rochester *Democrat Chronicle*, April 6, 1890.

6. New York *Evening Telegram*, April 5, 1890.
7. *The Newsdealer: The Organ of the Trade*, March–December 1890, Vol. 1 (San Francisco: Price, 1890). The edition of June 1890, Vol. 1, no. 4, mentions the appearance for the first time in the journal of *Sporting Critic*. It is listed in July 1890, Vol. 1, no. 5; August 1890, Vol. 1, no. 6; September 1890, Vol. 1, no. 7; and then the death of *Sporting Critic* is listed in October 1890, Vol. 1, no. 8.
8. Francis Richter, "The Press and Sport" in Harry Clay Palmer, James Austin Fynes, Francis C, Richter, and William Ingraham Harris, eds., *Athletic Sports in America, England and Australia: Comprising History, Characteristics, Sketches of Famous Leaders, Organization and Great Contests of Baseball, Cricket, Football, LaCrosse, Tennis, Rowing and Cycling* (New York: Union, 1889), 570.
9. John P. Rossi, *The National Game: Baseball and American Culture* (Chicago: Dee, 2000), 52.
10. "It Was a Draw: The Battle Between Jim Butler and Pat Cahill," *Brooklyn Daily Eagle*, December 17, 1891.
11. Frederic J. Haskin, "Prize Fight Legislation: Federal Government and Many States Rule Against the Fascinating Game," El Paso *Herald*, June 17, 1910. This paper was in partnership with "*The Daily News, The Telegraph, The Telegram, The Tribune, The Graphic, The Sun, The Adviser, The Independent, The Journal, The Republican*, and *The Bulletin*," and was a member of the Associated Press and American Newspaper Publishers' Association.
12. San Francisco *Call*, June 16, 1910, addressed the concept of "beating each other" in an article dealing with the laws on prize fighting. The Fort Worth *Gazette*, October 23, 1895, listed issues in boxing coming before the Supreme Court.
13. Edward James, *The Complete Handbook of Boxing and Wrestling; with Full and Simple Instructions on Acquiring these Useful, Invigorating, and Health-giving Arts* (New York: Clipper, 1878), p. 11.
14. *Brooklyn Daily Eagle*, April 26, 1930, mentions June writing for the Associated Press at the Corbett-Sullivan Championship.
15. *Brooklyn Daily Eagle*, March 20, 1892.
16. http://research.sabr.org/journals/jim-corbett-playing-first-base.
17. June Rankin, "The Sporting Point of View: As Seen by June Rankin in the Metropolis," Los Angeles *Herald*, November 20, 1892.
18. New York *Clipper Annual* for 1893 (New York: New York Clipper, 1893), 33–48.
19. An example of this is "Reporting Time is Here," *Brooklyn Daily Eagle*, March 11, 1898.
20. As per Ruth Rankin Leaper to author on November 21, 2011.
21. H. B. Martin, *Fifty Years of American Golf* (New York: Argosy-Antiquarian, 1966), 348.
22. Ibid., 149, citing the New York *Herald*'s October 1895 coverage of the game.
23. H. L. Fitzpatrick, "Amateur Golf Championships," *Outing: The Magazine of Amateur Sport and Pastime*, November 1898, 132.
24. Martin, 25–26.
25. Ibid., 25.
26. Ibid., 44–45, 116.
27. Kenneth G. Chapman, *The Rules of the Green: A History of the Rules of Golf* (Chicago: Triumph Books, 1997), 9.
28. Ibid., 45–59.
29. Ibid., 124.
30. As per Ruth Rankin Leaper, granddaughter of June Rankin in a letter dated July 5, 2012.
31. Ibid., 134.
32. H. L. Fitzpatrick, "Early American Golf Reporters, *Golf Illustrated & Outdoor America*, January 1916, 31–34.
33. New York *Herald*, November 8, 1896, and September 30, 1896.
34. Examples might be he New York *Evening World*, April 7, 1922; July 26, 1921; and October 9, 1919.
35. Martin, 137.
36. Ibid., p. 27.
37. Excerpt from "New York Wins Four Games Out of the Six from Cincinnati–Results Elsewhere," New York *Clipper*, September 11, 1897.
38. New York *Clipper*, March 30, 1895, as per Jean-Pierre Caillault, *The Complete New York Clipper Baseball Biographies* (Jefferson, NC: McFarland, 2009), 247–248.
39. Albert Goodwill Spalding, *America's National Game* (Memphis: General Books, 2010), 111.
40. Graham, 26.
41. *Brooklyn Daily Eagle*, June 17, 1897.
42. *Sporting Life*, March 26, 1898.

43. "Concentrated Movement of Troops to the South," New York *World*, Thursday, May 15, 1898.
44. Spalding, 111; and Frank Deford, *The Old Ball Game: How John McGraw, Christy Mathewson, and the New York Giants Created Modern Baseball* (New York: Grove Press, 2005).
45. Martin, 28.

Chapter Eight

1. W.M. Rankin, "Base Ball's Birth," *Sporting News*, April 8, 1905. Ibid., "Game's Pedigree," *Sporting News*, April 2, 1908. A copy of "Early History of Baseball" by William Rankin is in the Charles W. Mears Baseball Collection of the Cleveland Public Library: Vol. 1, 1853–1870.
2. "Baseball Biography on Robert Ferguson," New York *Clipper*, July 14, 1888.
3. W.M. Rankin, "Base Ball's Birth. Wadsworth Made Diagram of Diamond," *Sporting News*, April 8, 1905, in Charles W. Mears Collection of the Cleveland Public Library, Vol. 8.
4. *Brooklyn Daily Eagle*, July 27, 1877; August 18, 1879.
5. W.M. Rankin, "Disgraceful End. Poor and Rowdy Ball at Polo Grounds," *Sporting News*, October 15, 1904, in Charles W. Mears Collection of the Cleveland Public Library, Vol. 8.
6. W.M. Rankin, "On Hospital List. Several Members of Clark Griffith's Team," *Sporting News*, March 30, 1907.
7. Curry was quoted by Will Rankin in "Base Ball's Birth," *Sporting News*, April 8, 1905.
8. Charles A. Peverelly, *The Book of American Pastimes* (New York: New York, 1866), 339–349.
9. John Montgomery Ward, *Base-Ball: How to Become a Player* (Lexington, KY: Filiquarian, 2011), 3–4.
10. W.M. Rankin, "Base Ball's Birth," *The Sporting News*, April 8, 1905.
11. *Sporting News*, May 27, 1905.
12. W.M. Rankin, "Game's Pedigree. Alex Cartwright was Father of Base Ball," *Sporting News*, April 2, 1908.
13. For a more complete history on the evolution of the game, see David Block, *Baseball Before We Knew It: A Search for the Roots of the Game* (Lincoln: University of Nebraska Press, 2005).
14. W.M. Rankin, "Infancy of Game," *Sporting News*, June 14, 1905.
15. Alfred H. Spink, *The National Game*, (Carbondale: Southern Illinois University Press, 2000), 56, makes mention of the July 5, 1853, Knickerbockers game which was recorded in the New York *Clipper* on July 16, 1853.
16. Ward, 3–4.
17. Peter Morris, *But Didn't We Have Fun? An Informal History of Baseball's Pioneer Era, 1843–1870* (Chicago: Dee, 2008), 24. Morris states that rounders as the parent of baseball "cannot be justified." Morris also states that it is one in a "family of games" related to baseball.
18. W. M. Rankin, "Final Struggle: Will Be Between New York and Pittsburg," *Sporting News*, June 25, 1904, in Charles W. Mears Collection of the Cleveland Public Library, Vol. 8.
19. John Thorn, *Baseball in the Garden of Eden: The Secret History of the Early Game* (New York: Simon & Schuster, 2011), 4.
20. Henry Chadwick, *Haney's Base Ball Book of Reference* (Boston: Applewood Books, 1867), v–vi.
21. Ibid., vi.
22. David Block, 4–14, 297–289; W.M. Rankin, "Our National Game," Box 8, "New York Clipper articles by Rankin, 1904–1912" in the Charles W. Mears Collection on Baseball at the Cleveland Public Library, and "Scrapbook of William Rankin's Weekly Base Ball Letters, 1904–1912," Part 9 of the Baseball Scrapbooks microfilm collection, University of Notre Dame Memorial Library, South Bend, IN. W. M. Rankin, letter dated March 25, 1908 (published April 2, 1908), "Rankin's Weekly Base Ball Letters." W.M. Rankin to Albert G. Spalding, January 15, 1905, John Doyle Papers, National Baseball Hall of Fame Library, Cooperstown, NY.
23. Block, 5, 288, as stated in a letter dated March 25, 1908, "Rankin's Weekly Base Ball Letters," published April 2, 1908. W.M. Rankin to Albert G. Spalding, January 15, 1905, John Doyle Papers, National Baseball Hall of Fame Library, Cooperstown, NY. William told Spalding that John Montgomery Ward, popular ballplayer and author in 1888, obtained his ideas about the origin of baseball from William's article. Block, 6. Will also mentioned Ward visiting his home in *Sporting News* articles.
24. Spink, 54–56.
25. *Syracuse Evening Telegram*, June 1, 1901, actually attributes the Native American origin for baseball to June Rankin. *Porter's Spirit*, December 6, 1858.

26. W.M. Rankin, "Base Ball's Birth: Invented and Introduced by the Dutch," *Sporting News*, December 17, 1904.
27. Thorn, 14.
28. Box 8, "New York Clipper articles by Rankin, 1904–1912" in the Charles W. Mears Baseball Collection of the Cleveland Public Library. Most of these are from the *Sporting News*. Also, Block, 287, 4–5.
29. Thorn, 29.
30. W.M. Rankin, "Game's Pedigree: Alex Cartwritght was Father of Base Ball," *Sporting News*, April 2, 1908.
31. As per Thorn, 304–305, quoting W.M. Rankin in a letter to A. G. Mills about January 16, 1908, from the Jack M. Doyle, Albert Spalding Scrapbooks, BA SCR 42, National Baseball Hall of Fame Library, National Baseball Hall of Fame and Museum, Cooperstown, NY.
32. Thorn, 22.
33. Ibid., 51.
34. American Turf Congress, *The American Racing Rules of the American Turf Congress ... January 1, 1888* (Cincinnati: Turf, 1888) gives the rules of the organization at that time.
35. David Daisley's obituary, *Brooklyn Daily Eagle*, August 1, 1913.
36. Abraham Mills, "Final Decision of the Special Baseball Commission," December 30, 1907, in *Spalding Official Base Ball Guide*, Henry Chadwick, ed. (New York: American Sports, 1908), 47, as per John Thorn forward in Monica Nucciarone, *Alexander Cartwright: The Life Behind the Baseball Legend* (Lincoln: University of Nebraska Press, 2009), x–xi.
37. Harold Seymour, *Baseball: The Early Years* (New York: Oxford University Press, 1960), 9–10.
38. Ibid., 19.
39. W.M. Rankin, "Game's Pedigree," Ibid.
40. Ibid., "Two Great Teams," *Sporting News*, April 16, 1908.
41. Andrew Schiff, *The Father of Baseball: A Biography of Henry Chadwick*, (Jefferson, NC: McFarland, 2008), 204–205.
42. "How Baseball Began: A Member of the Gotham Club of Fifty Years Ago Tells About It," San Francisco *Examiner*, November 27, 1887.
43. Block, 152–162.
44. Harry Katz, Frank Ceresi, Phil Michel, et al., *Baseball Americana* (New York: HarperCollins, 2009), 3.
45. David Q. Voigt, *American Baseball: from the Gentleman's Sport to the Commissioner System*, Vol. 1 (University Park: Pennsylvania State University Press, 1992), xxv–vii.
46. Block, 131.
47. Ibid., 161.
48. Ibid., 134.
49. Ibid., 132.
50. Ibid., 161.
51. Mark Rucker, *150 Years of Baseball* (Lincolnwood, IL: Publications International, 1989), 6–8.
52. Block, 67–78, refers to Johann Christoph Friedrich Gutsmuths, *Games for Exercise and Recreation of Body and Spirit for the Youth and His Educator and All Friends of Innocent Joys of Youth* (Schrepfenthal, Germany: Verlag der Buchhandlung der Erziehungsanstalt, 1796).
53. http://www.german.about.com/library/bltrivia_windsor.htm
54. Nucciarone.
55. *Sporting Life*, April 5, 1913.
56. Voigt, p. 199.
57. Ibid., 6.
58. Spink, 356–359.
59. *Brooklyn Daily Eagle*, February 17, 1879.
60. "Henry Chadwick — The Father of Baseball," Washington *Star*, July 2, 1906, Chadwick Scrapbooks, 18, as per Andrew J. Schiff, *The Father of Baseball: A Biography of Henry Chadwick* (Jefferson, NC: McFarland, 2008), 6.
61. Jules Tygiel, "The Mortar of Which Baseball is Held Together: Henry Chadwick and the Invention of Baseball Statistics" in *Past Time: Baseball as History* (New York: Oxford University Press, 2000), 20.
62. Schiff, p. 144–145, and 209.
63. Frank Phelps, "William M. Rankin," in *Baseball's First Stars*, edited by Frederick Ivor-Campbell, Robert L. Tiemann, and Mark Rucker (Birmingham: Society for American Baseball Research, 1996), 134.

Chapter Nine

1. As per Arthur Rankin, great-grandson of William M. Rankin, in biographical information mailed May 29, 2012, to the author.
2. W.M. Rankin, "First Match Game: Played in Hoboken, NJ, in June, 1846," *Sporting News*, April 6, 1907.
3. W.M. Rankin, "First Fixed Game," *Sporting News*, January 5, 1907.
4. W.M. Rankin, "Hurts Base Ball," *Sporting News*, January 12, 1907.
5. W.M. Rankin, "More Room Needed: Polo Grounds Too Small for Crowds," August 20, 1908.
6. New York *Clipper*, March 10, 1894.
7. As per Ruth Rankin Leaper and Lois Rankin Prior, June's granddaughters, on November 1, 2011, to author.
8. As per Ruth Rankin Leaper, daughter of Andrew Brown Rankin VI, November 21, 2011.
9. As per Ruth Rankin Leaper and Lois Rankin Prior in December 2011.
10. Harry Brownlow Martin, *Fifty Years of American Golf* (New York: Argosy-Antiquarian, 1966), 213–214.
11. *Brooklyn Daily Eagle*, May 21, 1900; June 16, 1900; and June 17, 1900.
12. Ibid., June 17, 1900.
13. Ibid., June 16, 1900.
14. Ibid., May 21, 1900.
15. Ibid., July 3, 1900.
16. New York *Daily Tribune*, April 8, 1900; August 18, 1901.
17. *Brooklyn Daily Eagle*, November 13, 1900.
18. *Ibid*., December 16, 1901; January 26, 1902.
19. New York *Clipper*, April 5, 1913.
20. *The Sporting News*, January 19, 1901.
21. New York *Clipper*, May 20, 1903.
22. Ibid., October 26, 1901.
23. Notre Dame Archives, *Francis P. Clark Sports Collection*, MFCS M3009 Group Baseball Scrap Books ca. 1853, part 9, has Will's *Sporting News* articles from 1903 to 1912 on microfilm.
24. W.M. Rankin, "Pleases Patrons: New York Fans Like American League Ball," *Sporting News*, July 23, 1904.
25. Ibid., "Brilliant Work. Patrons Pleased at Playing of Yankees," *Sporting News*, August 19, 1905.
26. Ibid., "Cinch For Giants. American Race A Perplexing Problem," *Sporting News*, September 10, 1904.
27. Ibid., "Had a Close Call. M'Graw's Admirers Sent Him to Hospital," *Sporting News*, September 17, 1904.
28. Ibid., "Never Equaled. Teamwork of Giants in 1905 World's Series," *Sporting News*, October 21, 1905.
29. Ibid., "Monetary Motive. Prominent in the Giant's Post-Season Plans," *Sporting News*, September 27, 1904.
30. Peter Morris, *A Game of Inches: The Stories Behind the Innovations that Shaped Baseball* (Chicago: Dee, 2006), 25, 62, 126, 131, 138, 151, 205, 211, 239, 261, 276, 292, 355, 437. Morris mentions *Sporting News* articles written by William Rankin in the May 25, 1901; July 1, 1905; July 1, 1905; February 13, 1908; December 24, 1908; February 25, 1909; September 2, 1909; September 9, 1909; November 4, 1909; February 3, 1910; and March 3, 1910, issues in which persons initiating innovations in baseball were named.
31. W.M. Rankin, "The Curve in Baseball," New York *Times*, September 26, 1900.
32. Ibid., "Some Small Stars. All Great Players were not Large Men," *Sporting News*, December 8, 1906.
33. Ibid., "Professional Baseball Summary for Week Ending May 13, 1911," Charles W. Mears Collection of the Cleveland Public Library, Vol. 8, p. 160.
34. Ibid., "Not Home Umpires," *Sporting News*, August 5, 1905.
35. Ibid., "Deserved to Win. Giants' Success due to Steady Playing," *Sporting News*, October 23–25, 1904.
36. Abe Yager, "Brooklyn Bits," *Sporting Life*, February 22, 1913.
37. John Thorn, *Baseball in the Garden of Eden* (New York: Simon & Schuster, 2011), 59.
38. Henry Chadwick, ed., *Spalding's Official Base Ball Guide*, Vol. 15, no. 172 (New York City: American Sports, 1903), 279.
39. Charles A. Peverelly, *The Book of American Pastimes: Containing a History of the Princi-*

pal Base-Ball, Cricket, Rowing, and Yachting Clubs of the United States (New York: New York, 2012), 83.
    40. Ibid., 355.
    41. Ibid., 400–401.
    42. W.M. Rankin, "First Match Game. Played in Hoboken, N.J., in June, 1846," *Sporting News*, April 6, 1907; Rankin, "Succeeded Bray: Chadwick Made Clipper Debut in 1858," April 13, 1907.
    43. *Sporting News*, April 6, 1907..
    44. United States Golf Association, *Golf* 15, no. 5 (November 1904), 306; ibid., vol. 17, no. 5 (November 1905), 290–291, with a photo on the last page.
    45. Quirin, 102.
    46. "Keatley Has Low Score in Newspaper Men's Golf," New York *Tribune*, September 14, 1921.
    47. William L. Quirin, *Golf Clubs of the MGA: A Centennial History of Golf in the New York Metropolitan Area* (Chicago: Golf Magazine, 1997), 102.
    48. Kevin Walsh, *Forgotten New York: Views of the Lost Metropolis* (New York: Collins, 2006), 31–32.
    49. Harry Brownlow Martin, *Fifty Years of American Golf* (New York: Argosy-Antiquarian, 1966), 226–227.
    50. Martin, 225.
    51. Quirin, 102.
    52. http://usgamuseum.com/memorable-moments/.
    53. *Brooklyn Daily Eagle*, July 23, 1905.
    54. *Golf Illustrated*, March 13, 1903.
    55. Quirin, 15.
    56. Los Angeles *Herald*, Tuesday Morning, October 10, 1905. San Francisco *Call*, October 15, 1905.
    57. W.M. Rankin, "Picks Home Team: Rankin thinks Giants Will Win World's Series," *Sporting News*, Saturday, September 30, 1905.
    58. Alfred H. Spink, *The National Game*, (Carbondale: Southern Illinois University Press, 2000), 342.
    59. *Sporting Life*, February 2, 1907.
    60. H.L. Fitzpatrick, "Early American Golf Reporters," *Golf Illustrated & Outdoor America* 4, no. 4 (January 1916), 31–34, mentions June writing on golf for the *World*, *Brooklyn Eagle* and other newspapers in 1896.
    61. *The Official Golf Record*, June 22, 1906.
    62. Ibid., 13.
    63. Ibid., November 16, 1906, 12.
    64. Harry Clay Palmer, et al., *Athletic Sports in America, England and Australia: Comprising History, Characteristics, Sketches of Famous Leaders, Organization and Great Contests of Baseball, Cricket, Football, LaCrosse, Tennis, Rowing and Cycling* (New York: Union Publishing House, 1889), 607.
    65. As per Ruth Rankin Leaper, October 20, 2005.
    66. "Spalding to Rankin," January 26, 1905; "Mills to Rankin," January 6, 1908, in the Jack M. Doyle, Albert Spalding Scrapbooks, BA SCR42 National Hall of Fame Library.
    67. *Sporting Life*, August 24, 1907.
    68. Ibid., September 7, 1907.
    69. *New York Daily Tribune*, August 18, 1901; and April 8, 1900, mentions the driving parties and June's stay in Brighton with other members of the press.
    70. *Brooklyn Daily Eagle*, April 20, 1908.
    71. *Sporting Life*, April 5, 1913.
    72. Ibid., April 30, 1908.
    73. Ibid., February 10, 1906.
    74. Ibid., March 14, 1908.
    75. Ibid., July 31, 1909.

Chapter Ten

    1. Alfred H. Spink, *The National Game* (Carbondale: Southern Illinois University Press, 2000), lxviii–lxix.
    2. W.M. Rankin, "Baseball Items: Gossip from Here, There and Everywhere," New York *Clipper*, December 23, 1911.
    3. Connie Mack, *My 66 Years in the Big Leagues* (New York: Dover, 2009 reprint), 127.

4. W.M. Rankin, "Three Good Teams," *Sporting News*, March 31, 1910.
5. Ibid., *Sporting News*, September 9, 1909; November 11, 1909; March 17, 1910.
6. Ibid., "Professional Baseball Summary." The columns for 1911 and 1912 are found in the Charles Mears Collection of the Cleveland Public Library, Vol. 8.
7. Ibid., May 6, 1911.
8. New York *Clipper*, April 5, 1913.
9. The Charles Mears Collection of the Cleveland Public Library, Vol. 8, last page, has a newspaper photo of Will's granddaughter, Mildred V. Rankin, taken in the Catskill Mountains. She was perhaps age six or seven.
10. W.M. Rankin, "Ebbet's Field: Enterprise Worthy of Brooklyn's Baseball Progress," *Sporting News*, August 17, 1912, in the Charles W. Mears Baseball Collection of the Cleveland Public Library, Vol. 8.
11. Ibid.
12. New York *Clipper*, April 5, 1913. "Mr. Rankin kept a record of professional baseball, and his records of the game are acknowledged to be the most complete in existence." *Sporting Life*, May 17, 1913. "When William M. Rankin, the veteran base ball writer, died recently in Brooklyn, he left one of the most complete base ball libraries in existence. It contained records of the diamond extending over a period of nearly 40 years. In all probability the National League will buy this library from Mr. Rankin's family."
13. Peter J. Nash, *Baseball Legends of Brooklyn's Green-Wood Cemetery* (Charleston: Arcadia, 2003).
14. *Sporting Life*, July 19, 1913.

Chapter Eleven

1. Edward Coffman, *The War to End All Wars: The American Military Experience in World War I* (Lexington: University of Kentucky Press, 1998), 13–14.
2. As per Ruth Rankin Leaper, July 21, 1990.
3. As per an email from William Rankin's great-grandson, Arthur Rankin, on May 23, 2012.
4. http://virus.stanford.edu/uda/.
5. John Rossi, *The National Game: Baseball and American Culture* (Chicago: Dee, 2000), 97.
6. Joe Hoppel, ed., *From the Archives of The Sporting News Baseball: 100 Years of the Modern Era: 1901–2000* (St. Louis: Sporting News, 2001), 56.
7. Harry Brownlow Martin, *Fifty Years of American Golf* (New York: Argosy-Antiquarian, 1966), 351.
8. Ibid.
9. *Brooklyn Daily Eagle*, April 26, 1930.
10. "Champions of Three Continents in Play for 'Met' Open Title: American, British and Australian Title Holders Included in Large Entry List," New York *World*, July 26, 1921.
11. *The American Annual Golf Guide* (New York: Golf Guide, 1931),17–19.
12. William L. Quirin, *Golf Clubs of the MGA: A Centennial History of Golf in the New York Metropolitan Area* (Chicago: Golf Magazine, 1997), 24–26.
13. New York *World*, September 15, 1923.
14. Ibid., 15.
15. V. Treanor, "High Cost of Golf Jeopardizes Popularity of Game," New York *World*, February 10, 1921.
16. Martin, 64.
17. *Brooklyn Daily Eagle*, April 26, 1930.
18. As per Ruth Rankin Leaper and Lois Rankin Prior, nieces of Elizabeth Rankin.

Appendix

1. New York *Clipper*, April 5, 1913.
2. *Sporting Life*, April 5, 1913. A number of pieces from the William M. Rankin library are now part of the Charles W. Mears Baseball Collection of the Cleveland Public Library.
3. "Rankin's Ability as a Base Ball Writer," Elmira *Telegram*, April 6, 1913.
4. *Brooklyn Daily Eagle*, Saturday March 29, 1913.
5. New York *Tribune*, March 30, 1913.
6. *Washington Post*, March 30, 1913; ProQuest Historical Newspapers, *Washington Post* (1877–1994), 51.

7. Boston *Daily Globe*, March 30, 1913; ProQuest Historical Newspapers *Boston Globe* (1872–1927), 15.
8. *Sporting Life*, April 5, 1913.
9. Ibid.
10. Frank Phelps, "William M. Rankin," in *Baseball's First Stars*, Frederick Ivor-Campbell, Robert L. Tiemann and Mark Rucker, eds. (Birmingham: Society for American Baseball Research, 1996), 134.
11. Andrew J. Schiff, "*The Father of Baseball": A Biography of Henry Chadwick* (Jefferson, NC: McFarland, 2008), 134, 192–5, and 197.
12. *Base Ball Magazine*, August 1909; September 1909; October 1909; November 1909; December 1909; January 1910; February 1910; March 1910; April 1910, as per http: //www.baseballindex.org.
13. Harry Clay Palmer, James Austin Fynes, Francis C. Richter; William Ingraham Harris, and Henry Chadwick, *Athletic Sports in America, England and Australia: Comprising History, Characteristics, Sketches of Famous Leaders, Organization and Great Contests of Baseball, Cricket, Football, LaCrosse, Tennis, Rowing and Cycling* (New York: Union, 1889), 607.
14. Alfred H. Spink, *The National Game*, (Carbondale: Southern Illinois University Press, 2000), 357.
15. *Base Ball Magazine*, March 20, 1913.
16. *Elmira Telegram*, April 6, 1913.
17. Ibid. *Brooklyn Daily Eagle*, March 29, 1913.
18. *Brooklyn Daily Eagle*, October 29, 1922.
19. Ibid., April 26, 1930.
20. *Brooklyn Daily Eagle*, June 11, 1916, notice on Herbert's wedding mentions that June was a "former writer" at that time on golf and baseball for their paper.
21. *Sporting Life*, February 17, 1886.
22. June Rankin, *The New York and Brooklyn Base Ball Clubs: Brief and Authentic Sketches of the Clubs with Portraits of the Managers and Individual Players* (New York: Fox, 1888) as per Steven Geiber, "Their Hands Are All Out Playing: Business and Amateur Baseball, 1845–1917," *Journal of Sport History* 11, no. 1 (Spring 1984): 11.
23. Spink, 342.

Bibliography

Books

Agg, John. "Proceedings and Debates of the Convention of the Commonwealth of Pennsylvania to Propose Amendments to the Constitution Commenced and Held at Harrisburg." *Pennsylvania Constitutional Convention*, Vol. 3. Harrisburg, PA: Pacher, Bariett and Park, 1837.
Ayers, Edward L., and Anne S. Rubin. *Valley of the Shadow.* New York: Norton, 2000.
Ayers, Edward L., and William G. Thomas III. "Two American Communities on the Eve of Civil War: An Experiment in Form and Analysis." Reprint from *The American Historical Review*, January 11, 2002.
Bakker, Pamela. "Franklin County, Pennsylvania, Abolitionist: Andrew Nerva Rankin, Esq." *Franklin County History*, Vol. 23, *The Civil War Issue*, Beate A. Schiwek, ed. Chambersburg, PA: Franklin County Historical Society-Kittochtinny, 2011.
Bates, Samuel. *History of Franklin County, Pennsylvania.* Chicago: Warner, Beers, 1887.
Block, David. *Baseball Before We Knew It.* Lincoln: University of Nebraska Press, 2005.
Brouwer, Arie. *Reformed Church Roots.* New York: Reformed Church Press, 1977.
Brunson, James Edward. *The Early Image of Black Baseball: Race and Representation in the Popular Press, 1871–1890.* Jefferson, NC: McFarland, 2009.
Butler, Jon. *New World Faiths: Religion in Colonial America.* New York: Oxford University Press, 2008.
Caillault, Jean-Pierre. *The Complete New York Clipper Baseball Biographies.* Jefferson, NC: McFarland, 2009.
Chadwick, Henry. *Beadle's Dime Base Ball Book of Reference.* New York: Beadle, 1860.
___. *Haney's Base Ball Book of Reference.* Boston: Applewood Books, 1867.
___, ed. *Spalding's Official Base Ball Guide*, Vol. 15, no. 172. New York: American Sports, 1903.
Chapman, Kenneth G. *The Rules of the Green: A History of the Rules of Golf.* Chicago: Triumph Books, 1997.
Coffman, Edward. *The War to End All Wars: The American Military Experience in World War I.* Lexington: University of Kentucky, 1998.
Conrad, William. *Gloryland: A History of Blacks in Greencastle, Pennsylvania.* Greencastle, PA: n.p., 1989.
Cort, Cyrus, ed. *Fort McDowell Monument Dedicatory Services, October 5, 1916.* Union Bridge, MD: Pilot Print, 1917.
___. *Memorial of Enoch Brown and Eleven Scholars Who Were Massacred in Antrim Township, Franklin County, PA., by the Indians During the Pontiac War.* Lancaster, PA: Hensel, 1886.

Crouthamel, James L. *Bennett's New York Herald and the Rise of the Popular Press.* Syracuse: Syracuse University Press, 1989.
Deford, Frank. *The Old Ball Game: How John McGraw, Christy Mathewson, and the New York Giants Created Modern Baseball.* New York: Grove Press, 2005.
Dickson, Paul. *The Joy of Keeping Score.* New York: Walker, 1996.
Fendrick, Virginia Shannon. *American Revolutionary Soldiers of Franklin County, Pennsylvania.* Chambersburg: Historical Works Committee of the Franklin County Chapter, 1944.
Fitzpatrick, H.L. "Early American Golf Reporters." *Golf Illustrated & Outdoor America* 4, no. 4 (January 1916): 31–34.
Geiber, Steven. "Their Hands Are All Out Playing: Business and Amateur Baseball, 1845–1917." *Journal of Sport History* 11, no. 1 (Spring 1984).
Goldstein, Warren. *Playing for Keeps: A History of Early Baseball.* Ithaca: Cornell University Press, 1989.
Golf Guide Company. *The American Annual Golf Guide.* New York: Golf Guide, 1931.
Graham, Frank. *The Brooklyn Dodgers: An Informal History.* Carbondale: Southern Illinois University Press, 1945; reprinted 2002.
___. *The New York Giants: An Informal History of a Great Baseball Club.* Carbondale: Southern Illinois University Press, 1952; reprinted 2002.
Gutsmuths, Johann Christoph Friedrich. *Games for Exercise and Recreation of Body and Spirit for the Youth and His Educator and All Friends of Innocent Joys of Youth.* Schrepfenthal, Germany: Verlag der Buchhandlung der Erziehungsanstalt, 1796.
Hardin, Coy Wayne. *The Sporting News: Its First Fifty Years: 1886–1936.* Columbia: University of Missouri, 1966.
Henderson, Robert W. *Ball, Bat and Bishop: The Origin of Ball Games.* New York: Rockport Press, 1947.
Hoke, J. *Reminiscence of the War.* Chambersburg: MA: Folte, 1884.
Hynd, Noel. *The Giants of the Polo Grounds: The Glorious Times of Baseball's New York Giants.* Dallas: Taylor, 1995.
James, Edward. *The Complete Handbook of Boxing and Wrestling; with Full and Simple Instructions on Acquiring these Useful, Invigorating, and Health-giving Arts.* New York: New York Clipper, 1878.
Katz, Harry, Frank Ceresi, Phil Michel, et al. *Baseball Americana.* New York: HarperCollins, 2009.
Kenny, Daniel J. *The American Newspaper Directory and Record of the Press: Containing an Accurate List of All the Newspapers, Magazines, Reviews, Periodicals, etc. in the United States & British Provinces of North America.* New York: Watson, 1861.
Kirsch, George B. *Baseball in Blue and Gray.* Princeton: Princeton University Press, 2003.
Kittochitinny Historical Society of Franklin County, Pennsylvania, Newsletter 21, no. 5 (May 2005).
Lee, James P. *Golf in America.* Reprint. Montreal, Quebec: St. Remy Media, 2001.
Leyburn, James G. *The Scotch-Irish: A Social History.* Chapel Hill: University of North Carolina Press, 1962.
Mack, Connie. *My 66 Years in the Big Leagues.* Reprint. New York: Dover, 2009.
Martin, Harry Brownlow. *Fifty Years of American Golf.* New York: Argosy-Antiquarian, 1966.
M'Cauley, I. H., and J.L. Suesserott. *Historical Sketch of Franklin County, Pennsylvania.* Chambersburg: Pursel, 1878.
McDonough, J.H. "The Centre of the War: Some Facts About the Scoring in New York — How Newspaper Reporters are Coerced Through League Influence and How Papers are Manipulated." *The Sporting Life,* June 7, 1890.
Metropolitan Golf Association, with Dr. William L. Quirin. *Golf Clubs of the MGA: A Centennial History of Golf in the New York Metropolitan Area.* Elmsford, NY: Golf Magazine Properties, 1997.

Mills, Abraham. "Final Decision of the Special Baseball Commission." *Spalding's Official Base Ball Guide*, ed. Henry Chadwick. American Sports Publishing, 1908.
Morris, Peter. *But Didn't We Have Fun? An Informal History of Baseball's Pioneer Era, 1843–1870*. Chicago: Dee, 2008.
___. *Catcher: How the Man Behind the Plate Became an American Folk Hero*. Chicago: Dee, 2010.
Nash, Peter J. *Baseball Legends of Brooklyn's Green-Wood Cemetery*. Chicago: Arcadia, 2003.
Nemec, David. *The Beer and Whiskey League: The Illustrated History of the American Association—Baseball's Renegade Major League*. Guilford, CT: Lyons Press, 2004.
Nichols, James H. *History of Christianity 1650–1950*. New York: Ronald Press, 1956.
Nucciarone, Monica. *Alexander Cartwright: The Life Behind the Baseball Legend*. Lincoln: University of Nebraska Press, 2009.
Palmer, Harry Clay, James Austin Fynes, Francis C. Richter, and William Ingraham Harris, eds. *Athletic Sports in America, England and Australia: Comprising History, Characteristics, Sketches of Famous Leaders, Organization and Great Contests of Baseball, Cricket, Football, LaCrosse, Tennis, Rowing and Cycling*. New York: Union, 1889.
Pearson, Daniel M. *Baseball in 1889: Players vs. Owners*. Bowling Green, OH: Bowling Green State University Popular Press, 1993.
Peverelly, Charles A. *The Book of American Pastimes: Containing a History of the Principal Base-Ball, Cricket, Rowing, and Yachting Clubs of the United States*. New York: New York, reprint 2012.
Phelps, Frank. "William M. Rankin." In *Baseball's First Stars*, Frederick Ivor-Campbell, Robert L. Tiemann, and Mark Rucker, eds. Birmingham: Society for American Baseball Research, 1996.
Quirin, William L. *Golf Clubs of the MGA: A Centennial History of Golf in the New York Metropolitan Area*. Chicago: Golf Magazine Properties, 1997.
Rader, Benjamin G. *Baseball: A History of America's Game*. Urbana: University of Illinois Press, 2008.
Rankin, June. Sports newspapers. *The Official Record—The Official Baseball Record*. 1885–1886; *The Sporting Critic*. 1890; *The Official Golf Record*. 1906–1907.
___. *The New York and Brooklyn Base Ball Clubs: Brief and Authentic Sketches of the Clubs with Portraits of the Managers and Individual Players*. New York: Fox, 1888.
___. *The New York Baseball Club*. New York: Fox, 1888.
___. "The Sporting Point of View: As Seen by June Rankin in the Metropolis." In Los Angeles *Herald*. Sunday, November 20, 1892.
Rankin, William. "Base Ball's Birth." *Sporting News*, April 8, 1905, page 2. "Game's Pedigree." *Sporting News*, April 2, 1908.
___. "Baseball Items: Gossip from Here, There and Everywhere." New York *Clipper*, December 23, 1911.
Richter, Thomas. *Richter's History and Records of Base Ball: The American Nation's Chief Sport*. 1914. Reprint, Jefferson, NC: McFarland, 2005.
Riess, Steven A. *Touching Base: Professional Baseball and American Culture in the Progressive Era*. Chicago: University of Illinois Press, 1983.
Rossi, John P. *The National Game: Baseball and American Culture*. Chicago: Dee, 2000.
Rowell, George P. *American Newspaper Directory*. New York: Rowell, 1887.
___. *American Newspaper Directory: Containing a Description of all the Newspapers and Periodicals Published in the United States and Territories, Dominion of Canada and Newfoundland, and of the Towns and Cities in Which They Are Published*, Vol. 32, no. 1. New York: Rowell, 1900.
Rucker, Mark. *150 Years of Baseball*. Lincolnwood, IL: Publications International), 1989.
Rupp, Israel Daniel. *The History and Topography of Dauphin, Cumberland, Franklin, Bedford, Adams, Perry, Somerset, Cambria and Indiana Counties*. Lancaster, PA: Hills, 1846.

Seitz, Don. *The James Gordon Bennetts, Father and Son: Proprietors of the New York Herald.* Indianapolis: Bobbs-Merrill, 1928.
Seymour, Harold. *Baseball: The Early Years.* New York: Oxford University Press, 1960.
Schiff, Andrew J. *"The Father of Baseball": A Biography of Henry Chadwick.* Jefferson, NC: McFarland, 2008.
Schneck, Benjamin Shroder. *The Burning of Chambersburg, Pennsylvania.* Memphis: General Books, 2010.
Shannon, Virginia. *American Revolutionary Soldiers of Franklin County, Pennsylvania.* Chambersburg: Historical Works Committee of the Franklin County Chapter, 1944.
Spalding, Albert Goodwill. *America's National Game; Historic Facts Concerning the Beginning, Evolution, Development and Popularity of Base Ball, with Personal Reminiscences of its Vicissitudes, Its Victories and Its Votaries.* 1911. Reprint, Memphis: General Books, 2010.
Spink, Alfred H. *The National Game.* Carbondale: Southern Illinois University Press, 2000.
Sullivan, Dean. *Early Innings: A Documentary History of Baseball, 1825–1908.* Lincoln: University of Nebraska Press, 1997.
Thorn, John. *Baseball in the Garden of Eden: The Secret History of the Early Game.* New York: Simon & Schuster, 2011.
Turf Publishing Company. *The American Racing Rules of the American Turf Congress ... January 1, 1888.* Cincinnati: Turf, 1888.
Tygiel, Jules. "The Mortar of Which Baseball Is Held Together: Henry Chadwick and the Invention of Baseball Statistics." *Past Time: Baseball as History.* New York: Oxford University Press, 2000.
United States. Bureau of the Census. 1790, Green Castle/Antrim, Pennsylvania, Nathaniel Rankin and John Ritchey.
_____. _____. 1820 Green Castle/Antrim, Pennsylvania, Andrew Rankin, Anne Rankin, William Ritchey, John Ritchey. Washington, DC: Government Printing Office.
_____. _____. 1830 Greencastle/Antrim, Pennsylvania, Andrew B. Rankin, Esq., Ann Rankin. Washington, DC: Government Printing Office.
_____. _____. 1840 Mercersburg, Pennsylvania, John Ritchey. Washington, DC: Government Printing Office.
_____. _____. 1860 Chambersburg, Pennsylvania, Andrew Nerva Rankin. Washington, DC: Government Printing Office.
_____. _____. 1870 Ramapo, New York, Andrew Nerva Rankin. Washington, DC: Government Printing Office.
_____. _____. 1880 Brooklyn, New York, Andrew Brown "June" Rankin. Washington, DC: Government Printing Office.
_____. _____. 1880 Brooklyn, New York, William M. Rankin. Washington, DC: Government Printing Office.
_____. _____. 1890 Brooklyn, New York, Andrew Brown "June" Rankin. Washington, DC: Government Printing Office.
_____. _____. 1900 Brooklyn, New York, William M. Rankin Washington, DC: Government Printing Office.
Van Every, Edward. *Sins of New York as "Exposed" by the Police Gazette.* New York: Stokes, 1930.
Vecsey, George. *Baseball: A History of America's Favorite Game.* New York: Modern Library, 2006.
Voigt, David Q. *American Baseball: From the Gentleman's Sport to the Commissioner System.* Vol. 1. University Park: Pennsylvania State University Press, 1992.
Wallace, W. Stewart, ed. "John Dougall," *The Encyclopedia of Canada.* Vol. II. Toronto: University Associates of Canada, 1948.

Walsh, Kevin. *Forgotten New York: Views of a Lost Metropolis*. New York: Collins, 2006.
Ward, John Montgomery. *Base-Ball: How to Become a Player*. Reprint. Lexington, KY: Filiquarian, 2011.
Ware, W. Powell, and A.N. Rankin. *Professor Ware's $10,000 Prize Rule for the Equation of Payments*. New York: Francis and Loutrel, 1890.
Warner, Beers. *History of Franklin County, Pennsylvania*. Chicago: Warner, Beers, 1887.
Woman's Club of Mercersburg. "Old Mercersburg: Mercersburg, 1786." In *The Journal of American History*, 1913; and in print form through *The Marketplace for Digital Content*, http://www.lulu.com, ID: 96497. 2005.

Journals and Newspapers

American Engineer: An Illustrated Weekly Journal 12 (Some of Andrew Nerva Rankin, Esq.'s, inventions are listed in this journal).
American Machinist (Some of Andrew Nerva Rankin Esq.'s inventions are listed in this journal), (September 3, 1881, and October 8, 1881).
Baltimore *Sun*. March 31, 1913.
Base Ball Magazine (William Rankin's baseball letters, 1909–1910), (August 1909, September 1909, October 1909, November 1909, December 1909, January 1910, February 1910, March 1910, April 1910, March 20, 1913).
Boston *Daily Globe* (William Rankin served this paper as New York correspondent), (August 1, 1889; December 10, 1889; March 30, 1913).
Brooklyn Daily Eagle (William and June Rankin both wrote for this paper from 1874 to about 1916), (February 6, 1873; July 16, 1874; August 17, 1874; March 15, 1875; May 24, 1875; June 3, 1876; June 14, 1876; July 22, 1876; October 5, 1876; November 16, 1876; July 27, 1877; November 19, 1877; December 14, 1878; February 17, 1879; August 5, 1879; August 18, 1879; August 24, 1879; December 12, 1883; October 25, 1885; February 28, 1886; April 23, 1886; August 16, 1889; December 17, 1891; March 20, 1892; February 29, 1896; June 17, 1897; May 21, 1900; June 16, 1900; June 17, 1900; July 3, 1900; November 13, 1900; December 16, 1901; January 26, 1902; April 7, 1905; July 23, 1905; March 20, 1913; March 29, 1913; June 11, 1916, October 29, 1922; April 26, 1930).
Central Press (February 9, 1830; August 5, 1864).
Chambersburg *Gazette* (June 19, 1798).
Chambersburg *Times* (June 19, 1843).
Commissioner of Patents Journal. August 21, 1874 (This lists one of A.N. Rankin's inventions).
Elmira *Telegram*. April 6, 1913.
Franklin *Repository and Transcript* (This paper became the *Repository and Transcript* during Andrew N. Rankin's ownership), (February 9, 1830; February 1864; May 9, 1864; July 3, 1864; August 25, 1864; August 31, 1864; September 24, 1890).
Golf (November 1904; November 1905).
Golf Illustrated and Outdoor America 4, no. 4 (January 1916).
Harper's Weekly, November 1, 1862.
Hudson *Evening Daily Register*, July 10, 1889.
Lancaster *Intelligencer*, August 4, 1864.
Los Angeles *Herald* (June Rankin was a New York correspondent), (November 20, 1892; October 10, 1905).
Mail and Express (William Rankin wrote on baseball from 1887 to 1888), (April 27, 1887; April 29, 1887).
The National Police Gazette (April 12, 1884; August 2, 1884; February 26, 1888; May 17, 1890).

The Newport Daily News. March 31, 1913.
The Newsdealer: The Organ of the Trade (Vol. 1, March-October, 1890).
New York *Clipper* (William Rankin worked for this paper from 1885 to 1913, covering baseball until 1901), (July 16, 1853; June 28, 1879; May 22, 1880; July 23, 1881; October 8, 1881; July 8, 1882; August 26, 1882; May 12, 1883; October 13, 1883; May 24, 1884; August 1, 1885; July 14, 1888; September 15, 1888; January 1, 1887; March 26, 1887; March 2, 1889; July 20, 1889; March 19, 1892; March 10, 1894; March 30, 1895; September 11, 1897; December 23, 1911; April 5, 1913).
New York *Clipper Annual* (1880, 1887, 1892, 1893, 1894), (February 14, 1885; July 20, 1889; March 2, 1889).
New York *Daily Tribune* (William Rankin wrote on baseball beginning in the summer of 1876. June is listed in the society pages), (April 8, 1900; August 18, 1901; March 30, 1913; September 14, 1921).
New York *Daily Witness* (William Rankin wrote for them from 1876 to 1878).
New York *Herald* (Andrew Rankin was baseball writer and editor from the spring of 1876 to the fall of 1889 and then wrote on many sports until 1898. He wrote about boxing from 1889 to 1898. His golf coverage was from 1895 to 1898), (September 16, 1876; May 18, 1908; October 7, 14, 21, 28, 1895; September 30, 1896; November 8, 1896).
New York *Press* (William Rankin's history of the Metropolitan Base Ball Club is in the July 30, 1905, issue).
New York *Sunday Mercury.* December 6, 1879 (Andrew Rankin was baseball writer and editor from 1875–1889).
New York Times (William Rankin wrote various articles on baseball beginning in the summer of 1876 through 1913. Andrew played on a baseball team with the baseball editor of the paper), (September 8, 1888; September 26, 1900).
New York *Weekly News and Democrat.* January 13, 1892.
New York *World* (Both William and Andrew Rankin wrote for the paper; Will wrote only on baseball beginning with the summer of 1876, and Andrew wrote on many sports from about 1892 to 1930, though they did not tend to list contributors), (April 14, 1885; October 14, 1890; March 28, 1897; May 15, 1898; February 10, 1921; July 26, 1921; September 15, 1923).
Nyack *Evening Journal.* July 28, 1877.
The Nyack Villager. September 2010; October 2011.
The Official Gazette of the United States Patent Office (Some of Andrew Nerva Rankin, Esq.'s, inventions are listed in this journal), (Vol. 36, July 6–September 28, 1886).
The Official Golf Record (Andrew Rankin published beginning in 1906 and through at least 1907), (June 22, 1906; November 16, 1906).
Official Record/Official Baseball Record (Andrew Rankin published this from 1885 to 1886), (September 3, 1885; April 24, 1886; May 3, 1886; May 17, 1886; June 15, 1886; July 26, 1886; August 6, 1886; August 9, 1886; September 28, 1886; October 4, 1886; October 7, 1886; October 9, 1886).
Porter's Spirit.(September 6, 1856; September 13, 1856; November 15, 1856; December 6, 1858).
Repository and Transcript (Andrew N. Rankin owned this from about 1856 to 1863), (May 5, 1860; July 18, 1860; August 1, 1860; September 5, 1860; September 12, 1860).
The Resister. March 4, 1876.
Rochester *Democrat Chronicle.* April 6, 1890.
Rockland County Journal (William Rankin wrote on baseball from 1870 to 1873), (July 14, 1866; August 4, 1866; August 11, 1866; August 25, 1866, September 2, 1866; September 29, 1866; January 5, 1867; April 20, 1867; May 25, 1867; July 27, 1867; August 10, 1867; August 17, 1867; August 31, 1867; September 21, 1867; October 12, 1867; October 19, 1867; May 15, 1869, p. 2; July 31, 1869; August 14, 1869; August 21, 1869; September

11, 1869; September 18, 1869; November 27, 1869; January 1, 1870; March 19, 1870; April 9, 1870; May 28, 1870; June 4, 1870; July 9, 1870; August 27, 1870; September 17, 1870; October 1, 1870; January 21, 1871; April 15, 1871; April 29, 1871; May 6, 1871; June 10, 1871; February 4, 1871; July 6, 1872; August 31, 1872; September 7, 1872; October 25, 1873; August 16, 1873; August 8, 1874; August 5, 1875; July 22, 1876; July 29, 1876; November 25, 1876; December 2, 1876; June 5, 1880; July 10, 17, 1880).

San Francisco *Call*. October 15, 1905.

The Sporting Critic (Andrew Rankin published this from June to October 1890).

Sporting Life (February 17, 1886; July 13, 1887; January 19, 1887; February 16, 1887; April 27, 1887; September 14, 1887; January 11, 1888; September 20, 1890; June 7, 1890; March 26, 1898; June 3, 1905; July 30, 1905; February 10, 1906; August 18, 1906; September 29, 1906; December 1, 1906; February 2, 1907; March 23, 1907; March 30, 1907; August 24, 1907; September 7, 1907; November 2, 1907; January 4, 1908; March 14, 1908; June 16, 1908; October 24, 1908; July 31, 1909; September 25, 1909; October 16, 1909; July 30, 1910; October 8, 1910; February 22, 1913; March 29, 1913; April 5, 1913; May 17, 1913; July 19, 1913; December 5, 1914).

The Sporting News (William wrote for this paper from 1903 to 1912), (September 15, 1888; March 27, 1897; January 19, 1901; May 25, 1901; November 21, 1903; June 25, 1904; July 23, 1904; August 20, 1904; September 10, 1904; September 27, 1904; October 15, 1904; October 23-25, 1904; December 17, 1904; January 7, 1905; April 8, 1905; May 27, 1905; June 14, 1905; July 1, 1905; August 5, 1905; September 30, 1905; October 21, 1905; November 24, 1906; December 8, 1906; December 29, 1906; January 5, 1907; January 12, 1907; March 30, 1907; April 6, 1907; February 13, 1908; April 2, 1908; April 16, 1908; April 30, 1908; June 16, 1908; August 20, 1908; December 24, 1908; February 25, 1909; September 2, 1909; September 9, 1909; November 4, 1909; November 11, 1909; February 3, 1910; February 17, 1910; March 3, 1910; August 17, 1912).

Sporting World (William Rankin wrote and edited baseball around 1886).

Syracuse *Evening Telegram*. June 1, 1901.

Valley Spirit. January 29, 1864; February 10, 1864.

Washington Post. March 30, 1913.

Letters

"William M. Rankin to Albert G. Spalding," January 15, 1905. Albert Spalding Scrapbooks in the Jack M. Doyle Collection, National Baseball Hall of Fame Library, Cooperstown, New York.

"Spalding to Rankin," January 26, 1905, Albert Spalding Scrapbooks in the Jack M. Doyle Collection, National Baseball Hall of Fame Library, Cooperstown, New York.

"Mills to Rankin," January 6, 1908. Albert Spalding Scrapbooks in the Jack M. Doyle Collection, National Baseball Hall of Fame Library, Cooperstown, New York.

Websites

http://www.baseballindex.org.
http://www.covehurst.net/ddyte/brooklyn/1890.html.
http://www.explorefranklincountypa.com/history/.
http://www.facstaff.elon.edu/dcopeland/mhm/mhmjour4-2.htm; Abstract: Anderson, William, "Creating the National Pastime: The Antecedents of Major League Baseball Public Relations." In *Media History Monographs* 4, no. 2. Baton Rouge: Louisiana State University Press, 2000–2001.
http://faculty.assumption.edu/aas/Reports/amunioncomorigin.html.

http://www.germanabout.com/library/bltrivia_windsor.htm.
http://rarenewspapers.com.
http://www.sonofthesouth.net/leefoundatio/civil-war/1862.
http://usgamuseum.com/memorable-moments/.
http://www.villageofossining.org/.
http://virus.stanford.edu/uda/.

Archival Collection

Cleveland, OH, Public Library. Charles W. Mears Baseball Collection. GV875.A1 B37x.
Notre Dame Archives. Francis P. Clark Sports Collection, MFCS M3009 Group Baseball Scrap Books ca. 1853. Part 9 has William Rankin's *Sporting News* articles from 1903–1912 on microfilm.

Index

Page numbers in **_bold italics_** indicate pages with illustrations.

Abbott, Rev. Dr. Lyman 26–28
Abbott, Margaret 144
Abell, Ferdinand 67
Abolition 15, 16, 19
Acherman, Peter 36
Acheson, Archibald 10, 11, 36, 37
Acheson, Lady Elizabeth *see* Ritchey, Elizabeth Acheson
Acheson, Thomas 11
Act of Union of 1707 6
Actor's Athletic Association 93–96
Adams, Daniel "Doc" 126
African American 13, 16–28, 52
Alaska Nine Base Ball Club 50–52
All American Team 88, 99–100
Allen, Myron 74
American Alliance 67
American Association of Base Ball Clubs 51, 63; early members 63, 70–71, 79, 87, 93, 98
The American Engineer 87
American Expeditionary Force 170
American Golf Association (AGA) 153
American Golf Association of Advertising Interests 153
American Indians 7–9, 18, 35, 48, 58, **_68_**, 129, 165
American League 142, 146, **_163_**
American League Park/Hilltop Park 146–147, 164
American Missionary Association 26–28
American Union Commission 22–28
America's Cup 35, 167
Anglican Church 6
annunciator 13
Anson, Cap 148
Anthony, Henry T. 126
Appalachian Mountains 6, 19
Armstrong, Col. John 7
Associated Press 2, 53–54, 167
Atlantic Base Ball Club (amateur) 29, 50, 69
Atlantic Base Ball Club (professional) *see* Brooklyn Base Ball Club, major league
automobiles 159

Averill, Gen. 23–**_24_**
Avery, Walter T. 126

Baltic Base Ball Club 29
Baltimore American 51
Baltimore Monumentals Base Ball Club 71
Baltimore Orioles Base Ball Club 120
Baltimore Terrapins 168
Barclay Street Ferry 123, 150
Barnes, James 168–173
Barnum & Bailey 168–169, 173
Barrymore, Maurice 95
Base Ball Association (Rockland County) 34
baseball: origins 122–138; signing 146–147; umpire 32, 39
baseball catcher 1, 29–30, 41, 64–65; injury 64–65; mask 65
baseball guides: Beadle 32, 125; De Witt 81, 86, 125; Haney 32, 128; Reach 125, 130; Spalding 125, 133, 149
Baseball Magazine 160
baseball scoring 1, 42, 48–49, 81, 85, 90; Orr-Edwards Code 96; Scorer's League 96
Baseball Wars (National League vs. Player's League) 1; *see also* National League War Committee
The Baseball Writers Association of America 160
baseballs 41, 112; dead ball 33–35, 44, 64; live ball 33, 64; regulation ball 64–65
Battle of Little Big Horn 48
Beadle and Adams 58
Becannon, Buck 75
Bechtel, George 49
Bedford Base Ball Club 29
Beer & Whiskey League 63–64, 87; *see also* American Association
Begley, Ed 75
Bell, Alexander Graham 48, 50
Bennett, James Gorden, Jr. 52–54, 61, 103–104, 150
Bennett, James Gorden, Sr. 52–54, 75
Bicycling 95, 106

Bird, Oliver W. 118
Black Sox Scandal 171
Blauvelt, John 31
Block, David 134–136
Booth, Eddie 49–50
Boston Americans 142, 171
Boston Braves 141
Boston Daily Globe 51, 97, 171
Boston Doves 141
Boston Herald 51
Boston Nationals 141
Boston Pilgrims 142, 171
Boston Plymouth Rocks 142, 171
Boston Puritans 142, 171
Boston Red Sox 142, 171
Boston Somersets 142, 171
Bowler's Day 158–159
boxing 1, 98, 108–112; International Boxing Hall of Fame 76; London Prize Ring Rules 108, 110; prize fights 111; Queensberry Rules 111
Braddock, Gen. 7, 9
Braddock's Road 7, 9
Brady, Steve 62
Briody, "Fatty" 62
Brody, Steve 93
Brooklyn, NY 39–40, 51, 69, 117; Brooklyn beaches 58; Brooklyn Bridge 66
Brooklyn Atlantics Base Ball Club (amateur) 124, 126
Brooklyn Base Ball Club/Grays/Atlantics (professional) /Bridegrooms/Trolley Dodgers/Kings/City Nine/Superbas/Dodger 66–71, **79**, 85, **91**–92, 120–121, 147; early rosters **68**–71; **68**–69, 83–84, 89, **91**
Brooklyn Citizen 51
Brooklyn Daily Eagle 1, 39–50, 56–57, 64, 66, 72, 81–95, 118, 121, 124, 145, 149, 159
Brooklyn Eagles Base Ball Club 29, 124
Brooklyn Enterprise Base Ball Club 50
Brooklyn Golf Club 117, 157
Brooklyn Tip-Tops Base Ball Club/Brookfeds 70, 168
Brooklyn Unions Base Ball Club 60
Brotherhood of Base Ball Players *see* National Brotherhood
Brown, Mrs. C.R. 116
Brown, E.H. 29
Brown, Enoch 9, 18; Enoch Brown Association 7; Enoch Brown Park 9–10
Brown, Jim 75
Brown, John (Harpers Ferry raid) 15–16
Brown, Willard 75
Brush, John 106, 146
Buffalo Bill's Wild West Show 58, 86
Buffalo Buffeds Base Ball Club 168
Bunnell, Frank 90
Butler, Jim 109–110
Byrne, Charles 67, 69

C&O Canal 21
Cahill, Pat 109–110
Calkins, Leighton 154
Calvin, John 7
Camden Merritts Base Ball Club 71
Cammeyer, William 47–50
Capitoline Grounds 61, 69, 89
Carson, Kit 58
Cartwright, Alexander 122–138
Caskin, Ed 74, 75
"cat" ball games 122–138
Cauldwell, William 44, 124, 126, 150
Caylor, Oliver P. 103, 159
Centennial Exposition **46**–48
Chadwick, Henry 32, 34, 40–49, 78–81, 85–88, 90, 96, 105, 120, 122–138, 149, 151, 158–159
Chadwick, P. Remsen 151
Chambersburg *Repository and Transcript* 2, 13–25
Chaplin, Charlie 167
Chapman, John 126
The Charles W. Mears Collection of the Cleveland Public Library viii, 128, 140–141, 166, 182
Charleston Golf Club 115
Chase, C. Thurston 27
Chase, Salmon P. 30
Chauncey, Daniel 107, 118
Chelsea Base Ball Club of Williamsburg, Long Island 34–36, 66
Chester, PA 6
Chicago Colts/Orphans/Cubs Base Ball Club 141
Chicago Whales/Chifeds Base Ball Club 168
Chicago White Stockings/Sox Base Ball Club 38, 49, 51, 142
Cincinnati Base Ball Club/Red Stockings Base Ball Club 38, 54, 69
Cincinnati Commercial 120
Cincinnati Enquirer 120
Cincinnati Outlaw Reds Base Ball Club 71, 142
Clapp, John 62, 74–75
Clemens, Samuel L. 44, 130
Cleveland, Elmer 75, **91**
Cleveland Blues/Bronchos/Napoleans/Naps Base Ball Club 142
Cleveland Forest Cities Base Ball Club Base Ball Club 38
Clinton, Jim 62
coaching (horse drawn coaches) 154
Cobb, Ty 160
Columbia Presbyterian Medical Center 146
Columbus Buckeyes Base Ball Club 54
Columbus Colts Base Ball Club 71
Commercial High School 169
Concord Stage Coaches 71
Conegogig Creek 6, 19
Coney Island 58
Confederate Army 13–25
Conner, Roger 74–75, **91**, 95–98, 106
Conococheague Creek 19
Continental Base Ball Club, NYC 29
Continental Base Ball Club of Spring Valley 31–33
Continental Conduit Company 66
Coogan's Hollow *see* Polo Grounds II

Corbett, James 111; Corbett-Fitzsimmons match 113, 114; Corbett-Sullivan match 111
Corcoran, Jack 70
Corcoran, Larry 75
Corkhill, John "Pop" 68
Couch, Maj. Gen. Darious 23
Cramer, Dick 74
Crane, Ed 75, 91
Crane, Samuel 62, 120
Crescent Athletic Club 117
Crescent Base Ball Club of Nanuet 30
Crescents Football Club 117
cricket 18, 40
Crickmore, Henry G. 131–132
Crouthamel, James 52, 54
Cumberland Valley, PA. 6, 7
Curry, Duncan 124, 131
Curtis, Lawrence 114
Custer, Gen. 48

Dakin, Thomas S. 29
Dacey, Billy 93
Daily, Hugh 62
Daisley, Ethel Lydia 121
Danforth, Tommy 93
Day, John B. *59*–63, 73, 84, 95, 99–103, 106–107, 146
deafness 13, 37, 142–143, 146–147
Deasley, Pat 75
Delancey, Jack 93
Delmonico's Restaurant 53
Dempsey, Billy 93
Dempsey, Jack 110, 174
Dempsey, Mike 93
Democrat 15–25
Detroit Free Press 51
Detroit Tigers Base Ball Club 142
Devery, William 146
Devlin, Jim 75
Dexter, Kathryn 169
Dodgers *see* Brooklyn Base Ball Club
Dolan, Tom 70
Donahue, P.J. 95
Donavan, Mike 93
Donegal Church, Lancaster, PA 7
Dorgan, Jerry 62
Dorgan, Mike 74–75, *91*
Doubleday, Gen. Abner 127–138, 158
Dougall, John 45
Douglass, Frederick 15–16
Doyle, John 62, 69
Doyle, Joseph 67
Driscoll, Denny 62
Dyker Meadows Golf Club 116, 118

Egan, Jim 69–70
Earp, Wyatt 114
Ebbets, Charles 70, 120, 166, 174
Ebbets Field 70, 165
Eckford Base Ball Club 29, 69
Eckhardt, John P. 93

Edison Picture Company 113
Eiffel Tower 144
electric light 56
Ellis Island 106, 111
Elysian Fields, Hoboken 123, 127, 150
Empire Base Ball Club 29
Endler, Charles 71
Enoch Brown Association 7
Enoch Brown Park 9–10
Erastus Wiman's Staten Island Amusement Company 76
Esterbrook, Dude 62, 75
Eurekas Cricket Club 30
Evening Journal of Detroit 51
Ewing, Buck 62, 74–75, 91, 98, 106
Excelsior Base Ball Club 29, 38, 69, 124
Excelsior Perpetual Almanac 22

Fairview Base Ball Club 34
Falling Spring, PA 19
Fallon, Jack 93
Farrell, Frank 146
Farrell, Joe 62
Farrow, John 62, 70
Federal League of Base Ball Clubs 70, 168; original members 168
Feitner, Lillian Hyde 161
Fennelly, Frank 70
Ferguson, Robert 124
Field Golf Club 116
financial panic 113
Firth, John 69
Fitzpatrick, Hugh L. 114, 116, 145, 154
Fitzsimmons, Robert James 113, 114
Fleming, William 11
football 112; American Professional Football League/National Football League 171
Force, Davy 49
Forest Park 117
Fort Duquesne 7
Fort Hamilton High School 117
Fort Loudon 7
Fort McDowell 6, 7; McDowell Mill 7, 8; McDowell Road 6
Fort Sumter 20
Fort Wayne Kekiongas Base Ball Club 38
Foster, Elmer 76, *91*
Foutz, David L. *68*
Fox, Richard K. 76–77, *91*–92
Fox Hills Golf Club 119
Franklin County, PA 5–25; Antrim Township 8, 10–13; Chambersburg 8–*24*; Greencastle 5–13, 20
Fraser, Alexa Stirling 169
free blacks 13
Free School Party 27
Freedman, Andrew 119–120, 146
Freedmen's Aid Society 26–28
Fulton Street 43, 66
Fulton Street Ferry 43, 58, 66
Fulton Street Prayer Meeting 46

gambling 38–39, 96
Geer, Billy 70
George, Bill 75–76, *91*
Gerhardt, Joe 75, 98
Germaine, William 108
German baseball 136
Gettysburg Address/Gettysburg Cemetery 21–22
Gettysburg, Battle of 21
Giants *see* New York Base Ball Club
Gillespie, Pete 74–75
gloves: baseball 29–30, 64–65; boxing 110–111
Goldstein, Warren 33–34
golf 1, 113–117, 152–154, 162, 168–178; golf balls 144, 173–174
Golf Illustrated magazine 116, 154
Golf magazine 118, 152
Golf Writers Association of nineteen hundred and twenty 172
The Golfer 117–118
Golfing magazine 117
Gordon, Joseph W. 146
Gordon Highlanders *see* The Greater New York Base Ball Club
Gore, George 76, 91, 106
Gothams Base Ball Club (amateur) 29, 44
Gothams/Giants (professional) *see* New York Baseball Club
Graham, Frank 98
Grant, Ulysses S. 32, 88
Graves, Abner 133
The Great American Egg Company 66
Great Britain 7–10; Act of Union 6; exportation laws 6; monarchy 136; Test Act 6; Ulster plantations 6
Great Depression 174
The Greater New York Base Ball Club/The Americans/ Highlanders/ Yankees 104, 146–147, 164, 171–172
Greencastle Kangaroos Base Ball Club 19
Greenwood, Bill 70
Green-Wood Cemetery, Brooklyn 89, 109, 166, 174, 177
Griffin, Sandy 75
Guelph Maple Leafs Base Ball Club 54
Gutsmoths, Schnepfenthal 136

Hagen, Walter 167, 173
Hagerstown, MD 8
Hamilton, Gen. Alexander 9
Hankinson, Frank 62, 74–75
Hanlon, Ned 69, 120–121
Harlem Base Ball Club 29
Harlem Railroad Depot 123
Harmar, Gen. Josiah 8
Harmony Base Ball Club 29
Harpers Ferry, Virginia 15–16
Harrisburg Base Ball Club 71
Hartfort Dark Blues Base Ball Club 45
Harvard Base Ball Club 65
Hatfield, Gil 75–76, 91, 106
Hatfield, John 49

Havemeyer, Theodore 115
Hawes, Bill 62
Hayes, John 62
Henrietta (yacht) 53
Herrman, August 142, 160
Heubel, George 49
Hickok, Wild Bill 58
Hill, Gus 93
Hilltop Park *see* American League Park
The History of the New York and Brooklyn Baseball Clubs *91*-93
The History of the New York Baseball Club *91*-93
Hoboken Yacht Club 150
Holbert, William H. 62–63, 91
Holdsworth, Jim 50
Hollins, H.B. 119
Hollins, Marion 174
Holzberger, John 71
Hopper, DeWolf 96
Hornbacker, Eugen 93
Householder, Charlie 70
Hoyt, Beatrix 116
Hubert, W. A. 45, 55
Hughes, Timothy (Rare & Early Newspapers) 83–84
Hulbert, William 49, 51, 138
Humphries, John 74–75
Hutchison, Jock 168, 173
Hynd, Noel 76, 103

ice skating 19, 48, 88–89
Independent Order of Odd Fellows 11–12
Indianapolis Blues 71
Indianapolis Hoosiers/Federals/Newark Peps Base Ball Club 168
industrial revolution 5
Internal Revenue Service (IRS) 32
International Association of Professional Base Ball Players (1877–1880) 54–55, 66; Judiciary Committee 54; original members 54, 66–67, 101
International Association of Professional Base Ball Players (1888–1890) 55, 67
International Boxing Hall of Fame 76
International League 163
Inter-State Association 67, 70–71; original members 71

Jack the Ripper 88
Jackson, James Randolph 56–57
Jackson, Theodore F. 29
Jenkins, Brig. Gen. Albert G. 21
Jews/anti-semitism 6, 171–172
Johnson, Ban 142
Jones, Bobby 174, 176
Jones, Charles W. 160
Jones, Joseph 29

Kane, Grenville 118
Kansas City Cowboys Base Ball Club 71
Kansas City Packers Base Ball Club 168

Keefe, Tim 62, 63, 75, *91*, 98, 106
Kelleher, Denny 93
Kelly, John 62
Kelly, Michael J. 48, 81, 86
Kennedy, Ed 62, 63
Kennedy, James C. 95
Kenny, Jack 93
Kerrigan, Tommy 173
Kilrain, Jake 108
Kimber, Sam 69, 70
Kirkby, Oswald 167
Kittanning 7
Knickerbockers Base Ball Club *see* New York Knickerbockers
Knox, Gen. Henry 9

Ladies Aid Society 20
Lancaster County 7
Larkin, Terry 62
League Alliance 50–52, 67
Leary, Jack 62
Lee, Col. James 125–126
Lee, Gen. Robert E. 16, 21
Liberty Base Ball Club 30
Lincoln, Abraham 17, 23, 28
A Little Pretty Pocket-Book 135
Lockhart, Robert 114
London Prize Ring Rules 108, 110
London Tecumsehs Base Ball Club 54
Loughran, Bill 75
Louisville Colonels Base Ball Club 63, 71
Louisville Grays 45
Los Angeles Dodgers 69; *see also* Brooklyn Base Ball Club
Luff, Henry 70
Lynch, Jack 62

MacDonald, Charles 114–115
MacDonough, John 94
Mack, Connie 42, 160, *163*
Madden, Billy 93
Madison Square Garden 93, 95
Magnolia Base Ball Club 137
malaria 73
The Manchesters Base Ball Club 54
Mandigo, John 90, 159
Manhattan Cricket Club 78
Manhattan Island 122–138
Manlove, Charlie 75
Manning, Tim 70
Mansell, Tom 62
Marine and Field Golf Course 116
Martin, H. B. 114–116, 152–167, 173
Mason-Dixon Line 13, 20
Massachusetts Game 122
Masterson, Bat 114
Mathews, Bobby 49
Mathewson, Christopher 146, 164
Mattimore, Mike 75
Mazeppa Base Ball Club 30
McAllen, Texas 169–170

McCabe, John 69
McCaffrey, Dominick 93
McCausland, Gen. John 22
McClellan, Gen. 20
McCullough, A.H. 17–18
McCullough, Archibald 18
McDermott, J.J. 161
McDonough, Glen 94
McDonough, J.H. 102–103, 105
McDowell, Elizabeth *see* Rankin, Elizabeth M.
McDowell, John 7
McDowell, Mary I. 6
McDowell, Nathan 8
McDowell, William 6, *14*
McGraw, John 73, 146, 147, 154, 160, *163*
McGunnigle, William *91*
McKinnon, Alex 75
McKnight, H. D. 63
McManus, M. 70
Meade, Maj. Gen. George Gordon 21
Meadow Brook Golf Club 118
Mechanics Cricket Club 30
medieval longball 135
Mercer, Hugh 7
Mercersburg, PA. 8
Mercersburg, Greencastle, Waynesboro Turnpike Company 10, 21
Meritts Base Ball Club, Camden 69
Methodist 40, 149, 172
Metropolitan Golf Association (MGA) 116, 118, 152; Met Am 119, 154, 167–168; Met Open 152, 161, 173; original members 118–119, 152, 154, 173; WMGA 161, 169
Metropolitans Base Ball Club *see* New York Metropolitans Base Ball Club
Mexican Punitive Expedition 169–170
militia 8
Mills, Abraham 130–138, 158
Milwaukee Brewers 71, 142
Minniscongo Base Ball Club of Haverstraw 34
Monongahela River 8
Morgan, Bill 70
Morris, Peter 147
Morris County Golf Club 118
Mott, John W. 126
Muldoon, Mike 62
Mulford, Ren, Jr. 90, 105, 159, 166
Munson, George 90
Murphy, Pat 75, *91*
Murray, Miah 70
Mutrie, James 59–61, 63, 75, 84–85, *91*, 95–96, 107
Mutuals *see* New York Mutuals

Nanuet Base Ball Club 34
Nassau Base Ball Club 29
National Agreement: 1870s 81; 1903 142, 147, 158
National Association of Base Ball Players (NABBP) 29, 34–38, 69
National Association of Professional Base Ball

Players (NAPBBP) 38, 49; original members 38
National Baseball Hall of Fame Museum and Library 92, 97; early New York members inducted 97
National Base Ball Reporters Association 90
National Brotherhood of Base Ball Players 85, 98–102; officers 85, 98; Players League 106–107
National Commission 142
National Defense Act 169
National Game 135, 161
National League and the American Association of Base Ball Clubs 107, 142
National League of Professional Base Ball Players/National League 98–104; Clubs 1, 45, 49–52, 55, 63, 66–67, 70–79, 93–104, 107–108, 120–121; Mills Commission 88, 122–138, 158; War Committee 1, 98–102, 157
National Police Gazette 76–77, 83–84, 92, 108
Neagle, Jack 62
Negro National League 172
Nelson, Candy 62–63, 75
Nemec, David 64, 103
Nereid Rowing Club 117
Nerva Pipe Protecting Company 66
Netherlands/Dutch 7, 39, 40, 129, 135–136; stoolball 129; golf 115
New England Press Association 51
New York Associated Press 1, 51–54, 111, 154, 174
New York Base Ball Club (amateur) 36
New York Base Ball Club/Gothams (professional)/New Yorks/Giants 62, **73**–75, 76, 81, 84–85, **91**, **94**–97, 107, 118–121, **163**, 165; original rosters 73–75, **91**, **94**, 97, 146
New York *Clipper* 1, 40–43, 62, 70, 74, 76–81, 86–**91**, 93, 106–107, 112, 140–145, 158, 170; *Clipper Annual* 81, 112
New York Courier and Enquirer 53
New York Daily Witness/Weekly Witness 45–48
New York *Evening Telegram* 108
New York *Express* 53
New York Gothams Base Ball Club (amateur) 124, 132, 134
New York *Herald* 1, 43–48, 52–54, 57–**59**, 70, 75–76, 81–84, 90–93, 97, 108, 114, 117, 123, 156, 158
New York Highlanders *see* Greater New York Base Ball Club
New York *Journal of Commerce* 53
New York Knickerbockers 18, 29, 44, 87, 122–138; early rosters 126
New York *Mail and Express* 89–90
New York Metropolitan Exhibition Company 60, 73, 81
New York Metropolitans Base Ball Club (amateur) 36, 61
New York Metropolitans Base Ball Club (professional) 1, 59–66, **73**–**79**, 85–86; early rosters 60–62
New York Mutuals 1, 38, 45–50, 54, 69, **79**, 124; early rosters 47, 49, 50, **60**, 62

New York National Guard 169–170
New York *News* 76–77
New York Newspaper Men's Golf Club 1, 151–153
New York Press Association 51
New York Press Tobogganing Club 88
New York Public Library 92
New York Reporter's Base Ball Club 1, 85–86, 93–96, 151–152; roster 95
New York *The Rider and Driver* 152–153
New York *Sporting Times* 92, 95
New York *Star* 102
New York *Sun* 51, 53, 84, 116, 120, 145, 159
New York *Sunday Mercury* 1, 43–44, 52, 55, **59**, 76, 83–84, 116, 123, 126, **155**
New York Times 40, 43, 51, 93, 95, 148
New York *Tribune* 51–53, 145
New York *World* 51, 75, 116, 118, 121, **155**–156
New York Yacht Club 53
New York Yankees *see* Greater New York Base Ball Club
New Yorks Base Ball Club 124
The Newsdealer 109
Norcross Company 168
North Western Press 51
Northwest Territory 8
Northwestern League 51
Norwood Base Ball Club 34
Nyack, NY 29
Nyack Sports Clubs: Eurekas Cricket Club 30; Liberty Base Ball Club 30; Mazeppa Base Ball Club 30; Mechanics Cricket Club 30
Nynn Live Oaks Base Ball Club 54

Official Gazette of the US Patent Office 87
The Official Golf Record ix, **155**–158
Official Record/Official Baseball Record **82**–85, 90–92, 103, **155**–156
Oldfield, Dave 70
Olympic games, Paris 1900 144–145; Paris Exposition 144
Olympics Base Ball Club of Paterson, New Jersey 34, 50
O'Neill, Tip 62, 74
O'Rourke, Jim 75–76, **91**, 98, 106
O'Rourke, John 62
Orr, David 62–63, 74, **91**, 106
Oxley, Henry 75

Panama Canal 168
pasteurized milk 113
Patton, Cap. James 8
Patton, Cap. Samuel 8
Pearce, Dicky 50–51
Pearl River Base Ball Club 34
Pearson, Daniel 100
Pelgram, Maj. 20
Peters Township, PA. 6, 8
Penn, William: heirs 6
Perry Base Ball Club of New York City 34
Peverelly, Charles A. 140, 150–151

Phelps, Frank 138
Philadelphia Alerts Base Ball Club 38
Philadelphia Athletics Base Ball Club 18, 42, 45, 50, 71, *79*, 142, 163
Philadelphia Keystones 71
Philadelphia Olympic Base Ball Club 18, 29
Philadelphia Phillies Base Ball Club 142
Philadelphia *Sunday Mercury* 79
Picked Nine Base Ball Club of Middletown 34
Pierce, Gracie 74
pitcher/pitching 30, 65, 69
Pittsburgh Alleghenys/Pirates Base Ball Club 54, 54, 63, 71
Pittsburgh Rebels Base Ball Club 168
Pittsburgh Stogies 71
Players League *see* National Brotherhood
polo: (horse) Manhattan Polo Association 61; (water) polo 111; *see also* Polo Grounds I
Polo Grounds I 52, 61, 73, 76, 84, 104
Polo Grounds II/Manhattan Field 76, 95, 99–100, 104, 107
Polo Grounds III 107, 164
Polo Grounds IV 164
Poorman, Tom 62
Postley, J. Ross 29
Potomac River 19
Pottsville Anthracites Base Ball Club 71
Powers, Phil 62
Pratt, Daria 145
Presbyterian 6; Covenanter 7; Westminster Confession 6
Princeton College 117, 127, 148; Base Ball Club 148; Diary of J. R. Smith 149
Princeton Theological Seminary 148
Printer 31, 33, 36, 39
Pritchard, Joseph 90
prize fights *see* boxing
Professional Golfers Association of America/PGA 168–172
protective gear 64–65
Pulitzer, Joseph 75, 118, 143
Pullman, Harry 160
Puritans 7
Putnam Base Ball Club 29, 69

Queen, Frank 78, 80, 129
Queensberry Rules 111

racism 13, 23, 52, 56–57, 67
radio 171
railroad: Baltimore & Ohio 76; Cumberland Valley 11, 18, 21, 42; Erie 42, 153; Franklin 11, 21; Mont Alto 11; New York Central 130; Southern Pacific 149; Southern Pennsylvania 11
Rainey, John 75
Rankin, Andrew B. (III) 8–*14*, 23, 43
Rankin, Andrew B. (IV)/Andrew Nerva 2, 9, 10, 11, 13–28, 36, 42, 58–*59*, 66, 87, 109, 159, 165; abolition work 13–28; justice of the peace 11, 13, *14*, 20–21; patents *14*, 22, 28, 42, 66, 186–187*ch*3*n*4; *see also* Chambersburg *Repository and Transcript*
Rankin, Andrew Brown (V)/ "June" 1, 2, 5, 13, *14*; baseball clubs played for 1, 30–38, 58, 64, 85–89, 93–*94*; books published 76, *91*–92, 183; family life 5, 13–25, 96, 111, 113, 142, 168–169, 172–177; death 176–177; golf club played for 1, 151–153, *162*; International Association Judiciary Committee in 1870s 54, 85, 101; newspapers published *82*–84, 108–109, *155*–158; newspapers wrote for 1, 43–44, 52–55, *59*, 76, 87, 90, 92, 98, 110–111, 113, 116, 118, 143, 153–157, *162*, 172, 174, 177; official scorer 1, 59–61, *73*, 76, 81, 85, 92, 97, 182; tobogganing club 88
Rankin, Andrew Brown (VI)/ "Drew" 14, 43, 96, 116, 142–143, 169, 172
Rankin, Andrew Charles/ "Andy" 14, 174
Rankin, Ann Brown (I) 8–9
Rankin, Ann Brown (II) 11
Rankin, Anne Swartz 172–173
Rankin, Annie Mitchel 89, 113, 143
Rankin, Arie Alcesta/ "Etta" *14*–15, 37, 72, 87, 145, 174, 177
Rankin, Arthur *79*
Rankin, Carl 93
Rankin, Charlotte Tracey 121, 139
Rankin, Cornelia Polhemus 36
Rankin, David F. 149, *163*
Rankin, Edmund Davidson 11
Rankin, Elizabeth/"Betty" 113, 142, 143, 168, 177; *Woman's Day* Magazine 177
Rankin, Elizabeth McDowell 5–26
Rankin, Ethel Daisley 121–149
Rankin, Harold E. 65, 89, 121, 139, 149, 165
Rankin, Herbert/"Hub" 111, 142, 169, 176
Rankin, John 11
Rankin, Lois C. 176
Rankin, Margaret Jane 11
Rankin, Margaret Ritchey 10–11, 43, 72
Rankin, Margaret Virginia/"Margie" 13, 37, 174
Rankin, Martha Fisher 11
Rankin, Marguerite 142–143, 176
Rankin, Mary 11
Rankin, Mary Adella/"Adda" 13, 18, 37, 42–43, 56, 72, 145, 174; public speaking 13
Rankin, Mildred (I) 121, 139, 149
Rankin, Mildred (II) 139
Rankin, Nathaniel 8, 9, 13
Rankin, Percy B. 39, 121, 139, 149
Rankin, Robert 169
Rankin, Ruth Ann 43, 176
Rankin, Sarah Elizabeth/"Lizzie" *14*–15, 37, 72, 174, 177
Rankin, Sidney I. 56, 139, 149, 170
Rankin, William M., Jr. (infant) 36, 89, 139
Rankin, William McDowell, Sr. 1, 2, 5, 13; baseball clubs played for 29–38, 64; baseball histories 36, 66, 93; baseball library 80, 125, 139–151, *163*, 166, 181; baseball origins 122–138; death 165–166; family life 5–25, 36–39,

56, 65, 89, 121, 139, 149, 163, 165; newspapers wrote for 2, 29–36, 39, *46*–47, 51, 90, 93, 124, 140–141, 147–151, 160, 177, 183; official scorer 1, *47*–49, 67–72, 81, 97, 182; printer 29–39; referee 158; umpire 32–39
Rankin, William Ritchey 11, *14*
Reading Actives Base Ball Club 71
Reagan, Johnny 93
Reconstruction Acts 26–28
Red Scare 171
Reed, Adeline 11
Reformed Church of Spring Valley, NY 36
Reid, John 114
Reilly, John 62
Reipschlager, Charlie 62
Repository and Transcript see Chambersburg *Repository and Transcript*
Republican 10, 15, 13–25
Rice, Grantland 152
Richardson, Danny 75–76, *91*, 98, 106
Richmond Virginias Base Ball Club 71
Richter, Francis 90, 154
The Rider and Driver 152–153
Ritchey, Elizabeth Acheson 10
Ritchey, John, Sr. 10–11
Ritchey, Col. John Lindsay 11
Ritchey, Margaret 10
Riverside Base Ball Club of Fort Lee 30
Roach, John 75
Robinson, David F. 11
Robinson, M.F. 11
Robson, Capt. Andrew 10
Rochester *Democrat Chronicle* 108
Rochester Hop Bitters Base Ball Club 60
The Rochesters Base Ball Club 54
Rockland County, NY, baseball clubs 26–37; Base Ball Association 34; Pearl River Base Ball Club 34; *see also* Nyack, NY, baseball clubs
Rockland County Journal 30–38, 66
Roman Catholic 6
Roseman, Chief 62
rounders 87–88, 122–138, 122; *see also* Rankin, William M., baseball origins
Rusie, Amos 107
Ruth, "Babe" 171
Ruthrauff, John 11
Ryan, Jimmy 93
Ryder Cup 173–174

St. Andrews, Scotland 114
St. Andrews, Yonkers 114, 144, 157; Apple Tree Gang 114
St. Louis Brown Stockings/Browns Base Ball Club 45, 63, 146–147
St. Louis Cardinals Base Ball Club 146
sanitation 28
Sarazen, Gene 173–174
Savannah Golf Club 115
Say, Lou 62
Schenck, Bill 70

Schiff, Andrew 42, 45
Seitz, Don 53
Shinnecock Hills Golf Club 115
silver ball 26–37
Sinclair, Sir John 7
Slattery, Mike 76, *91*, 106
slavery 12–16
Smith, Edgar 70
Smith, John Rhea 149
Society for American Baseball Research (SABR) x, 2
Soden, Arthur 107
South Carolina Golf Club 115
Spalding, Albert Goodwill 39, 51, 65, 88, *91*, 93, 98–1–2, 120, 129, 134, 138, 144
Spalding & Brothers Company 51, *91*, 116–117, 144
Spanish Flu 170
Sparkill Base Ball Club of Piermont 30, 34
Spartans and Alerts Base Ball Clubs of Warren Village 34
Spink, Alfred 30, 35–36, 98, 128, 161
Sporting Critic 108, 155
Sporting Life 39, 81, 90, 102–108, 121, 145, 154, *155*, 157–159
The Sporting News 51, *60*, 67, 69, 78, 90, 126, 129, 136, 150–151, 159, 161
Sporting Times and Theatrical News 129
Sporting World 88–89
Spring Valley Base Ball Club of Cornwall 34
Springfield Cemetery, Queens 113, 177
Stackhouse, George 90, 159
Standard Oil Company 144
Staten Island Cricket Club 119
Staten Island Ferry 76
states in the Union 58
stationer 31
Statue of Liberty 88
Star Base Ball Club of Brooklyn 30, 33
"Star Spangled Banner" 48
Stars Base Ball Club of Spring Valley 34
Steel, John 7
Steiner, Simmons 71
Stevens, Thaddeus 26–28
stoolball 129, 135
Stuart, Gen. J.E.B. 16, 20–21
subway 139
Suck, Tony 70
Sullivan, Dan 62
Sullivan, John 77, 108, 111
Sullivan, "Sleeper" 62
Sunnysides Base Ball Club, Sing Sing 35
Swarback, Bill 75
Sweeney, Rooney 62
Swipes the Newsboy 93

Talcott, Edward 107
Talmadge, Henry 114
Tammany Hall 120; *see also* New York Mutuals
Tappan Zee Base Ball Club 30, 31, 34
Tassie, Thomas 126, 129, 131, 132

Index

Taylor, Billy 62
Taylor, George 67, 70, 88
Taylor, Luther Haden "Dummy" 146–147
telegraph 28, 50, 53, 167; American Telegraph Company 28
telephone 167
teleprinter 167
teletype 50
temperance/alcohol 96, 170; Volstead Act/Prohibition 170; Woman's Christian Temperance Union 170
Terry, Adonis 69
Thayer, Frederick 65
Theosophy Society 134
Thompson, Arthur 71
Thompson, Rev. Dr. James P. 27
Thorn, John 131–135
Thorpe, Jim 165
Tidal Wave (schooner) 35
Tidal Waves Base Ball Club of Nyack 35–38
Tiernan, Mike 76, 97
Timothy Hughes Rare and Early Newspapers 83–84
Titanic 165
Titcomb, "Cannonball" 75, **91**
Toledo Blue Stockings 71
townball 18, 122–123
Tracey, Charlotte M. 121
trap-ball 135
Travers, Jerry 154
Travis, Walter 144
Trenton Base Ball Club 71
Troy, John "Dasher" 74
Troy Unions Base Ball Club 38
Tucker, Abraham 125
Tucker, William 123, 125
Tuttle, Charles 70
Tuxedo Golf Course 118
Twain, Mark *see* Clemens, Samuel L.
Tweed, "Boss" 38, 49; *see also* New York Mutuals
typewriter 65

Ulster, Northern Ireland 6, 8, 10–11
Underground Railroad 19
Union Army 13–25
Union Association of Base Ball Clubs 71
Union Base Ball Club 29, 150
Union Club 53
Union Skating Grounds 48, 54, 61
United Press 2, 51, 113
United States Golf Association/USGA 1, 114–115, 152–154, 169, 172–174; original members 115; US Open 115, 167, 169, 172–174; USGA Museum Library ix, 184
urinal 28

Valley Spirit Newspaper 13–25
Van Cortlandt, Jacobus 152
Van Cortlandt Park 152–153
Van Cott, William H. 29, 129
Van Riper, Frank 32

Vardon, Harry 143–144
Vare, Glenna Collett 174
Villa, Joe 102–104
Villa, Pancho 169
Voight, David 41–42, 63
Volstead Act/Prohibition 170
Voorhis, William 35

Wadsworth, Louis 131–133
Walker, George Herbert 174
Walker, James John 110
Walker, Oscar 70
Walker, Terry 70
Walker Cup 174
Walker Law (boxing) 110
Wanamaker, Rodman 168–169
Ward, John M. 74–76, 80, 85, 90–95, 98, 104, 106, 126–127, 133
Ward's Wonders Base Ball Club 95, 106
wars 1, 5–10, 13–28, 115, 121, 169–170
Washington, George 8–10
Washington, DC, Nationals/Senators Base Ball Club 71, 142
Washington, DC, Olympics Base Ball Club 38
Washington Park 70, 160
Waynesboro First Nationals Base Ball Club 19
Welsh, Mickey 74–75, **91**, 98
Welsh Run, PA 5, 13, **14**
West, Billy 49
West, Harry 70
Western League 142
Westmoreland County, PA. 8
Wheaton, William 125, 134
Whig Party 10
Whiskey Rebellion 9
Whitney, Art 106
Whittier, "Polly" 144–145
Wickey's Soluble Chemical 66
Wide Awakes 17
Wiedman, "Stump" 75
Williams, Richard H. 118
Williams, Wash 70
Wilmington Quicksteps 71
Wilson, Pres. Woodrow 169, 170
Woman's Christian Temperance Union (WCTU) 170
Women's Day magazine 177
Wood, Spencer 30
World Series 147, 154
Wright, Alfred 78, 83, 112
Wright, Harry 38–39
Wright's Ferry Raid *see* Brown, John
Wrigley Field/Weegham Park 168

Yankee Stadium 171
Yankees (professional) *see* Greater New York Base Ball Club
Yankees Base Ball Club of Nyack (amateur) 30
YMCA 170
Youghiogheny River 8
Young, N.E. 29

www.ingramcontent.com/pod-product-compliance
Lightning Source LLC
Chambersburg PA
CBHW032053300426
44116CB00007B/721